THE BATTLE OF TOMOCHIC

OXFORD

THE BATTLE OF TOMOCHIC

The Battle of Tomochic
MEMOIRS OF A SECOND LIEUTENANT

by Heriberto Frías

Translated from the Spanish by
BARBARA JAMISON

With an Introduction by
ANTONIO SABORIT

OXFORD
UNIVERSITY PRESS
2006

OXFORD

UNIVERSITY PRESS

Oxford University Press, Inc., publishes works that further
Oxford University's objective of excellence
in research, scholarship, and education.

Oxford New York
Auckland Cape Town Dar es Salaam Hong Kong Karachi
Kuala Lumpur Madrid Melbourne Mexico City Nairobi
New Delhi Shanghai Taipei Toronto

With offices in
Argentina Austria Brazil Chile Czech Republic France Greece
Guatemala Hungary Italy Japan Poland Portugal Singapore
South Korea Switzerland Thailand Turkey Ukraine Vietnam

Copyright © 2006 by Oxford University Press, Inc.

Published by Oxford University Press, Inc.
198 Madison Avenue, New York, 10016
www.oup.com

Library of Congress Cataloging-in-Publication Data

Frías, Heriberto, 1870–1925.
[Tomochic. English]
The battle of Tomochic : memoirs of a second lieutenant / by Heriberto Frías ;
translated from the Spanish by Barbara Jamison ; edited with an introduction
and notes by Antonio Saborit.
p. cm. — (Library of Latin America)
Includes bibliographical references.
ISBN-13: 978-0-19-511742-4

ISBN-13: 978-0-19-511743-1 (pbk.)

1. Tomóchic (Mexico)—History—Fiction. I. Jamison, Barbara.
II. Saborit, Antonio, 1957– III. Title. IV. Series.
PQ 7297.F75T613 2002
863'.5—dc21
2001035906

Printed in the United States of America
on acid-free paper

Contents

This effort is dedicated to E.B. for her fine literary eye, to Diana Hembree, *comadre* of words and children, and to my daughter Isabel Estrada, dancer, scholar, muse, without whose variegated intensities neither life nor literature would be so rich.

Series Editors'
General Introduction

The Library of Latin America series makes available in translation major nineteenth-century authors whose work has been neglected in the English-speaking world. The titles for the translations from the Spanish and Portuguese were suggested by an editorial committee that included Jean Franco (general editor responsible for works in Spanish), Richard Graham (series editor responsible for works in Portuguese), Tulio Halperín Donghi (University of California–Berkeley), Iván Jaksić (University of Notre Dame), Naomi Lindstrom (University of Texas–Austin), Francine Masiello (University of California–Berkeley), and Eduardo Lozano of the Library at the University of Pittsburgh. The late Antonio Cornejo Polar of the University of California–Berkeley was also a founding member of the committee. The translations have been funded thanks to the generosity of the Lampadia Foundation and the Andrew W. Mellon Foundation.

During the period of national formation between 1810 and into the early years of the twentieth century, the new nations of Latin America fashioned their identities, drew up constitutions, engaged in bitter struggles over territory, and debated questions of education, government, ethnicity, and culture. This was a unique period unlike the process of nation formation in Europe and one that should be more familiar than it is to students of comparative politics, history, and literature.

The image of the nation was envisioned by the lettered classes—a minority in countries in which indigenous, mestizo, black, or mulatto peasants and slaves predominated—although alternative nationalisms existed at the grassroots level. The cultural elite were well educated in European thought and letters, but as statesmen, journalists, poets, and academics, they confronted the problem of the racial and linguistic heterogeneity of the continent and the difficulties of integrating the population into a modern nation-state. Some of the writers whose works will be translated in the Library of Latin America series played leading roles in politics. Fray Servando Teresa de Mier, a friar who translated Rousseau's *The Social Contract* and was one of the most colorful characters of the independence period, was faced with imprisonment and expulsion from Mexico for his heterodox beliefs. When he returned after independence, he was elected to the congress. Domingo Faustino Sarmiento, exiled from his native Argentina under the dictatorship of Juan Manuel de Rosas, wrote *Facundo: Civilización y barbarie*, a stinging denunciation of that government. He returned after Rosas' overthrow and was elected president in 1868. Andrés Bello was born in Venezuela, lived in London where he published poetry during the independence period, settled in Chile where he founded the university, wrote his grammar of the Spanish language, and drew up the country's legal code.

These post-independence intelligentsia were not simply dreaming of castles in the air, but vitally contributed to the founding of nations and the shaping of culture. The advantage of hindsight makes us aware of problems they themselves did not foresee, but this should not affect our assessment of their astonishing energy and achievements. Although there is a recent translation of Sarmiento's celebrated *Facundo*, there is no translation of his memoirs, *Recuerdos de provincia* (Provincial Recollections). The predominance of memoirs in the Library of Latin America Series is no accident—many offer entertaining insights into a vast, complex continent.

Nor have we neglected the novel. The Series includes new translations of the outstanding Brazilian writer Machado de Assis' work, including *Dom Casmurro* and *The Posthumous Memoirs of Brás Cubas*. There is no reason why other novels and writers who are not so well known outside Latin America—the Peruvian novelist Clorinda Matto de Turner's *Aves sin nido*, Nataniel Aguirre's *Juan de la Rosa*, José de Alencar's *Iracema*, Juana Manuela Gorriti's short stories—should not be read with as much interest as the political novels of Anthony Trollope.

However, a series on nineteenth-century Latin America cannot be limited to literary genres such as the novel, the poem, and the short story. The literature of independent Latin America was eclectic and strongly influenced by the periodical press newly liberated from scrutiny by colonial authorities and the Inquisition. Newspapers were miscellanies of fiction, essays, poems, and translations from all manner of European writing. The novels written on the eve of Mexican independence by José Joaquín Fernández de Lizardi included disquisitions on secular education and law, as well as denunciations of the evils of gaming and idleness. Other works, such as a well-known poem by Andrés Bello, "Ode to Tropical Agriculture," and novels such as *Amalia* by José Mármol and the Bolivian Nataniel Aguirre's *Juan de la Rosa*, were openly partisan. By the end of the century, sophisticated scholars were beginning to address the history of their countries, as did João Capistrano de Abreu in his *Capítulos de história colonial*.

Memoirs such as those by Fray Servando Teresa de Mier or Sarmiento frequently offer the descriptions of everyday life that in Europe were incorporated into the realist novel. Latin American literature at this time was seen largely as a pedagogical tool, a "light" alternative to speeches, sermons, and philosophical tracts. Especially in the early part of the century, the readership for novels was small because of the high illiteracy rate. Nevertheless, the orally transmitted culture of the gaucho and the urban underclasses became the linguistic repertoire of some of the most interesting nineteenth-century writers—notably José Hernández, author of the "gauchesque" poem "Martin Fierro," which enjoyed an unparalleled popularity. For many writers the task was not to appropriate popular language but to civilize, and their literary works were strongly influenced by the high style of political oratory.

The editorial committee has not attempted to limit its selection to the better-known writers such as Machado de Assis; it has also selected many works that have never appeared in translation or writers whose works have not been translated recently. The Series now makes these works available to the English-speaking public.

Because of the preferences of funding organizations, the series initially focuses on writing from Brazil, the Southern Cone, the Andean region, and Mexico. Each of our editions will have an introduction that places the work in its appropriate context and includes explanatory notes.

We owe special thanks to the late Robert Glynn of the Lampadia Foundation, whose initiative jump-started the project, and to Richard Ekman and his successors at the Andrew W. Mellon Foundation, which generously supported the project. We also thank the Rockefeller Foundation for funding the 1996 symposium "Culture and Nation in Iberoamerica," organized by the editorial board of the Library of Latin America. The support of Edward Barry of Oxford University Press was crucial in the founding years of the project, as was the assistance of Ellen Chodosh and Elda Rotor of Oxford University Press. The John Carter Brown Library at Brown University in Providence, Rhode Island, has served as the grant administrator of the project since 1998.

—*Jean Franco*
—*Richard Graham*

Introduction
Accusations, Confessions, and
Proclamations

Who knows what a man hides, even from himself, when he is telling
the truth for his survival?

—*John Le Carré*

Eyewitness

The manuscript of this novel disappeared in Mexico City. That would
correspond to all twenty-four installments of *Tomochic! Episodios de
campaña*, published by *El Demócrata* between March 14 and April 14,
1893. Each episode claimed "to be written by an eyewitness."
"Rigorously edited and enlivened with historical detail," the novel circulated in the capital city until 1894. The veteran publishing house of
Jesús T. Recio, an ex–comrade in arms of Porfirio Díaz with a string
of three terms as president of Mexico behind him, printed the book.
At that time, Recio was a resident of Rio Grande City, Texas. The
novel was first published outside the country in a shabby edition. In
Mexico City it was sold in La America, a tiny shop in the Portal de
Mercaderes, across the street from the bohemian Café del Cazador.

When it was printed in book form, the novel was subjected to the
usual process of editing, additions, and changes without initially alter-
ing its strategy of attribution. For example, it retained the anonymity of
the supposed "eyewitness," but from the outset the novel arrived in the
hands of its readers with a slightly modified title: *Tomóchic! Episodios de
la campaña de Chihuahua: 1892*. The new historical details consisted
of several paragraphs that added a note of political irony aimed at the

government; a number of lines suggesting that the conflict between the "pure-hearted, simple souls" of the mountain fighters and "the sad heroism of federal bayonets" had been artificially stirred up; several paragraphs that pointed to the possibility of armed rebellion against Díaz in the north in the mid-1890s, and a new chapter, "Sotol and Kerosene." The prestigious Maucci Brothers publishing house brought out the next edition of this unusual work under the abridged 1899 title *Tomochic*. In 1906, another edition came out under the auspices of the Valdés publishing house. It was "unique . . . the whole work, edited and expanded, with annotations and previously unpublished chapters written by the author for publication in *El Correo de la Tarde*," the prestigious Mazatlán newspaper published in the city's northern state of Sinaloa. By that time Díaz had served six presidential terms. Writer José Ferrel, one of *El Demócrata's* principal contributors (thirteen years previously the newspaper dared publish the book in fragments) added a prologue to the Sinaloan edition. This was the edition which the Librería, owned by Charles Bouret's widow, reprinted in 1911, titled *Tomochic: Novela histórica mexicana*. Even then the author preferred to remain anonymous. The 1906 edition was the most heavily edited, adding several paragraphs in the following chapters: "Heroic Troops," "The Hand of General Díaz," "Ready to Kill or Be Killed," "Apparent Causes," "Crossing the Sierra Madre." Additionally, there were three new chapters: "Recalling the Campaign against the Apaches," "The Dogs of Tomochic," and "The Saint of Cabora." The most casual comparison reveals the sequence of the various editions. That "Los perros de Tomochic" originally appeared in story form in the elegant and exclusive *Revista Moderna* in January 1900 points to the ongoing interest in the work and also touches on its authorship. At the time, a few Mexican books were printed in many (and varied) editions. This explains the appearance of a sequel, *El triunfo de Sancho Panza: Novela de crítica social mexicana*, published in 1911 by Luis Herrera's press. Even though there was no manuscript (although military authorities and police agents of President Díaz were enthusiastically looking for it in the first weeks of spring 1893) but rather an original version of an edition published in *El Demócrata*, the definitive text was established after fifteen years of its intense life by going back to the five earliest editions. The testimonial intent of the work perhaps explains its initial broad success.

The action, writing, and publication dates for *Tomochic* all point to its incontrovertible testimonial slant. For example, let's take a look at one part of its internal chronology: Miguel Mercado, a young second lieutenant of the 9th Battalion appears in the sun-drenched plaza of Guerrero City at some point after September 2, 1892, "when General Rangel attempted to attack the town of Tomochic." In the plaza's immediate vicinity, in the "inn" frequented by officers of the 5th Regiment of the 11th Battalion and the Public Security Corps of Chihuahua State, the talk is of "the inexplicable betrayal of Santa Ana Pérez. He had shamelessly defected to the enemy side, it was said, along with more than sixty men from the Chihuahua State forces."

The government's defense also comes up in the conversation, and General Díaz is toasted in gratitude for "order, which means peace and progress." How did they get there? Miguel Mercado, along with "half a battalion," left Mexico City by train the night of October 3, arriving in Chihuahua "after traveling two days and two nights." There the young second lieutenant joined ranks "with his two companies" and learns that "an isolated group had taken up arms against the government and was making a defiant stand in the heart of the Sierra Madre mountains; military might had been used repeatedly to no avail. Many officers had died, and Colonel Ramirez of the 11th Battalion had been taken prisoner." In Chihuahua State's capital the Tomochic rebellion was the vital issue of the day. On the tenth of the month "the march began" on horseback toward the city of Guerrero. The "two companies arrived in Concepción on the fifteenth, having traversed the lonely wild lands and inhospitable rocky hills." The two companies of the 9th Battalion pitched camp "along the Alameda, eager for the order to push on into the Sierra Madre, whose dark silhouette undulated majestically just ahead." From there, the companies pushed forward "in the dawn hours of October 16" making their "their slow ascent toward the west," on their way to Tomochic, where they arrived after three days on the road. Gunshots, raids, and voices of death filled the valley of high rocky ridges during all nine days of confrontations between federal forces and the civilian population of Tomochic until the place was transformed into a landscape of desolation, silence, and death. "The campaign was over. The last stronghold was burning, engulfed in immense, whistling flames that the harsh morning winds fanned. The bugles' disorderly reveilles vibrated convulsively one after the other in the cold air, their thunderous martial joy contrasting darkly with the devastated landscape." The tale ends amid "deadly bursts of flames [from] the piles of corpses" and dawn breaking over the occupied valley.[1]

Three months and a few days after the massacre, on February 2, 1893, from its offices in Mexico City, *El Demócrata* advised its readers that it had sent reporters to collect particulars for a detailed account of the Tomochic campaign.

The initial chronicle, written immediately after the campaign and published in *El Demócrata*, implicated and reproved Mexico's leaders in an unprecedented manner. How did they interpret it? As an accusation? A settling of accounts with General Díaz and his supporters, instigated by a political minority such as the one headed up by local strongman Luis Terrazas in Chihuahua? The chronology in *Tomochic* is a good indicator in this respect. Despite certain discrepancies between the campaign and the literary version, the cataloguing of unfortunate events that befall Miguel Mercado (a literary character in his own right with his own motivations) justifies the surprise of the important political personalities named and alluded to in the book. It is a fictional account, told in the third person. Indebted to European war novels, it is a historical account of facts. It is open and sensitive to the atrocious realities of a confrontation between a professional army and a handful of civilians, and it exploded like a bomb in the presidential palace. Consequently Díaz ordered legal proceedings against Lieutenant Heriberto Frías. First he ordered him to be arrested and held incommunicado, declaring that he had reliable information that Frías was the author of the chronicle of the military campaign against the people of Tomochic.

"If it were possible to have the original reports from *El Demócrata* and Frías's letters, this would strengthen the investigation," wrote Chihuahua's governor in response to the president's orders. The general of the military zone also insisted on proof to Díaz; he suggested searching *El Demócrata's* printing press and editorial offices "in the hope of finding original manuscripts."

But obviously *Tomochic* didn't astound only the powerful. It held intense appeal for *El Demócrata's* faithful readers, who were partisans and friends of the opposition in Mexico City. The fact that the events and their subsequent narration occurred almost simultaneously contributed to its mass appeal. Both the powers that be and the average reader of the day would tend to interpret a narrative like this literally, and believe it to be written by a flesh-and-blood eyewitness. A character like Miguel Mercado didn't need realism nor was he taken for real. Events of the bloody military campaign precluded any accusation of implausibility, obviating the effort to give it a purely fictional interpretation. The facts had been established in the manuscript published by *El Demócrata*. This isn't an incidental strategy but a tentative incursion into the modern novel itself, its treatment of an immediate, contemporary reality.

The chronicle's author, by erasing himself from the map, excited more public interest than any other Mexican writer of the nineteenth century, whether or not he was working in the genre of the testimonial historical novel.

Clausell Declares

The author's anonymity was the key to *Tomochic*'s existence.

The public never objected to the author's decision to keep his identity secret, devouring the chronicle's different editions throughout the 1890s—especially following the Díaz government's last gasp at the dawning of the twentieth century. If, for readers less familiar with General Díaz's modus operandi, the importance of *Tomochic* was that it related the essence of political truth of the moment, this is because literary conventions of the day had initiated even the most naive readers into pondering the dual faces of art and history in testimonial accounts. And as with countless other similar works, even in early editions *Tomochic* overflowed fiction's borders. On the one hand, interpreting books written in this particular code as fiction had not been customary for several generations—writers themselves contributed to the blurring of poetry and history. On the other hand, an account of events written in a deliberately literary prose, which narrated the campaign of a professional army against a population of its same people—however remote and unknowable the north and the Sierra Tarahumara might seem—didn't fall into the same category as the historical novels of Vicente Riva Palacio, Juan Antonio Mateos, and Manuel Payno. Despite its painstaking plot construction, from the outset *Tomochic* wasn't received as fiction, or presented as a work produced exclusively from the imagination. This is why, from its very first printing in *El Demócrata*, its author's name was omitted to emphasize the protagonist–witness Miguel Mercado.

Anonymity allowed *Tomochic's* author to render a work that went beyond mere fiction, with or without a few elements added or played down. It is an account of events that is "carefully edited and embellished with historical details." That it was first printed in a newspaper contributed to the meaning and honesty of the text. We can imagine the first readers' reactions to detailed descriptions of the time spent by federal troops in Guerrero City's "deserted plaza" ("the desolate plaza, resplendent with sun"), and to the spectacle of the military forces lazing around before departing for the rebellious town of Tomochic. Through the experiences of the apocryphal Miguel Mercado, the "young second lieutenant of the 9th Battalion," readers had a chronicle they could trust. Moreover, the chronicle's development over various installments would have alerted readers that this wasn't just any eyewitness. Nor was the account's exposition customary or expected. In the pages of this exposé of a state massacre, there was no room for abiding values or bravery.

Thus its anonymity separated the facts of the fiction from the fiction about the facts, allowing for the construction of an account, which, because of its painstaking attention to detail, seemed not only to distance itself from real emotions and common sense, but also conferred upon Díaz's government a sense of unreality. Moreover, given the political and literary climate of the times, the eyewitness anonymity contributed to the narrative's singular power while it protected the author's physical integrity from the powers that be. Anonymity is an age-old strategy; here it introduces an uncomfortable truth under the rubric of the historical narrative, a genre the political classes of the nineteenth century were well acquainted with.

Identifying the author became a point of vital interest. General Díaz and his supporters couldn't read *Tomochic* without an author. Subjective interpretation wasn't enough, as it had been for the novel's initial readership. They had to know, and to know beyond a shadow of a doubt. Toward this end, they employed several strategies.

One has already been mentioned. Lieutenant Heriberto Frías was arrested in Chihuahua and indicted on charges that he had violated various articles of the Military Justice Code. Once the lieutenant and his dwelling in the hamlet of Las Quintas had been searched on April 15, 1893, Díaz ordered that the disrespectful and treasonous officer be imprisoned and held incommunicado.[2]

His objective was to establish, with convincing proof, that the "eyewitness" was none other than Frías. To accomplish this, they harassed him with endless questions and the testimony of various witnesses. He continued to maintain that he had no communications with anybody in Chihuahua, that he lived far away from the city where he, at one time, casually spoke about the Tomochic campaign with "a few residents of insignificant standing." Yes, he had contributed articles to several newspapers, such as *El Combate* and *El Eco de Chihuahua*, none of which could be interpreted the way his interrogators might wish. Also, he had written "some three letters" in January 1893 to his friend Joaquín Clausell, telling him of his promotion and submitting his poem "Gritos" to him for publication. In the opinion of the court this contradicted the testimony of one of the witnesses, a local journalist who not only said he heard Frías censure orders from superiors, but heard him comment that he maintained a correspondence with Clausell, whose *Demócrata* would publish a chronicle of the Tomochic campaign "rendering it in a similar style as French novelist Emile Zola's *La Débâcle.*" The lieutenant's trial lasted four months. It was an unprecedented proceeding. How could a legal body hope to identify the author of a piece of writing whose strategy of attribution was to deny the author's existence? In the end, nothing came out of the trial that could be used as proof against Frías.

But the mention of Clausell leads to one of the other routes by which General Díaz tried to identify the author of *Tomochic.* Above all he wanted to ascertain who, among his political enemies and adversaries, would plot against his growing political prestige by accusing him—by means of this narrative—of one of the most serious crimes carried out by state forces to date. The chronicle began to appear in the pages of the newspaper four and a half months after the massacre. Tomochic was of strategic importance to the Díaz administration because it was on the road over which treasures extracted from the mineral mines of western Chihuahua passed daily. Two or three days on horseback separated the fifty voters of Tomochic from Guerrero City, the district capital. The efficient train system connected this capital and the state capital by 300 kilometers of rails. Telegraph cables also connected Guerrero City to the state capital. But Guerrero City didn't have sufficient resources to entertain petitions, calm fears, or flame the hopes of the 6,000 voters who comprised the impoverished district of Guerrero.

At the beginning of the 1890s, Chihuahua was experiencing a severe agricultural crisis that threatened to damage the social and political order of its capital. Guerrero City was about 200,000 kilometers from Clausell's office in the political center of the country on 169 Avenida Oriente or 26 Calle 2 in San Lorenzo, according to different designations. Neither distance nor communication problems dampened the new *El Demócrata* director's interest in recording in exhaustive detail the events of the military campaign against Tomochic in a novelized account. In those days a common adage was that abuse of power leads to the strength of the opposition. It was because of one of those abuses that Clausell was arrested and held incommunicado three weeks before Frías in the municipal jailhouse of the Federal District. The motive: criminal judges of Mexico City initiated legal proceedings against *El Demócrata.*

When Frías's trial in Chihuahua didn't go anywhere—the second lieutenant continued to insist he was not the "eyewitness" to whom *El Demócrata* attributed the episodes of *Tomochic! Episodios de campaña*— federal authorities issued Clausell a court summons. Responding to two separate rogatory letters, Clausell declared that as newspaper director he conceived the idea of writing and publishing a novel, using the events of the Tomochic war and appropriating the style of Emile Zola's *La Débâcle.* He claimed that the topical nature and the writing style would certainly draw an audience. Furthermore, he claimed to have carried out his objectives: he wrote the novel and then published it in several issues of *El Demócrata.* All the facts were culled from the news in the Mexican and American press as well as from private letters he had received from people in Chihuahua, among whom he remembered Señor Pedro Ortega, others from Leoncio Buenfil, and a Señor Sánchez.

To pointed questions Clausell responded that despite the novel's title or subtitle, which referred to an eyewitness, no such witness existed. Designating one, he claimed, gave credibility to the events. He also affirmed that before beginning to write the novel he collected as many news items as possible and educated himself on the terrain and people of Tomochic. As to the original manuscript of *Tomochic,* Clausell indicated that he wrote all the episodes—by machine first, then by hand. Once the typesetting was finished, they were thrown away along with the reams of paper waste from the printing press and the editorial offices.

This inquiry resulted in a visit to the press and editorial offices as well as the deponent's residence, in search of the original texts of the novel and letters. This search, carried out in Clausell's presence as well as that of authorized court personnel, only brought to light a few notebooks, the list of subscribers in Chihuahua, and four letters from the same state. None mentioned events in Tomochic.

In one last rogatory letter, Clausell had to respond to a new set of more exact questions. Was he acquainted with Lieutenant Heriberto Frías of the 9th Battalion? If so, why and for how long? Did he receive letters from Frías? On what dates, and what did Frías recount in them? Had Frías given him facts on the operations carried out by federal forces in Tomochic? How? Had Lieutenant Frías sent him some verses and travel impressions for publication? Which ones?

Clausell declared that he had known Frías for seven or eight years. They had studied together in the National Preparatory School, and Frías had sent him some four or five letters in January, February, and March, 1893. He clearly remembered that in his first letter Frías mentioned hearing about the founding of *El Demócrata* and its publishing a novel about events in Tomochic. He asked for the corresponding issues to be mailed to him. In Frías's second letter, he thanked Clausell for a gift subscription to the newspaper, and in the third—and the last to Clausell's recollection—Frías complained that *El Demócrata* didn't always arrive. Clausell also declared that Frías had not sent him any facts, directly or indirectly, about the operations carried out by military forces in the town of Tomochic. Frías didn't send anything directly, Clausell insisted, since Clausell took the verses from the newspaper's literary section published directly from *El Eco de Chihuahua*. Lieutenant Frías hadn't sent him verses or travel impressions, or any other literary, scientific, or artistic work.

In the end, Clausell was asked who had supplied him with the facts on which he based the articles in *El Demócrata* relating to events in Tomochic. He reiterated that he obtained the facts from various newspapers published on the U.S. border—since little was mentioned in the Mexican press in the capital, Clausell added—from reports given to him by two previously mentioned persons in Chihuahua, but above all from Agustín Páez, a native of Parral and student at National Preparatory School who maintained many connections in Chihuahua. All this information was put into archives and sent to the Chihuahua courthouse to be used in the ongoing proceedings against Lieutenant Frías.

Beyond Dreams

To be alive in Emile Zola's day, in the imagination of some Mexican writers, was to be lucky beyond belief. He had everything that was lacking in Mexico: an audience, recognition, and success. *La Débâcle*, the novel Zola published in 1892, sold more copies than any of his previous works and challenged the literary sophistication of more than just one reader.

The reigning imperious writer on wide-ranging topics, Ignacio Manuel Altamirano, experienced the publication of *La Débâcle* as Mexican consul in Paris, the capital of Europe in the nineteenth century. His almost contemptuous indifference to the French narrative was countered by novelist Federico Gamboa's enthusiasm. The latter cultivated his fame as an incurable and a decided admirer of Zola.

The aspiring writer Joaquín Clausell, though more measured in his admiration than *Santa's* author, from his position in the literature-friendly editorial offices of *El Universal* newspaper, was responsible for familiarizing Mexico City readers with the furious literary machine called Zola. Clausell worked on *El Universal* under Rafael Reyes Spíndola. The latter directed this powerful daily paper, which was later promoted and financed by the state in its attempt to commercially squash all who gave voice to the capital city's political minority groups. At that time, however, *El Universal* was home to a heterogeneous mix of literary generations and temperaments as divergent as the last of the romantics and the first modernists.

In a note published anonymously in *El Universal* toward the end of October 1892—and which, given the tumult that greeted the publication of *Tomochic* some five months later, we have to attribute to Clausell's pen—the writer produced an annotated commentary that was one of the most incisive works of criticism ever written on *La Débâcle*. According to the article that *El Universal* published in a front page column, Zola confessed to his friends that the importunate observations of one Captain Tanera, an officer of the German army's general staff, had affected him more than all the other censorious attacks flung at his most recent novel: "I who have read *La Débâcle*," added the anonymous and knowledgeable Mexican editor, "and have observed that my modest assessment of it coincides with that of several more or less worthy critics, even I hadn't considered this work, nor had they, from the point of view of the German officer."

The Mexican editor translated and cited the paragraphs in Tanera's criticism where this informed military man pointed out that Zola might be overlooking the obvious since he had never actually been engaged in the thick of battle: "What the soldier is thinking about when he's fighting and what he forgets." Despite *La Débâcle's* intense human interest, things are described that never happened, Tanera observed: "He adulterates facts and demonizes an army which has been disgraced, ineptly led, but has fought with valor at every turn and hasn't lost its honor in defeat."[3]

Zola tweaked a raw nerve when he narrated a sensitive event in France's contemporary history in *La Débâcle*: the burial of Napoleon III's Second Empire in the inferno of the 1871 commune, through the empire and Napoleon's entanglement the preceding summer—three years after his daring Mexican venture had come to naught in a useless war against Prussia's King William. After seven weeks and his humiliating defeat in the Sédan, a century and a half of arrogance in the French army was canceled out.

In addition, Zola made the coffers rattle. According to another article published in *El Universal, Le Figaro* made an unofficial accounting of how much money Zola made on the nineteen novels in the Rougon-Macquart series and came up with an astounding sum. Three novels had sold more than 100,000 copies: *L'Assommoir, La Terre*, and *La Débâcle.* To give some idea of the latter's fantastic reception: Stacked one on top of the other, the 120,000 copies of *La Débâcle*—Le Figaro claimed— with their 2.7-centimeter width, would have formed eleven columns the height of the Eiffel Tower. (Inexplicably, only *La faute de l'abbé Monret* and *Nana* sold less than 20,000 copies.) But even these titles, in a professional career spanning several decades, earned their author nearly Fr 1.5 million.[4]

Therefore it seems almost natural—to the extent that anything in the arena of literary representations appears natural—that some Mexican authors would take to heart the anecdote about Zola or even assume his tactics in the rustic capital of the Díaz era, which thought itself modern, elegant, and rich but daily woke up beneath its poor man's mantle.

Juan Antonio Mateos, according to rumors in the journalistic community of the capital, set out to see for himself. Between November 1892 and January 1893, various Mexico City newspapers claimed that this popular Parliament delegate, novelist, and playwright was working on the libretto for a play inspired by *La Débâcle* to be staged in the Arbeu Theater.[5] It seems likely that news of Mateos's play would appear in the editorial columns, along with the many other items of interest that made Díaz's capital such a colorful place. An example in point would be the imaginative groupings of velocipedes making their way through colonial streets of fin-de-siècle modernity, the trolley transportation in the Federal District, the Melcocha collisions (the fashionable bus of the day), the new silver-gray mares of Ignacio de la Torre, Ivy Baldwin's tour in the dirigible Mars, and the dances in some houses.[6]

It's difficult to know whether the play was good or not, since Mateos's librettos still need to be compiled. But even without seeing it on stage, to those in the know its title, *Sédan*, signaled its main intent.[7] Nevertheless, it seemed improper to Mateos to acknowledge his debt to Zola's work (as well as Zola himself), or he must have considered that the polite gesture would distance himself completely from it. It's hard to understand why the sixty-year-old Mateos would want to erase all traces of his relationship to Zola. His public clarifications were only vaguely literary in nature, and were largely indifferent to the complexities of the literary text. They ended up minimizing the enigma of author identity by dismissing the literary reality that went beyond authors who were exalted, profaned, or copied through parody or plagiarism. The fragile idea of authorship can be gleaned as we attempt to explain to ourselves Mateos's attitude toward Zola. What's this? The "author" isn't only a manner, style, or tone but a condition, a mood—part critical habit and part anguish. The author is usually the sum of these two incomplete pieces: that which he believes to be or identifies as the nerve of his unique temperament, on the one hand, and on the other, something to do with courage, enthusiasm, commitment, and the intelligence to live a vocation. Authoring alone shouldn't be an important property; it's having an avid readership that makes it a fortunate state. It's an effrontery to pity an author who toils without gain without first wondering if he has an affinity for certain authors or just bad habits. Reading's cultural weight is a nineteenth-century inheritance that can stun us if we're aware of the "brilliant things" (as Stendahl called them) that the nineteenth century bequeathed us: decency and hypocrisy. Writers' values have weight. Their opinions are taken seriously and their words assign rank.

It was because of Zola and particularly *La Débâcle*, which arrived in the Mexico City bookstores in a Spanish edition toward the middle of 1892 and was translated in the *Diario del Hogar* literary supplement, that the military campaign against Tomochic entered history. As always, the written word bestowed an urgent importance on the facts.

Authorship is a mask. To get behind it, one has to try and see from the other side of the polished surface of the mirror.

El Demócrata

While Lieutenant Heriberto Frías organized his own defense in Chihuahua, out of touch in a jail cell, the case against him gained strength through the secrecy of its proceedings.

Porfirio Díaz ordered these measures in an attempt to undermine the young lieutenant's version, break the silence, expose his fraud in a military court, and resolve the question of the anonymous witness of the Tomochic campaign. A rogatory letter was discreetly dispatched to the first judge of Mexico City, giving him the authority to order a "scrupulous search" in the printing plant as well as the editorial offices of the newspaper *El Demócrata* "or at the home of its writers or editors" with the objective of collecting the original pages of the published material that appeared in its columns under the title of *Tomochic* "as well as all the manuscripts and letters that referred to the military operations in this town." With the aid of military justice, the judge would be able to question the editorial staff of *El Demócrata* and subpoena all pertinent material. As already mentioned, the newspaper's director was the first to appear in court.

Only a few people had any idea who the guy testifying behind bars was. And if the respondent appeared at his appointment in a timely fashion, it was for the simple reason that he found himself isolated in the dank cells of Belem, in one of fourteen isolated cells on the second floor of the special wing of the prison. Joaquín Clausell had been living in the capital city since the beginning of the 1880s. In the beginning, he eked out an existence as a dishwasher in a pharmacy. This was how he paid for his weakness for politics and the effrontery of having confronted the governor and strongman of Campeche, where he was born on June 16, 1866, the son of the merchant José Clausell and Marcelina Troconi.

Life in the capital provided Clausell with a broad community of young people, with and without funds, with liberal ideas and radical ways, and more or less tenuously affiliated with existing political organizations. Some of the less fortunate made their living in printing presses and type-setting shops. Others, young educated people from every corner of the country—apprentices in everything and masters of nothing, as Clausell was—lived from day to day contributing for brief periods to the magazines and newspapers of the hour. Nobody had a steady job; the only stable occupation was studying. Clausell entered the Escuela Nacional de Ingenieros and then left for law school, where he met up with Frías the schoolmate who would make him take an irrevocable step. In those classrooms he finished up the course of studies he'd carried out in the streets of the capital, from the conversion to nickel coins in 1883 to the popular forums against the judgment on the conversion of the English debt presented to congress by the Treasury Commission. He was an impassioned orator. According to what he told his friends, he later received a silver medal in the Teatro Arbeu that a group of ladies bestowed on the most eloquent street orators. The Treasury Commission prize was suspended after a brutal confrontation between students and police. There was Clausell, just another student in worn clothes who taught classes, jotted down notes in the cafés, took on insignificant jobs in the library, cabinet, and courthouse. Mutual help functioned between friends; housing costs were shared, and it wasn't so difficult to get used to eating once a day, and whatever else it took to survive.[8] The anti-reelection cause became a crusade for these young people, a way to confront General Díaz and his supporters in the 1888 presidential elections. Clausell made the rounds with Alberto García Granados, Diódoro Batalla, Jesús Rábago, Enrique María de los Ríos, and Gabriel González Mier. Living together as a group, they shared similar worries, passions, hopes, and convictions. Politics seduced them. The death of ex-president Sebastián Lerdo de Tejada in New York in April 1889, and above all the arrival in Mexico of his remains, stirred the political mood of these anti-reelection youths. They transformed the dubiously exquisite corpse into a cruel mirror that they held up to General Díaz, the same military man who years before led the rebellion which defeated and exiled Lerdo by sabotaging the insincere official ceremony in his memory. This daring deed put Clausell behind bars in the Belem prison for six months, and when he emerged again he took up a career in journalism. Juan Pérez was one of his first pseudonyms. He dreamed of directing a publication of his own; the name *La soberanía de los Estados* was as far as he got. But he began by reporting for *El Monitor Republicano* and *El Universal.*

With a bit of boasting and a lot of modesty, Clausell exhibited his bachelorhood and his admiration for the poets Salvador Díaz Mirón and Gaspar Nuñez de Arce. Sporting their badge of anti-reelectionism, the opposition got together to talk at all hours on street corners, in cafés, in the rooms of guest houses, and at school. Despite his various careers, Clausell managed to finish his law studies.

All this activity didn't unseat Díaz. And after the 1892 presidential elections, which reaffirmed his power, Clausell and his supporters started up a newspaper in February 1893 and called it *El Demócrata.*[9] Its publication was announced on posters all over the capital. The young director availed himself of talented new writers for the four pages of the newspaper and favored investigative pieces.[10]

According to Clausell, a journalist was a public man who pledged himself to his country, truth, and justice. Thus he thought it strange that in Mexico the press had only minor importance. He reproached the lack of honor in the press, its inclination for lying, calumny, illicit speculation. Moreover, he claimed that the press didn't influence opinion. In those days the press sold itself for any tidbit and belonged to a few clever characters who functioned like bureaucrats. That's the way they were, if we believe the description in *El cuarto poder* by Emilio Rabasa.

The press as a whole played to the tune of the editorial and gossip columns, short items, clippings from other publications, filler.

Clausell set out in *El Demócrata* what he considered to be the plagues besetting the nation: tax stamp revenue, typhus, gambling houses, beggars, the semiofficial daily papers, the municipal council, psychology, postal service, coachmen, velocipede riders. His idea of journalism was ascetic.[11] "I judge the press to be a formidable machine which can forge either the monstrous or the sublime," said Clausell. Putting his strong convictions to work, he conceived of an unprecedented project that he voiced in the newspaper's second edition. *El Demócrata* sent reporters to collect particulars for a detailed account of the Tomochic campaign, "an event shrouded in silence," that had been given some coverage in the newspapers of the City of Palaces ever since October 1892.[12]

But before publishing the first campaign installment March 14, Clausell unleashed a short-lived crusade against the gambling houses of the capital.[13] This resulted in a lawsuit and robbed him of his liberty. A few days before the newspaper completed its second month in circulation, on March 29, at eleven o'clock in the morning, the director and owner of *El Demócrata*—Clausell and Francisco R. Blanco—gave themselves up voluntarily to the Third Correctional Court.

The Mexican police had been looking for him since March 24, the eve of Palm Sunday. Saturday afternoon, the chief of police reserves apprehended one of the two directors and, hours later, one of the editors in the editorial offices of the paper. Mexico City's criminal judges filed a formal lawsuit against Clausell's newspaper, citing a series of articles that appeared injurious to them and gratuitously accused ten judges, the same who then signed the lawsuit. *El Demócrata* criticized the gambling houses but above all governmental tolerance of them. The magistrates' lawsuit demanded reparations that would soothe the wounds and erase the wrongs done them. First, they demanded that their adversaries prove and justify their claims. The petition covered not only the author of the damning articles, Querido Moheno, but the author of the series "A General and Political View of the Ministers," and the editor and director (or the editor in chief) of *El Demócrata*.[14]

The Good Soldier

From the outset, the Tomochic military campaign mobilized a column of tens of soldiers from the troops of Porfirio Díaz against a population of 300 souls. Heriberto Frías, born May 15, 1870, in Querétaro, participated in "the campaign against the mountain rebels of Chihuahua State during the month of October 1892, where he engaged in the combats unleashed from the 20th to the 29th of the same month in the town of Tomochic," according to his service record.[15]

This was the only warfare the good soldier Frías knew. His tour of duty in Tomochic was the only period when Frías submitted to military discipline—a truce he maintained with his enemy, the army, for a brief stint.

The soldier's literary inclinations, or rather the debauched inclinations that sparked his idea of a literary vocation, got him into constant trouble with military discipline from the moment he was promoted to second lieutenant of the infantry on January 24, 1889. Frías was one of the few writers from the Military College who decided to join the army. He wrote poems in the romantic style of his ardent era, rhetorical, always shaken by moral crises that some writers of the day felt were akin to what brought about the demise of the classical world. His military conduct left a lot to be desired.[16]

In four years of service Frías worked at developing a very poor reputation. In May 1889, after just five years of service, the Honor Committee admonished Second Lieutenant Frías for poor grooming and for "disrespecting his military garments and accoutrements." He was imprisoned for inadequacies of service for twenty-nine days in the Santiago Tlatelolco Prison.[17] This prison, on the outskirts of the capital, wrote Concepción Lombardo de Miramón in his *Memorías*, had previously served as a seminary for Franciscan friars: "After Independence the friars emigrated and the government converted the cloisters to house troops or prisoners of the state."[18] This call to attention improved the second lieutenant's comportment. He won a place on the honor roll during the following three months. But the turn of events was ephemeral. From then on, Frías atoned for his lack of discipline with extended guard duty and Sunday stays—he was lax in bed making, fell asleep during guard duty, arrived late for roll call, left his cape lying around, was poorly groomed, was absent from gym activities and the ranks of his unit. In other ways, his abilities were average.[19]

Toward mid-1891, two years after his experience in Santiago Tlatelolco, Frías was accused of the crime of inflicting injuries, the most serious charges against the second lieutenant yet. He served his sentence from July to September. What injuries could this twenty-one-year-old boy have inflicted? He hadn't even served in one military camp; his mettle was still to be tried. His service record registers the fact that his trial fell into the hands of civil authorities. But musician, poet, literary critic, and historian Rubén M. Campos—his friend, contemporary, and colleague—wrote in an article that Frías was charged with "splitting open someone's head with a saber blow while defending his sword." We don't know whether this would have had a favorable impact on college officers who were familiar with the poor poet's military disaster; however, it did link him to a hobby of the day: the spurious refinement (excessive refinement) of dueling.[20]

One triumph of Frías's military career was to escape with his life in the Tomochic campaign. When his battalion took the strategically vital Cerro de la Cueva, their triumph was assured. Consequently he was promoted to infantry lieutenant and awarded a monthly salary of sixty pesos beginning on Día de los Muertos, 1892.[21] Tomochic also meant Frías's last arrest in the army. Two days after *El Demócrata* published the last of the anonymous episodes of a novel about the campaign of federal troops against its population he was taken into custody.

His buddies kept guard over him, all quartered together in the remote capital of Chihuahua State. General Díaz suspected Frías of authoring the novel published in *El Demócrata* and gave leave to the civilian and military command in Chihuahua to prosecute the second lieutenant. If the president was right, the young creative officer had violated several articles of the new Military Justice Code put into effect in January 1893 related to the duties of respect, silence, and loyalty. Colonel Miguel Ahumada, governor of Chihuahua, and José María Rangel, chief of the military zone, descended on the remote hamlet of Las Quintas, the home of Lieutenant Frías.

It could be said that the military campaign invited mythifying. And it wasn't a single author but a literary genre—the novel—that got Díaz and his supporters up in arms.

And this was not just any novel, as we have seen. This was a Mexican novel with a strong French influence that countered Ignacio Manuel Altamirano's writings. He questioned the benefits of the influence of French literature on Mexican literature.

In Spain as well as in Spanish America, the French novel introduced certain French flourishes into the conversation and affected writing style. Many peninsular as well as Spanish American critics have protested this despicable state of affairs. Although we may not desire a static language, closing the door on all the locutions that can enrich it (even though they derive from extraneous languages), we do want to guard against

corrupting its character. We don't want our lovely national language to
degenerate into a dialect of foreign tongues . . . The second problem with
reading foreign novels, French ones in particular, is that our people are
so drawn to the history and geography of other countries that they have
disdained their own.[22]

In light of the evidence of the novel, the military campaign against
Tomochic alerted Joaquín Clausell primarily because it was the first hot
news item of the administration newly elected to another four-year term.
Second, a friend and confrere was mobilized to Tomochic in October
1892: Frías, who had opted for a career in the army after graduating from
preparatory school in 1888. For anyone familiar with Zola, warfare's literary potential was obvious.

Writer José Juan Tablado was the first to point out that *Tomochic*
was a war novel, although he couldn't have realized what for us today
is fundamental: *Tomochic* was the first novel of its kind written by an
author of his generation. In his comments of 1895, he mentioned the
first edition of *Tomochic* in book form, published a year earlier in Rio
Grande City, Texas. "Let the battle begin. It's mystical, unbelievable, epic."

"War has been studied from every possible perspective," wrote
Amado Nervo in an 1898 column for *La Semana*. "Economic, political,
philosophical, etc. . . . But apparently nobody thought of it as literary
potential." France's example served to illustrate the obvious. Since the
battle of Sédan in 1870, Nervo wrote, war "has contributed its quota
to a huge library, even counting only the wealth of novels, poems, and
stories inspired by the epochal conjunction of Frederick the Great's
descendants." He added, "Without counting *La Débâcle, El Año
terrible*, and *Napoleón el pequeño*, along with all the other books as
fervent as those which have enjoyed the high privilege of becoming
universal, there is an entire literature which is fever-inducing, picturesque, suggestive, and at times tendentious as well. It emerged out of
the great European conflagration the way the opulent transparency of
glass emerges from powerful flames."

Written the year preceding Maucci's inaugural edition of *Tomochic*,
Nervo's comments went to the heart of the matter when he pointed out
"that those who set their criteria by the facts have written exquisite truths."
Going even further, he writes, "War is a great source of divine and horrible tragedies, admirable poetry, grand events: a red factory of episodes
that are always new and thrilling."[23]

The novelized chronicle was a source for protagonists and a text for
history in literature's glass decanter. In the gesture that confers the past's

future on the word, impotence in the face of power is gleaned. As we know, the past has a future only in so far as the word that preserves it does. Memory was at the center of numerous writings that authors sent walking down the tightrope of letters: remembered stories, rescued, invented. This explains the indifference to literary formulas among authors of some of these writings. To preserve before recreating and constructing meaning was the watchword in hundreds of historical/testimonial pages that only loosely fit within the category of novels. Even when the greatest took up their pens to write within this form divided between document and the literature, they considered themselves first preservers, then creators. These are works that retain the instinctive emotion of the witness, chock-full of external facts, sources for the theatrical and the true. Apparently Vicente Riva Palacio commented favorably that one could find information in the works of Juan Antonio Mateos unavailable in Mexican history books.[24] It was different for strictly literary works; in them, when real adventures occur, the writers of the nineteenth century rarely used anything from the history of their moving and dangerous present.

The influence of Zola and the *La Débâcle* imprint on *Tomochic*, revealed so lucidly by Clausell, instilled the new work with exceptional qualities. Not only did it reveal that Zola was the model, but that *Tomochic* was more literature than history, although both had brought it into being. More often than not, reality with all its imperfections inspired our writers to imagine scenarios that were distinct from their surroundings and improved them. The three-month run of *El Demócrata* is emblematic of such optimism. Back then, the reality of being a public figure familiarized writers with a disenchantment that became a stimulus: total marginalization. Notwithstanding the knowledge, enthusiasm, and culture of the literary youth at the end of the century, their access to a public forum was negligible. They spent their early years in the usual artistic stupor of their projects and hangouts. Art for art's sake was less artistic credo than it was social alibi. With the fractiousness of Mexican society during the century, especially its last decade, the intelligentsia's activities were perceived as superfluous. Then there was illiteracy, indifference. Intellectual property rights didn't exist. There was no marketplace of books, no readers, no readings. As José Antonio Tablada pointed out, in Mexico, as in Russia, "France mitigated much crudeness and softened the blows of many barbaric acts."[25] What's more, in the case of *Tomochic*, this influence allowed barbarism to be named, known, and interpreted.

The Other Side and the Plot

Military officials involved in the interrogation that kept Lieutenant Heriberto Frías, a member of the 9th Infantry Battalion, locked up and isolated for more than four months, were confident that exposing the identity of the writer of *Tomochic* would be easy. Joaquín Clausell resolved the matter of the anonymous authorship that had initiated the legal proceedings when he assumed responsibility for writing *Tomochic* at the first interrogation. Clausell's answers exonerated the imprisoned Lieutenant and pointed to the case's resolution.

Nothing could have been easier for Clausell than explaining the origins of this up-to-the-minute novelized chronicle. One thing was Tomochic in the mountains, the hamlet that federal shrapnel almost decimated, and another was the Tomochic in the unexpected literary representation in the newspaper *El Demócrata*. Clausell not only expressed himself forthrightly behind Belem bars as many times as he was called on to testify, but showed the investigators his hand in the creation of *Tomochic* by referring to Zola's narrative model.

Once the debt to Zola was acknowledged, the investigator with sufficient patience to compare the two stories—in the pages of *Diario del Hogar* and *El Demócrata*—wouldn't have found a direct correlation with *La Débâcle* in *Tomochic's* installments.

At first glance, this investigator would have determined that Clausell's answers contradicted themselves. To attempt a parallel reading of both writings would have made the case for the individual features of each. Abundant unique details point to a clear distinction between the two. In the first place, what could a three-volume novel of 400 pages each in the *Diario del Hogar* have in common with the account in twenty-four installments in *El Demócrata*?[26] The investigator would have noted immediately the difference in the tens of thousands of soldiers mobilized in the war between France and Germany and the tens of hundreds of federal soldiers deployed in the war against Tomochic. These differences were readily available in the two works, emblematic of the imbalance in military might of the two countries. Without a doubt, the latter would have also brought to mind the unexpected Mexican military victory over the French several decades earlier.

The heart of the military episodes is so similar that that the modest investigator wouldn't have been surprised at finding echoes in *Tomochic* of the judgments and descriptions of the unpreparedness and disaffection of the mobilized forces in *La Débâcle*. If Zola proclaimed that "the all-pervasive demoralization finalized the job of converting this army into an undisciplined mob that didn't believe in anything, carried along haphazardly to the slaughterhouse," in *Tomochic* one read that "the greatest anguish of that terrible situation—more than the atrocious uncertainty about the enemy's position, force and number—was the lack of guidance, orientation, and orders from above." It's worth wondering if the investigator would perceive the similarities between the scene in chapter 5, where the soldier Maurice Levasseur, posted to guard duty in "a night black as ink," waits much as Lieutenant Miguel Mercado does in the middle of the account, stiff from fear, the arrival of an enemy column that turns out to be from his own company.

A parallel reading of the two stories might have put the two narrative modalities in *Tomochic* into relief; one corresponding to a fraternal voice, "full of indulgent affection" (Zola) toward all the soldiers of the federal army involved in this campaign (the same tone of the two poems Frías wrote in the military camp), and the other tonality, a voice more critical toward the acts described and revealed. For example, in one of the first encounters, we read, "The smoke of the gunpowder, clamor of gunshot, whistling of bullets and the ferocious cries of the enemy surrounding him on all sides made that corner of the mountain a vertiginous country, a disaster zone."

The merit of the twenty-four installments, if one concedes they have merit, was to make a consistent whole from disperse and contradictory information. The example of *La Débâcle*, to which Juan Antonio Mateos had already succumbed in his musical *Sédan*, helped interpret the news and war dispatches that came from Tomochic.

The force of verisimilitude in *Tomochic* is taken for granted. But one must remember that in the eyes of military officers involved in this judicial knot and held up to the critical view of the rest of society, this didn't just work against the prestige of the military but went against the version told by official war records. As reported in *El Monitor Republicano*, toward the end of May 1893, a colonel and a second captain from the special forces of general staff left for Chihuahua together to draw up maps of Tomochic and Temósachic.[27] The fictional mountains in *Tomochic*—as these emissaries must have discovered if they found out why they were drawing the maps—not only didn't correspond with some of the details given by military chiefs about the battles against the rebels, but they didn't even coincide with the geography of the scene. Of course, accuracy would have been expected were Frías the eyewitness alluded to in *El Demócrata*—indeed the author of *Tomochic*, as the investigators wanted to prove. When they reread, reevaluated, and reinterpreted a past episode in the light of pressing current concerns, these two emissaries from general staff were doing precisely what historians do. What's more, a hundred years after the emissaries' cartographic mission, historian Fernand Braudel reminds us that scenery and topography are more than simple present realities; they are remnants from the past: "We constantly redraw and re-create yesterday's lost horizons; the earth, just like our skin, is condemned to bear the scars of ancient wounds."[28]

At a century's remove from this chronicle written by an "eyewitness" in the pages of *El Demócrata*, how can we explain the discrepancies between the minutely detailed descriptions of certain scenes and the topographical evidence? The discrepancies between reality and the description should have been so numerous as to be apparent to the eyes of the general staff emissaries. The colorful, woody disorder of the mountains is not apparent today in the Cordón de Lino foothills where the first column succumbed to the Tomochic fighters. Maybe we should see its aridity today not as an error of the account but rather a scar over an old wound, to follow Braudel. But how do we explain that in the description of so decisive a moment as the assault on the so-called Cerro de la Cueva—where Pedro Chaparro and his forces kept the federal forces at bay—it is said that the church tower at a certain point disappeared "behind the first hills of the mountain . . . entering into the blind spot of the line of fire," when those hills don't exist. And it was from that same tower that the Tomochic fighters could have opened fire freely on the troops of the daring Captain Eduardo Molino in their ascent, since the blind spot didn't exist. How to explain this error if Frías, who not only camped several days in Tomochic but participated in the capture of Cerro de Cueva on Tuesday, October 25, 1892, was really the anonymous witness?

This situation can perhaps be explained by considering the possibility that someone like Clausell, different from the eyewitness Frías, completed the account somewhere else, far from Chihuahua and the mountains. Clausell's words were the key. And that is how it has remained ever since.

The literary re-creation of the military campaign gave the geography of the terrain an important role in the text. The details of the setting were more relevant in *El Demócrata* than in any official report. Besides sometimes contradicting the territorial realities, the novelized geographical descriptions sought to exercise an explicit function that operated outside the factual evidence: to represent the historicity of the nineteenth-century moment in a form that could attain the prestige of art. The historian's faithfulness couldn't compete with the novelist's, no matter how naturally or realistically the former laid out his cards. The cultural prestige of literature went beyond the could-be of history. With Clausell's admissions, the legal inquiry made little sense. According to Clausell's confession, the eyewitness, initially introduced as the author in *El Demócrata*, was part of the fiction. How to prove to Clausell that *Tomochic* hadn't come from his pen? Literature re-creates with authority without the obligation of looking at things the way they really happened. Clausell's sources were verifiable—it was enough to take a glance at the press in the capital. What's to be done, Frías's military investigators would have asked themselves, when even the official Chihuahua State paper published a war dispatch signed by General Rosendo Márquez? The references to Zola must have meant little to the law, but that didn't make Clausell's idea any less plausible. In terms of material evidence the first inquiry at *El Demócrata*, as well as at Clausell's house, only delivered up a pair of typewritten fragments of the Tomochic campaign, plus four letters from Chihuahua—one signed by Francisco Montes de Oca, perhaps the newspaper's anonymous correspondent, that related the news of the uprising led by Simón Amaya. The letters written by the people cited by Clausell—Pedro Ortega and Leoncio Buenfield—never surfaced, nor did the whereabouts of these two informants.

Finally, the inquiry tacitly recognized Clausell as the author of *Tomochic* since there were no grounds to insist on Frías's responsibility. Given the subsequent history of the novel and the discrepancies already mentioned between the campaign scenes and the written version that fixed it in memory, it's practically impossible to overlook the close collaboration between Clausell and Frías in the creation of *Tomochic*, the young classic of Mexican literature.

The Novel and the Shadows

Gradually Heriberto Frías's shadow fell across the pages of the novelized chronicle of the campaign. The author of the first commentary on *Tomochic*, in the newspaper *El Tiempo* (1894), reflected on the calculating, singular silence of anonymity. He also indicated that it was "an almost disgraceful edition (since it's from Río Grande City), and very humble." He went on to say, "Because *Tomochic* is really an unpolished gem, a work of art that lacks perfection in the details, however it is not beyond repair." What a pity, said this anonymous critic, that the author won't reveal his name. Shortly thereafter, José Juan Tablada commented on the book's author. He's a young man, he claimed, "given to the linguistic improprieties suggestive of Zola, which sometimes undermines his syntax; nevertheless he doesn't enter competitions, nor does he spy on the workings of other people's brains, nor is he the furtive recorder of long-winded conversations. And he doesn't thread into the intrigues in his writing the phrases that fall from the lips of friends." Indeed, feeling, boldness, and originality place this author in the first rung "of young literary voices who have recently written novels," Tablada claimed. Inevitably dated by *El Universal's* novel-writing competition, for readers unaware of the journalistic secret of the day, Tablada's comments helped color in a picture of *Tomochic's* author. José Ferrel wrote a less useful commentary that was published on February 16, 1895. It was also published in the new *El Demócrata*, as were Tablada's comments. After a year and four months of prison time, Ferrel was released from Belem on a Monday in 1894, along with Antonio Rivera and Jésus Huelgas y Campos. Shortly thereafter, he announced his intention of returning to the editorship of the paper at the behest of Clausell.[29] Using the pseudonym Fidias, Ferrel posited four possible authors for *Tomochic*: Emilio Rabasa, Rafael Delgado, Emile Zola, and Alphonse Daudet.

The Texas edition of *Tomochic* did little more than stir the waters in which the trial to resolve the identity of its author floated. For many years the author remained anonymous, despite the fact that the new *El Demócrata's* editors permitted themselves the indiscretion of suggesting that Frías was its author. First the paper reproduced various chapters from the book, affixing the ex-lieutenant's name at the bottom between question marks. Then when publishing installments of *Naufragio*, the long novel Frías wrote in Belem, the newspaper accompanied the heading with a notice to entice readers by identifying it as a work by the author of *Tomochic*.[30]

The novel reappeared on the turn-of-the-century literary scene when Rubén M. Campos dedicated ten long articles to authors and works of Mexican realism. Published in *El Nacional* beginning on the first Sunday of April 1897, these notes compiled a list of realistic authors as seen through the eyes of a peer and set forth an interpretation of realism in light of the death of Mexican romanticism.

The great Romantic concepts such as love, duty, charity, sacrifice, abnegation were swept away in the Realist hurricane and banished from the reflections and analysis of the combative young generation. Only evil, vice, poverty, death and nothingness remained.

Humanity's great consolations disappeared: the great ideals of the sane and the insane, the glad and the unfortunate, the good and the bad among men, all were reduced to cinders. The last vestiges of hope were ripped from hearts, misfortunes were deprived of the last glimmers of their dreamlike clarity, perfection, and redemption. At last even love of life was banished from reality!

The cases under scrutiny were monstrous, terrible. The characters who entered into action were all criminals and corrupt, forged by perversion or illness. The women prostituted themselves and the men were traitors. The children begged alms for vice. Old people succumbed throwing their cynical futility at life.

What was the rationale behind the new school? To patent human misery?[31]

The articles by Campos attempted to respond to this query. He looked at the works of Ciro B. Ceballos, Alberto Leduc, Amado Nervo, José Ferrel, Federico Gamboa, Luis G. Urbina, Manuel Larrañaga Portugal, Rafael Delgado, and, of course, Heriberto Frías. The latter had just published his novel *El último duelo*—Frías's version of the scandal that shook the Diaz capital when Francisco Romero and José Verástegui fought a duel in 1894. He kept the eighty-eight installments of *Naufragio*, published between June and November, under wraps. Frías's confreres knew about his work, as well as the information that was first made public in Campos's third article of the series on April 15 commenting on *Tomochic*:

The novelist's first creative flurry was spontaneous, unexpected, impassioned, and explosive. It went off like a grenade and *Tomochic's* dazzling, brilliant, breathless stanza-chapters burst out over the inhuman strategies of warfare like the crumbling cliffs of the Tarahumara Mountains. Its overpowering and honest narration exalted the courage of an obscure town where William Tell could have been born.

It was a merciless war of extermination, to the death; it was a hothouse where the novelist's early flowering and his eagerness for terrible events was tested. He made of the tragic episode a Homeric feat in which the burning of Tomochic is reminiscent of Troy.

Aeneas escaped from Troy with his father Anchises on his shoulders and his son Ascanius in arms. From this humble, razed, and plague-stricken Mexican village not one of its heroes escaped alive.

Campos's comments are more or less correct in terms of Tomochic. The few survivors wandered through Díaz's country like ghosts or maybe at some point they returned to their little valley. Those who had taken up arms died in combat or were shot. The town was destroyed and the female victims of the catastrophe were incarcerated. Even worse, and Campos didn't say this, toward the end of 1895—a crucial year for the disinherited nationals who were incorporated into the slave market through a Díaz administration initiative—the transfer of petty thieves and vagrants to Tomochic to repopulate and work the lands of this valley of death came up.

Campos continued:

Despite the discrepancies visible to criticism's wise eye, the novel of *Tomochic*, though disorderly and written in the bivouac, in the marches, and in moments stolen from guard duty, displays an intense truthfulness, a radiant clarity, and a quick unfolding of events. It exhibits a clairvoyant grasp of the heroic act judged as rebellion, single details are wisely studied to personify character, and apt brush strokes draw the landscape. Its psychological analysis is achieved with brevity and synthesis, with creativity, truth, and reality.[32]

But Frías's name didn't appear on the cover of *Tomochic* until 1899 in the Maucci edition of Barcelona. Finally, thanks to this book, the identification of its author came to a clear, satisfying resolution.

Ramón Gómez de la Serna wrote that the number of reprintings a book goes through is the novelist's gauge of literary success. Did the Maucci edition of *Tomochic* have that significance for Frías? Or, in the darkest hours, what did it mean to this unusual Mexican writer? In reality, we can hardly say. In 1893, when Joaquín Clausell's *El Demócrata* was born and Ignacio Manuel Altamirano died, copies of the first edition of *Clemencia* were still available, printed thirteen years earlier.[33] Nevertheless, the seven years between the military campaign and the Spanish edition of the account of Tomochic was a long span of time for the state as well as for vulnerable Citizen Frías. Perhaps by the end of the century this massacre appeared to be another barely intelligible fact in the slow decade leading to the modern world of the twentieth century.

During those years, Frías dedicated himself full-time to journalism in the capital. As far as we know, he earned his daily bread from the skimpy benefits obtained from the coffers of the Díaz-backed press writing articles on whatever came his way.

Frías had already assumed the venal vitalist diversions of the press, making its volunteerist bitter tone his own. He lived the fabulous promise of the rotary printing press and the severe punishments of serving the charter imposed by the government on the bold brotherhood of the pen. Frías took the raucous, artistic, self-destructive path, but despite his literary pretensions, week after week he cranked out stories, legends, and Mexican military episodes. Frías tried to rescue national stories and events from oblivion, first in *El Combate*, beginning in May 1897, and then in Rafael Reyes Spíndola's *El Imparcial* beginning in September of the same year. He did it as well as he could in the beggared style that the poorly paid journalism of the day earned, intoxicated by the fumes of morphine and his serious, sentimental, declamatory, incurable nationalism. The fuel for Frías's fervid passion for his country's history lasted until 1898. His immediate work consisted in putting together a portfolio of these odds and ends, which he then transformed into strange new titles, acknowledging them as his.

Maybe it was the Maucci Brothers edition of *Tomochic* that sent Frías back to the mountains, to the unnamable hamlet. In January 1900, the stylish, incendiary *Revista Moderna* printed a previously unpublished story by Frías, "Los perros de Tomochic," which was subsequently added as a chapter to the next edition of the novel. Later, in Frías's lifetime, Bernardo Ortiz de Montellano included the story in his 1924 *Antología de cuentos mexicanos*.[34]

The year 1900 was a good one for Frías. Maucci brought out his *Leyendas históricas mexicanas*, a compendium of his columns from the journalistic enterprises of Emilio García and Reyes Spíndola. Enjoying absolute freedom since the War Council's resolution of August 1893, Frías sued for a discharge from military service to the 3rd Infantry Battalion around the middle of November 1901. On orders from Porfirio Díaz, according to a communication from Bernardo Reyes, Secretary of War and Navy, to the captain of said battalion, Martín Luis Guzmán, Lieutenant Frías remained a commissioned officer in the infantry department of the war and navy ministry. He worked there until the beginning of February 1903.[35]

The identity of *Tomochic's* author resurfaced with the publication of the first edition of Francisco I. Madero's declaration on *La sucesión presidencial de 1910*, where in commenting on the proof of absolute power in Mexico he mentions the events of Guerrero, Chihuahua. Without mentioning him by name, he cites the brave, honorable officer who narrated the military campaign against the civilian population.

What edition was Madero referring to? The Rio Grande City one? The Spanish one? A collection from *El Demócrata?* Madero probably didn't read the novel, nor was he familiar with the Spanish edition. He must have passed over the Texas edition and the first national edition as well, put out in 1906 by Valdés publishers for El Correo de la Tarde in Mazatlán, Sinaloa. This is the only explanation for the manner in which Madero wrote to Frías on Wednesday, February 24, 1909:

Honorable Sir,
 I have just received your gracious fifteenth installment which I have read with great emotion because of its eloquent poetry.
 I already knew that you were the officer involved in the Tomochic affair. And if I didn't say anything more, it was because I hadn't known that you had also been on the point of being condemned to death.
 If I bring out another edition, as is very probable, then I will be very careful about making that fact known.[36]

Madero kept his word. The subsequent editions of *La sucesión presidencial de 1910* did Frías no injustice. In the meantime the author became a shadow of himself. He was the owner of a speaking mask that one day spoke under the name of Heriberto Frías.

NOTES

1. The theses of two graduates of the National Autonomous University of Mexico, David López Peimbert ("Tomóchic," 1963) and José María Lujan ("Relato de un incidente," 1965) undoubtedly contributed to the renewed interest in the events in Tomochic, although the main stimulus was in large part due to the edition prepared by James W. Brown, *Tomóchic* (Mexico: Porrúa, 1968). Together they attracted new readers, new research, and readings of the main literature. Examples include: Aguirre, Lauro. *Peleando en Tomóchic* (El Paso, 1896); Almada, Francisco R. *La rebelión de Tomochi* (Chihuahua: Sociedad Chihuahense de Estudios Históricos, 1938); Chávez, Josè Carlos, *Peleando en Tomochi* (Ciudad Juárez: Imprenta Moderna, 1955); Chávez Calderón, Plácido, *La defensa de Tomóchic* (Mexico: Jus, 1964). Paul J. Vanderwood, who dedicated a few pages to the matter in *Disorder and Progress: Bandits, Police and Mexican Development* (Lincoln, NE: University of Nebraska Press, 1981), took up the theme again in "None but the Justice of God; Tomóchic, 1891–1892" in Jaime O. Rodríguez (ed.) *Patterns of Contention in Mexican History* (Wilmington, DE: Scholarly Resources, Inc., 1992). Some more recent studies are Pozo Marrero,

Acalia, *Dos movimientos populares en el noroeste de Chihuahua* (Universidad Iberoamericana, 1991); Osorio, Rubén, *Cruz Chávez: Los tomoches en armas* (Chihuahua: Universidad Autónoma de Ciudad Juárez, 1991); *Tomóchic en llamas* (CNCA: Mexico, 1995); Illades Aguilar, Liliana, *La rebelión de Tomóchic* (Mexico, 1993); Vargas Valdés Jesús (ed.) *Tomóchic: La revolución adellantada* (Ciudad Juárez, 1994); Saborit, Antonio, *Los doblados de Tomóchic. Un episodio de historia y literatura* (Mexico: Cal y Arena, 1994). Vanderwood again took up the theme in *The Power of God and the Guns of Government: Religious Upheaval in Mexico at the Turn of the Nineteenth Century* (Stanford University Press, 1998).

2. For the details of Heriberto Frías's military career, see Saborit, *Los doblados de Tomóchic*, pp. 55–74, 88–107, 137–148, and 165–169.

3. "Juicio de una alemán sobre *La débacle*. Opinión de *Le Figaro*," *El Universal*, October 26, 1892.

4. "Las obras de Zola," *El Universal*, November 22, 1892.

5. Sr. Mateos is writing a drama that will be called *Sedan: A stimulus*. Zola writes *La débacle* and Mateos calls him a *tecolote* in his play, "Un poco de claro oscuro," *Mexico Gráfico*, August 14, 1892.

6. Ángel Pola, "How Pedro Castera wrote Carmen," *El Partido Liberal*, January 15, 1893.

7. "Sedán," *El Universal*, January 7, 1893.

8. Mathilde Reyes, "Joaquín Clausell, pintor, periodista y luchador incansable de la no-reelección." *Querétero*, May 1990. This article is based on a piece by Gabriel González Mier, a friend and contemporary of Clausell, although the author did not divulge her sources.

9. Information on the anti-reelection demonstrations comes from "La manifestación antirreeleccionista de los estudiantes," *Diario del Hogar* (April 8, 1893), and the quotation on the Gabriel González Mier episode and the rest of the biographical information come from "Centenario del nacimiento de la libertad en Francia, 1793–1893—Mexico. Centenario de la libertad de pensamiento en el mundo moderno. Joaquín Clausell." *Diario del Hogar*, June 25, 1893.

10. "El Demócrata," *El Monitor Republicano*, February 1, 1893.

11. "Las diez plagas de México," *El Demócrata*, February 14, 1893.

12. "La campaña de Tomóchic . . . Soon to appear in the columns of El Demócrata," *El Demócrata*, February 2, 1893.

13. "Tomóchic! Episodios de campaña (Relación escrita por un testigo presencial)," *El Demócrata*, March 14, 1893.

14. "Episodios de la campaña de Tomóchic," *El Monitor Repyblicano*, March 12, 1893.

15. Secretaría de la Defensa Nacional. Dirección General de Archivo e Historia, Archivo de Cancelados, Frías Alcocer, Heriberto (henceforward SDN/DGAH/AC/FAH)XI/111/9-144457), f. 19.

16. José Emilio Pacheco, *Poesía Modernista: Una antología general* (Mexico: SEP/UNAM, 1982) pp. 5–6. See also his prologue to Marcel Schwob, *Vidas*

imaginarias. La cruzada de los niños (Mexico: Porrúa, Colección Sepan Cuantos 603, 1991).

17. SDN/DGAH/AC/FAH, XI/iii/9-14457, f. 4.

18. Concepción Lombardo de Miramón, *Memorias*. Prologue and some notes by Felipe Teixidor, 2nd edition (Mexico, Editorial Porrúa, 1989), pp. 33–34.

19. Frias's aptitude test and his civil and military conduct are found in SDN/DGAH/AC/FAH, XI/iii/9-14457, ff. 23–80.

20. Rubén M. Campos, "La literatura realista mexicana iii. Tomóchic, Naufragio, El último duelo de Heriberto Frías," *El Nacional*, April 18, 1897, pp. 2–3; SDN/DGAH/AC/FAH, Xi/iii/9-144457, f. 12; in f. 110, the letter according to which Sublieutenant Frías—accused of assault—was remanded in the custody of the prison judge from Thursday, July 2, 1891.

21. SDN/DGAH/AC/FAH, iX/iii/9-14457, f. 175.

22. "Revistas literarias de México (1821–1867)," José Luis Martínez (ed.), *Escritos de literatura y arte*, volume i of *Obras completas* (Mexico: SEP, 1988).

23. Amado Nervo, "10 de mayo de 1898," *Obras completas* i, p. 792.

24. See the prefatory notes by Clementina Díaz y de Ovando in Juan A. Mateos, *El Sol de Mayo. Memorias de la Intervención* (Mexico: Porrúa, Colección Sepan cuantos 197), p. xi.

25. José Juan Tablada, "La feria de la vida," *Lecturas Mexicanas* 22, Tercera Serie (Mexico: CNCA, 1991), p. 148.

26. "El Desastre," in *Diario del Hogar*, August 4, 1893. In this note the journal announced the end of the second part and the beginning of the third in the magazine section, as well as advertising the publication of the complete work in three volumes at a price of 50 centavos. However, the *Diario del Hogar* suspended the publication of Zola's novel on January 31, 1894, on page 166 of the third part.

27. "Tomóchic y Temósachic," *El Monitor Republicano*, May 23, 1893.

28. Fernand Braudel, "History and Environment," *The Identity of France*, volume i, trans. Sian Reynolds (New York: HarperCollins, 1988), p. 31.

29. "En libertad," *Diario del Hogar*, August 1, 1894.

30. "Naufragio. Novela del autor de Tomóchic. Costumbres mexicanas," *El Demócrata*, June 21, 1895, to November 7, 1895.

31. Rubén M. Campos, "La literatura realista mexicana," *El Nacional*, April 4, 1897.

32. Rubén M. Campos, "La literatura realista mexicana iii. Tomóchic, Naufragio, El úlltimo duelo," *El Nacional*, April 18, 1897.

33. Advertisements in *Diario del Hogar*, July 1893.

34. Heriberto Frías, "Los perros de Tomóchic." *Revista Moderna*, January 1900.

35. SDN/DGAH/AC/FAH, Xi/iii/9-14457, ff. 138, 139, 141, 144, and 147.

36. Francisco I. Madero. Archive of don Francisco I. Madero 2, Epistolario (1900–1909), eds Agustín Yáez and Catalina Sierra (Mexico: Ediciones de la Secretaría de Hacienda, 1963), p. 325.

THE BATTLE OF
TOMOCHIC

CHAPTER 1

Truth and Falsehood

A molten sun beat down on the decaying plaza, inducing a deathlike peace in the furnace of the day.

It was two o'clock in the afternoon. Miguel Mercado, a young second lieutenant with the 9th Battalion, stood at the far end of a side street leading into the desolate square and squinted at the city gates to his left. He wore a uniform of light cotton twill, and his shoes were white with dust; a kerchief was draped down over his shoulders to ward off the scorching sun.

Directly in front of him stood the ancient fortress walls. More than anything, they struck Miguel as gloomy and sad. To his right, the uneven profile of the squat church steeple was outlined against an azure sky. A few houses with sparkling white facades rose up alongside the small, neglected church.

At the center of the deserted plaza was a square bench surrounded by a garden of eight to ten skeletal trees whose scrawny branches sought the sky. Some garden! Holding his baby-smooth, sunburned face rigid, Miguel contemplated the desolate plaza, the only one in Guerrero City, with an air of wrath and ennui.

"And they call this a city," muttered Miguel.

Half dead with hunger, the second lieutenant set out looking for an inn or a shop. With each strutting stride, his saber rattled as rhythmically as clinking coins in its sheath. Passing through the shady archway of the town gates, Mercado caught sight of a few ramshackle shops with shelves stacked with glistening, multihued bottles.

The second lieutenant went in the double doors of a spacious shop swarming with weathered, long-haired men dressed in white shirts, coarse cloth pants, and antelope-hide boots. When he asked for a shot of tequila, it was silently set before him along with a glass of water.

"Say, friend, where can I find an inn?" said Miguel to a man who drained his tequila in a single gulp. The giant of a man with rumpled hair and a matted beard shrugged and turned away.

"Couldn't say," the man replied contemptuously, swigging back a glass of sotol.

Miguel could hardly contain his sense of outrage. Since their arrival in Chihuahua, he and every other officer had been treated to the same combination of brutish contempt and arrogance.

The man's boorishness enraged Miguel. After eating nothing but flour tortillas and roasted beef for six days, he was looking forward to broth, beans, chili—the plainest of meals. Today he'd had nothing to eat except a thick flour tortilla for breakfast. There was nothing for him to do but drink up. Trembling with a ferocious thirst, he drained his tequila in one gulp.

The sound of spurs clanking against flagstones and the familiar metallic rattling of a saber made him turn around. There was Gerardo, a boyish, good-natured lieutenant from general staff, whom he'd known in Mexico City. Framed by his cap and the protective white kerchief tucked into his black hussar's jacket, Gerardo's face was broad, with high color. He sported white pants and stiff riding boots, and he was so short his saber almost dragged behind him on the ground. Recognizing Miguel, Gerardo approached and called out joyously:

"Hey, Mercado. I didn't think I'd meet you here!" The two embraced affectionately, slapping each other heartily on the back as though knocking off the dust of the road.

"What are you having, brother? What will it be?"

"Nothing more to drink, but can we eat something around here?"

"I'm headed for the inn. But first you and I are going to drink a couple of tequilas. Two tall ones, Don Pedro!"

Talking a mile a minute, Gerardo enthusiastically waylaid the officer from the 9th Battalion, who was growing more irritated by the moment. "You must know this already! I'm over at general staff with General Rangel. Now we're going to get to show what we're made of. You'll see how we thrash those Tomochic devils. They're a brave bunch of men. That can't be denied. I swear I thought they were all bluster at first. But they are brave, and quick as deer. One moment they're here, and the next they're way over on the mountaintop. 'Glory to God and death to the soldiers,' and then *pow* . . . damn, and they don't even take aim. One glimpse and they'll shoot you dead. I swear that for every empty cartridge there's a dead man. Just imagine the state I was in when they put the general and me to the test. Here's to your health, brother."

"Here's to yours." Still overwrought, Miguel ordered another round. Grudgingly he gave in to the consolation afforded by the vile Chihuahua tequila.

Miguel leaned on the damp, dirty countertop as the little lieutenant's booming voice carried over the jokes and general revelry of the other officers as he recalled his many misadventures. He felt his cares melt away.

Then Miguel listened to the following account, as told by Gerardo, without comment:

On September 29, 1892, General Rangel attempted to attack the town of Tomochic. General Ramírez had already been wounded in the fray and Major Prieto and Lieutenant Manzano had been killed. Amid the confusion of the defeat, when General Rangel went in search of refuge, his horse was killed. Then some Tomochic fighters approached him, disarmed and then insulted him by whacking him on the ass.

"We don't fight little boys. Go back home to your mama," they told him, and left him swooning with fear.

Mercado smiled at the irreverent tale. He knew that even though it was based on the facts of the defeat, it could be considered slanderous.

Miguel retorted, "They say you all took a real beating on September 2."

"They're lying! What beating? What happened was they shot my horse. The bullet came out of the blue. I fell on the mountainside and hit my head, and was left for dead. It's a miracle that I'm alive to tell it."

"Well, that's not what they told us in Chihuahua. But it just goes to show. People will say anything! Now let's eat. This damned tequila is going to my head."

"Tequila! Dream on! It's raw sotol and rotgut. Okay, let's get going. I should warn you that the guys from the 11th Battalion will be there

3

and from the 5th Regiment as well. You don't know them, but you'll see soon enough what a rowdy time they can have."

The pair left the shop revitalized, talking a mile a minute. Together they crossed the forlorn plaza shimmering in the heat beneath an intense blue sky.

CHAPTER 2

How Lovely!

Second Lieutenant Mercado stopped inside the doorway of the inn and listened to the pleasant sound of loud voices and laughter surging above the clatter of dishes and the clinking of forks and knives on plates and glasses.

He balked when he saw some twenty military men seated at a long table. Their faces gritty and dark, all but a few of the men talked, ate, and drank.

The place was more of a shop than a tavern or an inn. The shelves were crammed with empty bottles and the long countertop, covered with a greasy cloth and crowded with plates and beer bottles, served as a table.

Miguel recognized the military men as high-ranking officers of the 5th Regiment, the 11th Battalion, and the public security forces of Chihuahua.

"This place is swarming with superiors," he said nervously to Gerardo, but the lieutenant grabbed Mercado by the arm and pulled him in. There was still plenty of room at one end of the long counter, and as the two sat down, the little lieutenant yelled out, "Cuca, two plates."

Nobody even noticed the arrival of the two young men. Thoughtfully, Miguel listened to the conversation that surged noisily in the wake of satisfied hunger.

As he cast his eyes around at the contented faces, Miguel recognized his worst enemy, Second Lieutenant Castorena of the 9th Battalion, a chubby adolescent with an unusually deep voice and a head of saffron-colored ringlets. For no particular reason, Miguel politely loathed him.

As appetites were sated, there was more drinking and talking as a mildly inebriated Castorena improvised toasts in rapid-fire verse. A smattering of applause came from some, while others continued to exchange desultory chatter.

Two overworked serving girls came and went carrying plates and bottles of beer. Fair and tall, they wore dresses of white percale and had red kerchiefs tied around their necks.

"One thing's for sure," began a lieutenant wearing a corsair's uniform and sporting a thick gray mustache, from the 11th Battalion. "Things are starting to heat up. The time is right. We've got enough men to make mincemeat out of them. Give us an hour . . . the dust won't even have time to settle."

"More like twenty minutes, comrade," countered a major.

"Colonel Torres is coming from Sonora with a hundred men from the 11th Battalion and a group of Pima Indians who are primed for action and know those mountains like the back of their hand."

Then he recounted the reasons for the September 2 defeat to the captain of the Ninth, who was sitting across from him. The attack had not been well planned and the terrain was unfamiliar. And then there was the inexplicable betrayal by Santa Ana Perez. It was said that he had shamelessly defected to the enemy side, along with more than sixty men from the Chihuahua state forces.

"Major, sir," chimed in Castorena. "Are these men actually what they're made out to be? Up and down the state of Chihuahua that's all you hear anymore . . . some even say that bullets don't penetrate their flesh."

"Comrade, they're ferocious. Their Winchesters are second nature to them. They've fought Apaches and outlaws their entire lives. They can run blindfolded through the mountains without faltering once. But they're an ignorant, insolent lot. They've never been truly educated, but they're determined to free themselves from the only two powers they've obeyed up to now: the clergy and the government. It's a mad fixation with them. Where do they get these ideas? They refuse to recognize any authority; attempts have been made to reason with them, but they ask for the impossible. We have to finish them off once and for all. It's cruel but necessary. They must be put down!"

At that moment the smiling Cuca, a plump little woman with beautiful black eyes, brought Gerardo and Miguel two bowls of steaming soup, which both men slurped up noisily. Then they waited patiently for the next course to be served, while listening to the major discuss the enemies they were going to vanquish in Tomochic.

Though the major expressed himself rationally and reasonably, Second Lieutenant Mercado remained perplexed. He couldn't imagine why that ignorant lot persisted in rebelling. By nature both skeptical and astute, Miguel Mercado thought he smelled a rat.

With beer running down his dusty jacket, his face purple, Castorena suddenly stood up, raised his glass, and cried out:

> Yes, indeed, we'll put an end
> To their fanatic prancing.
> To Tomochic! We'll win the day
> Then do our own hard-won dancing.

This vulgar toast was enthusiastically received by all except Second Lieutenant Mercado. Castorena's crude humor was not to his liking.

Glasses were next raised in honor of the brave men who were defending the government, which, according to the major, represented "order, peace, civilization, and so forth." Then the major respectfully toasted "General Porfirio Díaz, the triumphant rebuilder of the fatherland, and so on."[1]

Miguel listened while devouring a bloody slice of roasted meat. He was still uncomfortable in these noisy reunions among comrades thrown together by fate—perhaps on the eve of a great catastrophe.

It had been two years since Mercado entered the ranks of the 9th Battalion. After completing three years of engineering at the military academy, he was forced by dire family circumstances to give up his studies, along with his melancholy bohemian existence, and go directly into military service.

A single fateful turn of events had forever cut him off from the beautiful future he had dreamed of. What had happened was this: His mother separated from her second husband, who had abused her. Sick and penniless, she was bound for the poorhouse when Miguel intervened, volunteering for the military so that he could relieve her destitution—on his miserable second lieutenant's wages. He had intended to continue his studies in his free time but found it was impossible. He fell into bad habits, hit the bottle instead of the book, and became a drunk.

The monotony of garrison life made him lazy, and for a long time he didn't even open a book. Under the rugged discipline of barracks life, Mercado sank into the lonely oblivion of alcohol.

His intelligence, his imagination, and his fine feelings didn't flourish amid the banalities of military life. He could solve problems involving the subtlest of calculations or debate the laws of war, but he was at a total loss when commanding a platoon of soldiers. Indeed, he cut a very poor figure as an officer.

Moreover, his physical makeup at that time was very delicate. He was exceedingly thin, pale, and nervous. His face was long like an old man's—how ironic for someone in the full bloom of youth—and sadness inhabited those large green eyes. In short, Miguel Mercado inspired nothing so much as pity and contempt.

With his eternal melancholy, he was something of an exotic flower in this happy-go-lucky atmosphere. The battalion was made up of boisterous youths and daredevils who were, nonetheless, gallant and dedicated servicemen, fine sons of the military academy.

Mercado vainly tried to be as jocular and fun loving as the other soldiers. Though they treated him with scorn, deep down they were fond of him. But try as he might, he could not fraternize with men who made him the butt of their cruel jokes even as he acknowledged them as superior soldiers. And their trivial conversations irritated him.

On that day Mercado contemplated his empty plate in silent melancholy amid the continuing blasts of beer kegs being opened. When a glass of beer overflowing with foam was passed to him, Mercado forced himself to his feet to make a timid toast, cup in hand: "Gentlemen," he said, "I toast to the triumph of our government forces, to the quelling of all rebellion, to law and order which represents peace and progress."[2]

Glasses clinked, splattering the coarse tablecloth. A heavy silence reigned in the warm, humid establishment while these noble sentiments hung in the air.

Just then a tall young woman came into the hall. Slender and agile, the girl wore her hair in a thick braid down her back. She was dressed in a berry-colored wool skirt, and a black- and red-checked shawl was draped across her shoulders. Miguel was unable to get a good look at this graceful girl's face as she quickly crossed the room and disappeared into the kitchen.

A serving girl removed the officer's empty plate, replacing it with another of beans, and murmured in his ear, "That girl is from Tomochic, and they say she is St. Joseph's daughter."

As Mercado prepared to ask for more details, a lieutenant from general staff, who was standing by the door next to Cuca, the proprietress, exclaimed, "There's a roll call at headquarters. Let's get going!"

There was a great flurry as the men rose, pushing back their chairs, downing the last drops of beer, and wiping their mouths on the tablecloth. Then the men paid Cuca three reales each.[3]

While waiting for his five-centavo bill in change, Miguel, who was the last to leave, approached the kitchen door.[4] Beneath the clatter of plates and silverware he heard a gentle voice tinged with melancholy softly intone these words: "Yes, Don Bernardo says that the day after tomorrow we're heading for Tomochic. Blessed Mary!"

As he turned to leave, letting his sword belt out a notch, Mercado carried the luminous impression of the graceful girl with him. So, St. Joseph's daughter was also on her way to Tomochic.

Thinking about her grace, her rhythmic walk, and all her adolescent charms, Mercado felt a breath of fresh air enter his lungs in the swelter of midday, and he murmured, "How lovely!"

CHAPTER 3

Heroic Troops

On the dreary afternoon of October 3, 1892, Mercado sat at the common table in a cantina in the Peralvillo district of Mexico City. After he had eaten, he put the finishing touches on an eloquent letter to his mother.

He cherished his mother, who was currently staying with a woman friend in Tacubaya, and had sacrificed his education at the military academy for her. Meanwhile, her second husband was in the grips of a newly acquired vice—gambling—and was leading the jaded, perverse life of an adventurer. To think of his mother in the arms of such a man!

Miguel, more pale than ever, was full of melancholy thoughts that October afternoon. On the verge of tears, he folded his letter, wrote the address on the envelope, and then, leaning his elbows on the table, he drifted into a reverie when suddenly a corporal appeared at his side. The battalion adjutant had ordered Miguel to report immediately to the barracks across the street from the inn.

Mercado was stunned to discover that half the battalion was leaving by train for Chihuahua that very night. Miguel asked no questions, however, and a few hours later, in a train compartment crammed with soldiers and their gear, he was traveling at top speed as the train devoured kilometers at an impossible rate. Dumbfounded, he listened to the clap, clap of the iron wheels on the rails whenever the sliding door opened in a cold flash of noise and shadows. Miguel had never traveled, and he was ecstatic to be thrust into new sensations, possibly a new life. After a trip of two days and two nights they arrived in Chihuahua. At eight o'clock on the second night he found himself in front of the deserted railway station, standing in formation for several hours with his two companies.

Flanked by the rows of soldiers, he finally crossed the city, where he found a good night's rest waiting for him. The next day, while talking with officers from another battalion, he reflected on what was going on in the state of Chihuahua.

A renegade group had taken up arms against the government and they were making a defiant stand in the heart of the Sierra Madre mountains. Many officers had died in the fighting, and Lieutenant Colonel Ramírez of the 11th Battalion had been taken prisoner.

What kind of rebellion was this?

The rebels' cause seemed just, although their political objectives were unclear. Their bravery and gift for warfare, however, were legendary throughout the state. What's more, they were admirable, heroic, and had unsurpassed skills as marksmen.

At that time the inhabitants of Chihuahua were ignorant though brave and haughty. Their sullen antipathy toward the officer corps was replaced by extravagant praise when they referred to the sons of Tomochic. In fact they spoke of little else.

The Tomochic fighters were demigods; they were brave, confident, and invincible. These tigers of the mountains would vanquish all comers. Throughout the state of Chihuahua admirers exclaimed, *Oh yes!* and *How great and grand they are!*

Miguel was convinced that they were truly fearless, almost unimaginably so; their strategy was to target officers and commanders. The Tomochic warriors knew that once the leadership was out of the way, the troops would disband of their own accord; this had proven painfully true in the combat of September 2. Their triumph made them even haughtier, and from that day forward they believed that victory was certain.

Their leader, Cruz Chávez, preached a strange religion, a nonclerical Catholicism combined with extravagant ideas of saintliness typical of ignorant people lacking in culture, but all the same credulous and fierce. For the moment this was all Miguel could determine, although

9

he continued to speculate on the nature of this unique rebellion, as fool-hardy as it was heroic.

He wondered if opportunists were exploiting the bravery of these backwoods men. Were they offering them protection while stoking ancient enmities in their fierce, simple souls? Were they provoking them into battle against the sad valor of federal bayonets?

This was the inevitable topic of conversation. Names were mentioned that insinuated themselves mutely, malevolently throughout the district of Rayón and major regions of Chihuahua, and even made their way into the ranks of the bright, youthful officers of the 9th Battalion.

After their recent defeat, the federal government was gathering considerable military forces in Guerrero against Tomochic, located some 180 miles away. From the Ninth, 250 men had been sent in, along with several squads of state security forces, the 5th Regiment, and a company from the 11th Battalion that had survived the September 2 disaster.

Moreover, a small-caliber Hotchkiss cannon had been brought from Mexico City for a trial in the mountains. It was accompanied by a hundred grenades and a hundred boxes of shells, as well as a lieutenant and his corps of six artillerymen. General Rosendo Márquez would command this small brigade; his second in command was General Colonel José María Rangel, chief of the Second Military Zone with headquarters in Chihuahua.

Colonel Gómez, head of the 5th Regiment, was charged with procuring saddle horses for the 9th Battalion officers. Fresh out of the military academy and engaging in their first foray, they would find the six-day march from Chihuahua to Concepción, Guerrero, no easy undertaking.

The march began on the tenth of the month, and the two companies arrived in Concepción on October 15, after crossing the lonely wild lands and rocky, inhospitable hills. At that time, the area was nothing but desert. Nowadays, with the advent of the railway, the area between Chihuahua and the Sierra Madre mountains was slowly becoming settled and farmed.

The troops resented these long days, and for good reason. For more than eight years the 9th Battalion had been sitting pretty in the capital city, strutting in parades or as honor guards, displaying their perfect formation and brilliant military appearance in marches and lineups. Those officers were a sight to see, promenading the gold on their uniforms through the halls of the palace or at table in the banquets of Plateros, spruced up and handsome, their jackets always buttoned and their sabers hanging from their belts—spanking new, clanking, virgin sabers. What a sight those officers were! To see them on the cracked, dry path as they rode, dusty, battered, and darkened by the sun.

They rode their horses side by side with soldiers shod in thick huaraches, their pant legs rolled up to the thighs and the ends of their underwear hanging out.[1] These foot soldiers carried bulky rucksacks on their backs; their kerchiefs protected their heads from the sun and their rifles were slung over their shoulders, as they tramped the dusty road stretching on, bitter, monotonous, interminable, toward the horizon. Not a single tree in that silent wasteland! Nothing but the motionless, unadorned hills on the vast horizon, their undulating ridges etched against the intense blue sky. And beyond the interminable steppes could be glimpsed the Sierra Madre towering over all.

Their day's march would end in some miserable *rancho* that was short on provisions but long on the surly arrogance of its inhabitants; a guard would be appointed and the rancho appropriated for the troops, who happily stretched out on the ground to ease their weary, aching, sweaty limbs.[2] Then the parched, ravenous off-duty officers would go in search of meat, bread, cheese, sausage, and sotol, which was sold to them— when it was sold at all—unwillingly, with icy reserve, sidelong looks, and surly gestures.[3]

Sometimes the poor devils came back with their hands and stomachs empty, railing against such stingy, inhospitable folk. On other occasions it was apparent that the natives were on the receiving end of the inevitable abuses that tired, hungry soldiers commit.

The miserable soldiers fought blindly for concepts as lofty and incomprehensible as national tranquility, order, peace, progress, duty. What fault was it of the troops if they gave in to hunger, if they appropriated or brutishly snatched up whatever lay in their path?

Freebooting soldiers—a term invented, no doubt, by well-fed men in spacious offices—thought Miguel indignantly. He understood now that these troops could not be blamed for acting out of hunger. It's what city people did out of perverse ambition, wearing their white gloves and affecting the best manners.

CHAPTER 4

Soldaderas

As the soldiers got closer to the Sierras, the melancholy officer realized that the Chihuahua peasants judged them with boundless rage and surly disdain while exalting the sons of Tomochic beyond all measure. He was stung to the quick.

Meanwhile, the *soldaderas*, women troop followers who alternately trailed their guys like slaves and hurried ahead to obtain food for them, told astounding tales.

Like a migrating horde, those dirty, dusty women, dressed in rags and shod, like the men, in huaraches, resembled wild dogs as they trotted ahead of the marching column hefting enormous baskets full of cooking pots and utensils on their shoulders.

The *soldaderas!* Miguel both feared and admired them; they provoked terror and tenderness in equal measure. In truth, he found them repugnant. Their gaunt, dark faces, harpies' features, and predatory hands tortured and befuddled him. He had seen them in the teeming squares of Mexico City's poor districts, where they seethed in their own filth and lust and hunger . . . not to mention their drunken stupors of sotol and *pulque.*[1]

Oh, he had seen them all right. Witnessing their senseless vices and crimes had wrung his heart and turned his stomach. And now he scrutinized them in wonderment. Their rough-hewn features stood out in epic relief as he contemplated their tranquil selflessness, undaunted stamina, and inexhaustible tenderness for their long-suffering "Juans," their men, who would live and die in abject suffering, oblivious to their fate.

On the road, the officers prohibited the *soldaderas* from fetching water for the soldiers. But they disobeyed and obstinately carried canteens full of water to the troops and laughed in the face of authority. The sweaty, breathless men drank and were envied by all who, beneath the implacable sun and enveloped in clouds of dust, had not been so fortunate.

The soldiers grumbled among themselves in their uncensored, ignorant conversations. "If they give water to the machine to keep it going," they would say, "why wouldn't they give some to the troops?"

In the terrible heat of the marches the *soldaderas* carried out works of mercy of the highest order. Openly defying the corporals' truncheons and even the officers' sabers, they went on giving drink to their thirsty lovers who, with the candid black eyes of the acquiescent Indian, gave their thanks in the ecstasy of their sated thirst. Every swallow of cold water was like manna from heaven!

Miguel turned a blind eye to these transgressions of the captain's strict orders and on the sly observed the relief of the troops and the staunch persistence of the women bringing them canteens and pitchers full of water.

Second Lieutenant Mercado liked to listen in on their conversations during the rest periods, in camps lacking even a single tent. The improvised encampments were roughly marked off by rows of stacked rifles bunched in symmetrical steel bouquets. The men flung themselves down in the shade of craggy overhangs, amid their gear and gusts of billowing smoke, indistinguishable from the women lying beside them.

"Just imagine, Don Chema," he heard a tall, gaunt woman say to a strapping lad who was wolfing down thick tortillas, the only food she had to offer. "Imagine! Teresita herself blesses the rifles, and every shot fired is a dead man, and the gringos have given them piles of artillery. Loads of it. *Ay!* My dearest . . ."

Don Chema stopped chewing and reflected a moment on the implications of all this. Then he resumed eating, as though resigned to his fate. "You're right! Why do we have to go? They'll kill us all, and here we are, marching on and on, just to die like sheep."

But others, disbelieving, countered this. The Fifth was beaten, all right, but the Ninth was different! They weren't going to be caught with their pants down. They'd see if the guys of the Ninth turned tail and ran!

As they descended the steep slope that snaked circuitously along a mountain ridge and made a switchback on a cliff jutting out over a dark chasm far below, Miguel learned what had happened at that site two months earlier. The 11th Battalion of Guerrero needed more munitions, and headquarters sent the shipment to them with an escort of a few men. Four or five Tomochic fighters routed the escort party and took possession of the munitions. Later on, the boxes had been sent back to the colonel of the 11th Battalion headquarters with the cartridges empty.

Whenever the little Hotchkiss cannon, which brought up the rear of the column, dropped out of sight, Miguel thought of this anecdote. Given the audacity of these mountain fighters, wasn't it logical to fear a similar assault? The roads were deserted. Why didn't they launch a surprise attack?

In Guerrero City the two companies of the 9th Battalion set up camp along the Alameda, eager for the order to push on into the Sierra Madre, whose dark silhouette undulated majestically just ahead.

CHAPTER 5

The Hand of General Díaz

That afternoon, after leaving the inn, as he was crossing the deserted plaza on his way back to camp, Miguel carried the memory of the lovely girl from Tomochic with him. He was still under her spell when he arrived at the Alameda, where stacks of arms had been set up to form an enclosure in which the troops could eat and rest.

It was a gloomy spot, dotted with spindly pine trees and crisscrossed by sewer pipes filled with fetid water. Stone benches lined the rectangular perimeter of the square, where cold winds from the Sierras bent back the ancient branches of the trees intoning reproachful laments in a single monotonous chord. It was a scene as irremediably forlorn as Miguel's soul.

Word spread that the federal forces had arrived, and the deserted Alameda came to life again as women selling meat, bread, flour tortillas, *gordas*,[1] peaches, apples, and sweets flocked to the area near the stockpiled arms.

That night, when the officers gathered at the inn for dinner, there was sensational news: the brash mountain fighters of Tomochic had unconditionally released the man who had been injured and taken prisoner in the September 2 battle, Lieutenant Colonel José M. Ramírez of the 11th Battalion.

This was astounding. What did it mean now, when they were planning a serious attack? In the event they were defeated, wouldn't a hostage be useful to them? Was it weakness, cowardice?

Certainly not! Anyone who had witnessed the courage of that indomitable people knew as much. No, certainly not!

The news—brought by the commander himself—indicated that they were more determined than ever to wait out the attack. They were well armed, and their ranks were swelling by the day with political refugees and the increasingly restless inhabitants of the mountain towns; even outlaws like Pedro Chaparro joined their ranks with money and men, drawn by the booty alone.

Their overture could only be seen as a noble, honorable gesture; they had thrown down the gauntlet in a challenge to their adversaries, like the fabled knights of antiquity. Multiple versions of the event circulated freely. Some said that the Tomochic fighters had been swayed by promises of money; others maintained that Ramírez had spoken with Cruz and then fallen to his knees before the image of the girl saint of Cabora. After praying for days on end, he pretended she had miraculously converted him, after which he was given his liberty to go and spread the word.

The official story was that Ramírez, unable to endure his treatment any longer or sustain himself on a regimen of roasted corn and water, had appealed to Cruz to shoot him rather than subject him to a slow death. The astonished Cruz had then provided him with food and four armed men and escorted him to the entrance of Guerrero City.

In any event, here he was among them to corroborate the rumors about the number of rebel forces, which he calculated at three hundred men or more. But all agreed that, without exaggeration, each rebel was worth ten ordinary fighters.

Suddenly a cold shock went through the heated atmosphere of masculine breath and a few officers went pale, when General Staff Lieutenant Réndon informed them that General Márquez had given the command to General Rangel. The latter would be operating on broad instructions from the general, who would be on the alert in Guerrero City, sixty miles away from the tragic scene.

"Lucky for him he's an honorary commanding general, with his name on campaign communiqués just for show," an indignant captain dared to remark, breaking the timorous silence of the men around him.

And in truth, in a confrontation with Tomochic, there was no need for that commander's presence. General Díaz would command the operations of the minor campaign via telegraph from his offices in the capital. "The president of the republic knows how to run these things while he drinks his mug of chocolate in Chapultepec Park," Mercado allowed.

"So why send important generals into combat?" put in Castorena.

"Right. It's enough to have General Rangel, who knows the terrain, receiving precise instructions from above. When you have men who know how to obey orders, what more do you need?"

The major who had spoken earlier in the morning chimed in, "What's more, Guerrero City is the center of a base of operations. In a formal campaign, if other mountain towns and mining settlements joined the uprising in support of Tomochic, it would be very useful to have General Márquez here to defend the plaza until reinforcements arrived from Chihuahua. To abandon Guerrero would be inexcusable!"

Then cocky Lieutenant Torrea asked disdainfully, "Come now, major, how likely are they to take Guerrero City?"

"With a leader of Cruz's intelligence and that pack of devils behind him, why not? It's a good thing for us that they have no strategy or military training, so they can be polished off quickly. But it will cost us dearly because they're brave as devils."

Meanwhile, the overburdened Cuca carried plates back and forth to the officers who, having washed up and combed their hair, calmly ate dinner. Their conversation had turned sober, with the most knowledgeable taking the lead while the rest listened in.

There were occasional moments of pained silence. Dark thoughts passed over the faces of the young men, who had no real grasp of the dubious drama fate had assigned them. Fate and the iron hand of General Díaz, sure and swift to act, merciless in meting out punishment.

The mere mention of the name Porfirio Díaz, who conveyed his thoughts and power from his headquarters in Mexico City, kept the unruly in check; he was quick to extinguish any errant spark, smother the faintest crackle, catch any drop outside the channel he had designated for the revolutionary torrent. The invocation of his name was enough to subdue the men's spirit, and they resigned themselves as victims of Duty.

The men understood vaguely that this was necessary, decreed by fate. They would go wherever they were sent, go and die, so that throughout the great Mexican nation others could flourish. To sacrifice oneself without protest, without uttering an angry word. One had to be prepared to render up body and soul, and the bodies and souls of loved ones as well, in their faraway homes. Sad, ingenuous, mute, the anonymous victims of Duty. While Mercado pondered these bitter, melancholy truths, his eyes clouded with defiant tears that evaporated silently, searing eyes and soul alike.

In contrast, Castorena, the short, husky officer with the tawny face and hair, turned everything into a joke. He drank tequila with the same verve that he improvised bad quatrains. He earned hearty applause as he proffered drinks, managing to kindle a senseless glee in the company.

He was a madcap boy of twenty, with a happy vitality that was undaunted by official reprimands, fatigue, or hunger. Playing the mordant buffoon in the officers' festivities, he made himself indispensable to gatherings and parties.

Though he was always drinking, he was rarely drunk, claiming to be gifted with "brains of bronze." He was wry, unruly, mocking, and querulous, and he had an inexhaustible eye for the ladies. He was also a late-night partier famous for his guitar playing, plus an atrocious singer and worse poet. He might have made an excellent officer, except that he was always decked out in full-dress uniform, complete with sword and pistol.

Like the jester who arrives on the scene just as catastrophe is imminent, Castorena blurted out fantastically, "They can drop dead with their *jolas*.² We'll show them how to have a good time. How much can you kick in, lieutenant? Grand! And what about you, Mercado? Hey, Cuquita, how much to rent your guitar?"

> Good sirs, we're more chilly by far
> And our woes and our worries are realer
> Than when we strike up the guitar
> And have us a round of tequila.

Basking in the admiration and high spirits of his comrades, Castorena, the official clown, the fool, the "brains of bronze," rose to his feet and took Cucas's guitar down from the wall.

The commanding officers had already left, and only the younger men remained. In a haze of cigarette smoke, they uncorked a bottle of tequila, clinked glasses, and took turns toasting, while the melancholy strains of the guitar told of distant sweethearts and love gone wrong. Castorena's voice sang out desperately, "Do you remember, my lovely, a certain afternoon . . ."

Meanwhile, outside, cold winds from the Sierras buffeted the desolate little plaza, bringing the rumblings of far-off storms from the high woods, portents of coming disaster.

CHAPTER 6

Ready to Kill or Be Killed

Reveille sounded in the silence of the predawn hours of October 16, waking the camp along the Alameda in Guerrero. Drums didn't roll. Only the bugles of the 9th Battalion's two companies blasted their victorious sounds: rapid, nimble, bursting with joy and warlike bravura. As soon as the first note sounded, sudden and unexpected as a stab wound, a bustle of grumbling, throat clearing, and laughter could be heard. Tin canteens clanged against steel rifles, and the sergeants on rounds yelled out, "Up! Up! Onward and upward!"

The *soldaderas* snuggled cozily with their comrades under their serapes, lost in the voluptuous consolation of their fate. Indolently, they stretched while their soldiers leaped up in one bound to carry out orders.

The officers, having slept in their uniforms beneath rough red blankets in the spaces between the rows of stacked weapons, started awake, momentarily flustered. On hearing the first notes of the reveille, they shook off the stupor of sleep, invigorated to their very marrow. They rose ready to command or be commanded.

Imperious voices and full-throated cries crisscrossed in the shadows above the metallic scraping of sheathed sabers. "In formation, corporals!"

"Out of the way, wenches!"

"With your permission, lieutenant, sir."

"Listen, comrade."

"To the right. In line!"

Miguel stood in front with the 4th Company, next to the first sergeant who rapidly shouted roll call. Completely enveloped in his cape, his hands gloved, the scarf under his hood wrapped up to his nose to protect him from the freezing night air, Miguel felt like he was on his last legs. Above him, the stars glittered through the naked branches of the trees.

He had gotten drunk the night before and—as he usually did when not on duty—and on waking from his dark binge, he felt diminished, apprehensive, ashamed, and infinitely sad. But the spirit of military discipline quelled all resistance, all rebelliousness, as it did in the others. He shook his aching head, burning from the previous night's tequila, and soon arrived at the command site, his saber at his side, steadfast and willing, like his comrades, to command and obey. Ready to kill. Ready to die. To die! Despite the oppressive feeling in his soul on that dark, icy dawn, he knew that deep within there was, and would always be, an uncanny fearlessness. It was a dangerous dagger lying inert in its sheath; at the right moment it would be willing and able to do anything, even to kill!

When roll call was over, he rushed to report to the company captain, Stanislav Tagle. When he returned and marched past the town's steaming cauldrons, a pale dawn was already soaking up the stars.

It was frightfully cold. Miguel watched the soldiers gratefully receive the hot, sweetened mud they called coffee, the meager compensation that was distributed to the miserable flock in the dull half light of dawn.

The troops were then ordered to wash their clothes in the river. Each man received a bar of soap, and they marched along in the morning haze, turning toward the right, chattering, singing, yelling out orders to their women. The officers kept the march in line as they walked alongside the column, chatting and joking, bundled in their capes, their hoods pulled up and their necks wrapped in the scarves they had bought in Chihuahua.

When they reached the narrow, shallow river that passed west of the town, the soldiers were permitted to break ranks, and each went off to find a stone that would serve for washing clothes.

The intense cold did not let up, and Miguel craved something that would warm his empty stomach, still queasy from the alcohol. He stared weakly at the soapy swirls in the river current and felt faint.

The half-dressed soldiers, their sunburned flesh bared to the cold Sierra winds, sang as they washed their grimy uniforms and shirts. Mingling with the men, the women helped them wring out their tattered garments or washed their own skirts.

Good-natured shouting, bursts of laughter, singing, and whistling traveled back and forth among the launderers. The riverbank, sere and rocky with nothing but a few scrawny bushes, seemed like an impoverished Bajío hamlet, nestled in the rural area around Jalisco, amid the hubbub of a fair.

Unaffected by the glacial waters, a naked Castorena, his golden hairs standing up on his squat body, was more clownish than ever. He looked for all the world like a plump blond monkey and sang as though still drunk from the night before: "Do you remember, my lovely, a certain afternoon . . ."

Seeing the regiment clown goofing off on the eve of a merciless battle with the wildcats of the mountains, Miguel felt his hatred evaporate. "He's just like me, like all of us, poor fools; naked, freezing, defenseless, absurd. He is ready . . . to die."

C H A P T E R   7

The Beast's Due

Hoping to slake his unbearable thirst, Mercado approached a native as he was dismounting to water his horse. "Friend, do you know where I can get a cup of hot coffee?" Without looking up, the man pointed to a squalid little shack next to the river.

Shivering with cold, Miguel asked Captain Tagle for permission to leave his position temporarily. Then, wrapped in his full cape, his hood pulled down over his forehead, Miguel approached the hut and peered through the doorway into the darkness.

Standing at the threshold, he asked a shabby old woman who was grinding corn on a *metate*[1] and patting out thick tortillas by the hearth to prepare him a large coffee—at any price. A thick, raspy drunkard's voice answered back. "Come in! Let's see here. Julia! A jug of coffee, lots of it, nice and hot, and be quick about it, quick as the devil!" The order ended abruptly with a curse.

In the dim light Miguel made out a figure swathed in thick serapes on a broad wooden bed: a boorish face with glassy, red-rimmed eyes and a hooked nose surrounded by matted locks and a long gray beard. At the same moment, the neat, graceful figure of a beautiful girl emerged from the opposite corner.

She walked across the room, passing by him with a rhythmic stride and downcast eyes. Taking a pitcher from the hearth, she filled it with water and placed it on the fire. Violent flames leaped up and illuminated the dark girl's profile. Stunned, wide-eyed, Miguel stared.

The old man sat up and motioned him toward a stool. "Sit down, chief," he said to the officer. "And while the coffee is on, hand this over to her for some sotol."

The unrefined rotgut from Chihuahua was not to his taste and Miguel responded, "Tequila, please. I don't care for sotol." Julia approached, trembling and subservient, and he gave her a twenty-five-centavo note.

As Miguel watched the graceful young woman, he became more captivated by the minute. Who was she? Where had he seen this loveliness before? He could imagine the atrocities committed in the dark lair, which reeked of tobacco and excrement. Could the bandit be the father of this lovely child?

With surprised delight he recalled her from the inn; she was the same young woman who had caught his attention the night before. One and the same! Once again he spontaneously murmured his praise, "Lovely!" Then, to himself, he added, "It's the same girl, the very same!"

He took another look at the bearded brute in the semidarkness.

The witless old woman, grinding away with the regularity of a machine, asked, "Are you getting up now, Don Bernardo? Shall I bring your boots?"

Without waiting for his reply, the old woman rose stiffly and approached his cot, her head bowed. Then she knelt before the ogre, who stretched his legs out to her. She dutifully fitted his dark, hairy feet into his rawhide boots. Humble as a slave, the crone slowly adjusted the boots, pinching and patting to be sure she accomplished her servile task to perfection.

Dumbstruck, Miguel continued to observe the scene from his chair. Julia approached with the bottle of tequila and offered him his coffee in a pewter cup, then handed him the sugar.

Trembling, Miguel poured the foul liquor into the blackish water that steamed up from the earthenware cup. He experienced a moment of nausea and then, shaking off a dark thought, brought the brew to his mouth with both hands and avidly drank it down.

Such sweet poison, as Castorena says, he thought to himself, and felt the first tonic caress of the alcohol coursing through his body. It was a miracle. The desolate fog that weighed on his spirit like a shroud began to dissolve into warm, crystalline clarity. Through this rosy lens the enticing figure of the beautiful, gracious girl in the miserable hovel was revealed.

And now she seemed to flame up before the officer's astounded eyes, displaying yet more charms, new wonders. He watched her walk about, so fresh and lively in comparison to the haggard corpse doing her mechanical chores, and the hairy ogre stewing in his own foul juices, amid the worn and dirty objects.

Nimble and pure, she passed the nauseating rags, and when she lifted her head with birdlike grace, she turned on him the full magnificence of her shy black eyes.

"Lovely! My god, how lovely!" he sang inwardly, transported to a poetic reverie. And in his poor enchanted soul, the officer blended ecstatic contemplation of the young woman before him with the sacred memory of his absent mother.

Suddenly he heard her rhythmic voice, resonant with the enchanting accent of the daughters of Chihuahua: "Auntie, have you seen my kerchief around? I always put it under the pillow when I go to bed. I can't seem to find it today. How silly I am!"

Swift and agile, she walked over to the unmade bed from which the hairy old beast had just risen, and there, flinging serapes and bedclothes, she turned around to complain prettily, "But I put it here last night. How very silly!" Incredibly, she was lifting the same pillow that had supported the old rascal's filthy hair.

There could be no doubt. He could discern the young woman's graceful curves outlined in the mattress. Once again, reality grabbed him by the throat.

First he sadly contemplated Julia, then turned to look at Don Bernardo, who was loudly slurping his strong, tequila-spiked coffee. Julia widened her big, dark eyes. Like Miguel's, her gaze expressed melancholy and resignation.

Being of a despondent nature, Mercado was not much of a Don Juan. But his arrogant youthfulness, the nervous movements of his body, the way he raised his fair, noble forehead—all had appeal. This mute suffering creature, the resigned and adorable Julia, was more than susceptible to his charms.

She couldn't hide it, either. In the presence of the officer who came from so far away, spoke such kind words, and looked at her so tenderly— the way no one in the world had ever looked at her—she fell into a confused dream of unimagined pleasures. She was incapable of concealing her feelings.

The boorish Don Bernardo stepped outside the hut to warm himself in the sun. Contemptuous but also curious, he watched the troops wash their clothes on the far side of the river.

"Do you want more coffee?" said Julia. She brought the officer another cup, which he took from her strong, beautiful hands.

"Is that your mother, the woman grinding over there?" asked Miguel.

She shook her head sadly and said, with lowered eyes, "My stepmother, sir."

"Well, then, is Don Bernardo your father?"

"He's my uncle," she sighed. And the girl's face blazed an intense red. "Well, that is," she stammered, "we're not married or anything . . . because she is his wife." And she could say no more. Her soft voice choked at the mention of such abominations.

How could it be! This gracious, lively adolescent was the ogre's own? He could do what he wanted with her? This sweet, humble creature was his mistress, this fresh rose in full bloom. Appalled, Miguel turned pale.

What foul web is this? he wondered. Silently enduring her misfortune, she gives herself hopelessly and joylessly, as a passive victim would, to a master who abuses her with the despotism of a Moorish pirate. Can it be true? That decrepit corpse the wife, this fresh girl the beloved!

He inhaled her strong yet shy youthfulness. Though disgraced, it was still healthy and firm. The generous heart of the officer overflowed with boundless compassion.

Julia leaned toward Miguel as she offered him the cup. Almost touching, the two mingled their breath and exchanged tender looks.

Poor girl! He saw purplish marks on her sleek bare arms and lovely dark neck and said, "He beats you, doesn't he? Does he? Do you love him? No? Then leave him, denounce him. Speak with the political head of Guerrero."

Terrified at the indignation that flared in Miguel's eyes, the girl exclaimed, "No, sir . . . I can't. My father has ordered it, and my father is a saint. Teresita sanctified him. They shot him down and he came back to life as Our Lord. Imagine! That's why you mustn't go to Tomochic . . . don't go. They'll kill you if you do. Cruz will finish off every one of you. Offer prayers . . . Don't go to Tomochic!"

CHAPTER 8

Apparent Causes

This is what Second Lieutenant Mercado later discovered about the roots of the strange rebellion in Tomochic.

The tiny villages of the Sierra Madre west of Chihuahua were in constant fear of the marauding Apache Indians; warfare broke out from the mountains to remote jungle areas. Everyone in the area carried guns and used them in raids to win back cattle stolen by the Indians, who were gradually retreating toward their northern stronghold.

The famous mountain dwellers of Tomochic, a hamlet of some three hundred inhabitants situated in a valley, had distinguished themselves again and again in bravery and daring. When they had neutralized the danger, they returned to cultivating their land, tending their livestock, and sitting like lords in the doorways of their huts, sunning themselves and cleaning their rifles.

The rich folk of the area were buried in the church courtyard. Next to the church was a convent founded by Jesuit missionaries in the era when colonizers exploited the area's rich mineral resources.

Both the government and clergy of Chihuahua had abandoned these aloof, inscrutable people. It was as though they had vanished within the vast republic. Although these institutions supplied no instruction, taxes rose with each passing day. Suddenly religious fanaticism spread through the land. With an almost medieval exaggeration, devotees invoked the Saint of Cabora. The miracles the girl worked were described in infinite ways.

Passing through Tomochic, travelers from Sonora spoke of miracles. Journeying to the state on their pack animals, the natives returned as though from Mecca.

The child whose paroxysms brought about cures in many suffering from nervous prostration protested in vain that she was not a saint. She only offered up thanks to God for the powers he occasionally bestowed on her. But sly political ambition and commercial savvy were fashioning the poor girl into a symbol.

When the repressed energy of the Tomochic people was channeled into religious fervor, what gushed forth erupted with volcanic force. One particular incident tipped the latent rage against the local government into outright fury. Governor Lauro Carillo visited the church on his way through Tomochic. Enchanted by the artistry of several paintings, he tried to take them back to Chihuahua with him. But when those proud, ferocious people got wind of his designs, their indignation caused the official to leave the paintings behind.

Forever afterward, Tomochics considered the government and its agents staunch enemies and referred to them as "ungodly sons of Lucifer." To add insult to injury, another government official, arriving in Tomochic to carry out a judicial inquiry, took advantage of an innocent local girl and left her pregnant. Later an official from the Pinos Altos mine accused the Tomochics of being insubordinate thieves, alarming not only the minerals consortium based in London but the interim governor as well. The powder keg was packed, the fuse in place, and the spark was not long in coming.

Word spread throughout the surrounding villages that Tomochic native José Carranza had been declared a saint. He decided to share his joy with the natives of the town by returning to Tomochic to live. Spirits were high as everyone awaited the arrival of "San José."

The Chávez clan was the town's most distinguished family. They had prevailed for many years through a combination of talent, character, and ambition. On a Saturday, in an elaborate ceremony, the three Chávezes formally received St. Joseph.

The old man arrived with his wife Mariana and his brother Bernardo, who followed behind with his rifle on his shoulder, proclaiming that he was a "soldier of Jesus Christ."

The following Sunday was a happy day. Mass was held and St. Joseph was ushered into the church amid a devout procession. The priest had been instructed to throw the "saint" out of the church after mass and forbid the people from practicing their unorthodox ideas and practices. He exhorted his parishioners to abandon their fanaticism and then belittled their ludicrous beliefs.

The inborn pride of that small town was dealt a heavy blow, and a scandalous protest ensued. The popular Cruz Chávez, who until then had opposed mystical shenanigans, made a rush for the pulpit and screamed at the priest, "In the name of the almighty power of God, as his divine majesty's *police*, I am telling you to leave!"

"Death to the priest!" seconded an old woman.

"Yes, yes . . . throw him out!" exclaimed one and all as the contagion spread, inflamed by the priest's ruthless admonitions. The priest took to his heels, declaring them all possessed by the devil.

Mayor Reyes Domínguez imposed a hefty fine on the Chávezes, who refused to pay. The employee in charge of military conscription in Pinos Altos threatened to have the rebels "sent off as soldiers." They replied that the valley of Tomochic would be flooded with blood before that day came. By the time the news reached the capital of Chihuahua, it had been blown out of all proportion, as though the mountain men were involved in an armed rebellion.

Then the high command dispatched an impressive contingent from the 11th Battalion, which was wiped out by gunfire. Some thirty Tomochic fighters headed toward Sonora, working their way down the mountain and defeating more than eighty horsemen dispatched by Colonel Torres. Now, with the booty they collected, the Chávez and Mendías fighters were better equipped and returned to Tomochic ready to stir up the entire Sierra Madre and initiate a major campaign against the government.

At that time, Cruz was about forty years old, a tall, burly man whose face was framed by a thick, black beard. His large eyes were also black, and gleamed with a fierce tenacity that matched his obstinate spirit. He imposed his will with a commanding voice that was as serene as it was clear and dynamic.

At eighteen years of age, Bernardo Carranza had disappeared from the village after stealing a few pesos from the Medranos, a wealthy family of the region. He had returned on several occasions, but because he disdained all work in favor of his romance with sotol, he had never been accepted again.

His brother José was an easygoing man who owned a bit of land. He always opened his hearth and home to Bernardo, who repaid him with acts of petty thievery. José's daughter, Julia, had been sent to Chihuahua to live with her godfather, a man José had worked for as a laborer on his hacienda near Cusihuiriachic.

Old José had caught the fever of religious exaltation in Cusihuiriachic. He abandoned his property and his wife and set out for Cabora, where Teresa cured him of a tumor and told him exultantly that he resembled St. Joseph.

A servant in the house of Teresa Urrea overheard a few words and began telling everyone that he was St. Joseph himself. A few days later the old idiot convinced himself that he was indeed none other than the saint, brought back to life by God. He must now go out and preach, to bring happiness to the world. He embarked on a regimen of zealous prayer, penitence, and fasting. Then he sent for Bernardo and bequeathed him his properties in Tomochic, including his second wife.

That fateful Sunday, Bernardo Carranza and Cruz Chávez decided that Tomochic would become the capital of the reform movement, a holy place that would draw flocks of pilgrims. Bernardo's niece Julia would be held up as a virgin with miraculous powers, and they would raise a great white flag with the slogan inscribed in red: *All power to God! Death to the children of Lucifer!*

They would be "living saints" and, rifles in hand, they would spread the word throughout Chihuahua, obeying no one but God, and no laws but those of his divine majesty!

The days went by, and not one tranquil spirit rose to bring light to the chaos, not one enlightened teacher or missionary preached to the blind, duped masses, nor were the political authorities anywhere to be found.

From Chihuahua, young Julia was sent back to her father while the Chávezes loaded up a fleet of mules and traveled through Sonora selling cargo and pack animals. When they reached the North American border, they bought Winchester repeating rifles that fired twelve to eighteen rounds at a clip.

It so happened that the official in charge of transporting minerals from Pinos Altos to Chihuahua had to pass through Tomochic. Fearing for his safety, he communicated the warlike mood of the town to the government. In the meantime, he resolved to avoid passing through the community altogether, giving it a wide berth as he passed through the Sierras. But those haughty mountain men were not common criminals and told the driver he had nothing to fear from them.

The cry of alarm spread and intensified.

In the end, a detachment from the 11th Battalion was sent in as a preventive measure and, if necessary, to put down aggressive actions while efforts were made to calm the populace. But abuses meted out by government forces aggravated the situation, spawning a mute rage that continued to simmer after calm returned.

So the Chávezes returned, bringing arms and clothing to the village. They appropriated the corn crop and cattle of a rich, widely detested landowner, stirring things up with their slogan, *Religion and Independence.* They radicalized the good people of Tomochic all over again and resolved "officially" to recognize no authority but God's. Never had there been a darker mass blindness.

A frenzied, mystical dementia possessed the fierce sons of the mountains. A fever made up of a confusing clamor for liberty and power swept through those ignorant souls, breathing barbarous impulses into the remote tribe, cut off from the life of the nation.

Wild atavisms were bred. Adding to the dark accumulation of rage and poverty, aggravated by the insolence of political leaders, perverse incitement was orchestrated from as far away as Chihuahua and even Mexico City.

A rebellion in the Sierra Madre mountains of Chihuahua would upset the hard-won peace of the nation. But what was that compared to the shady ambitions of men as impotent as they were cowardly?

What did these remote hill people want? They had no notion of the fatherland or its government, the church or its clergy. And strangest of all, this was no uncivilized tribe. They were *criollos*.[1] Spanish and Arab blood, cruel fanaticism, and knightly valor flowed in the veins of that superb race, part Tarahuma and part Andalusían.

Tomochic presented the Mexican Republic with the rare spectacle of a small town gone mad. The sad truth was that the religious fanaticism of the Tomochic people had the potential to fire up other remote villages of the Sierra that suffered the same dark stirrings. They too were ready to throw themselves into outright rebellion.

C H A P T E R   9

By Divine Miracle

Cruz Chávez sent Bernardo to establish a household with his niece Julia and Mariana, the ex-wife of St. Joseph, in Guerrero. From there, Bernardo could freely spy on the government's military installations in the little village nestled in the foothills—a vital base for any strategic operation in the Sierra.

On the eve of their recruitment drive, Cruz arranged a pilgrimage. His men escorted the new "St. Joseph" through the surrounding villages while several "soldiers of God" welcomed last-minute enlistments into their ranks.

Persuaded by brother Bernardo, "St. Joseph," the old idiot, called in his wife Mariana and daughter Julia to pontificate about "God, his Son," and the afterlife. "In the name of God," he blustered, disavowing all ties to them, "you are no longer my family. My wife is the Virgin Mary. But you will obey my brother; you three will be married, so that I will be the Father of the Holy Trinity. You the Father," and he pointed to Bernardo, "you the daughter, and you the Holy Spirit," he said, pointing to the two women.

That was the black night of the first savage attack, the girl child sacrificed on the altar of fanaticism—the night of the tragic nuptials of the ogre and the damsel. The next day Julia developed a fever. Tied to her mule for the two-day journey, faint and delirious, she arrived in Guerrero City. Bewildered, she was crushed under the weight of her disgrace.

Julia was precocious for her age, her body a young woman's, though she was only fourteen. She was a well-groomed, industrious girl and dutiful in her domestic chores, first in her father's house and later in her uncle's.

She did the grinding, cleaned and patched her father's coarse pants, brought water to the animals, and even chopped firewood on glacial winter nights in the Sierra. Then she would light and stoke the fire in the chimney where she cooked meat for the evening meal and boiled coffee so her father wouldn't fall asleep when Cruz and prominent neighbors convened to recite the rosary, interspersed with strange prayers, fantastic litanies, cries of hate, and belligerent proclamations invoking the "almighty power of God."

Nearly all the women in the area carried out the same tasks, but they performed them passively, like beasts of burden. Julia had been something of a dreamer since tasting civilization while living in her godfather's house in Chihuhua. She became good friends with his daughter, whose enchanting tales thrilled her. Once her friend told Julia, "You are so lovely. Girls like you are born to be queens." She never forgot those words.

On serenade nights in Chihuahua, when the 5th Regiment or the 11th Battalion played music in the garden of the Plaza de Armas, Julia tagged along with her godfather's family. They were always sympathetic to her plight. Though still a child, Julia caught a glimpse of high-class Chihuahua society, with its haughty airs and trappings of luxury. She was dazzled by the beautifully dressed women and enchanted by waltz music, which she had never heard before. It awakened vague longings in her, and her childlike curiosity was aroused by the spectacle of modern, comfortable city life.

She was introduced to her friend's fiancée, a second captain in the 5th Regiment, a kind young man who wore his moustache curled like a musketeer's and his hussar's coat cinched tight. His uniform glinted with the martial splendor of its silver buttons, reflected in the steel of his saber and his shiny silver spurs. This was how princes looked in fairy tales! The dreamy girl of fourteen looked at herself in the mirror, wondering if she might be worthy of such a man.

Later, in Tomochic, she wept and sighed for those happy hours that would never come again. She understood intuitively that the men around her were mad, but she resigned herself to her fate, enduring her woes with the heroism of a martyr. Eventually her face softened, her gaze grew serene, and the smile returned to her delicate lips.

Then came the attack, sending a jolt through her body that sickened her. Then an immense, dark melancholy clouded her fevered brain, and after a while all her dreams and aspirations quietly faded.

A virgin spirit continued to shine through the concubine's spoiled flesh, handled by the old brigand night after night. Life passed sadly in the old adobe hut by the riverside where she was beaten down by her uncle's brutality. Julia endured the daily torment with unwavering resignation. At night when the drunken beast returned to his lair, he would lay next to her adolescent body and poke his stinking beard into the melancholy face of his lovely slave, grasping her to him in the same incestuous bed where once he had slept with Mariana.

And yet—happy consolation of her bewitched state—the monstrous transgression barely touched the ineffable transparency of the girl's spirit. The daily assault left her youthful spirit intact. The grinding of her flesh did not sully the high mirror where her clear, sad spirit resided or cloud her eyes, swell her hips, or age her firm round breasts. Once the first fever passed, the acts of violence and the rapes no longer gnawed at her thoughts or feelings. Her unshakable faith in the Virgin Mary and her constant activity kept Julia's body fresh and healthy.

The lovely Julia, daughter of "St. Joseph" and indentured wench to the old drunkard, was, by some miracle, a sainted child.

CHAPTER 10

Cruz of Tomochic, High Chief

In Guerrero City, far from Cruz's sobering influence, Bernardo fully indulged his predilection for drink. He sold off his livestock one by one to get by while spying on the infantry that the federal government had sent into Guerrero in August to attack Tomochic. The forces were composed of a twenty-five-man squad from the state security troops under Captain Antonio Vergara, thirty men from the 5th Regiment under the command of Captain Lino Camacho, and sixty-five men culled from the 11th Battalion.

Sixty men from the outlying towns were recruited as volunteers into the auxiliary forces, all experts in the local topography and afraid of nothing. Santa Ana Pérez, a courageous adventurer who was popular throughout the state of Chihuahua, was named commander. General José Rangel served as commander in chief of the entire force, bringing three officers with him from general staff and one Francisco Arellano, a major in the military medical corps. All together, there were 130 men.

Bernardo communicated this information to Cruz, and an emissary was sent to discuss matters with Bernardo. The two of them went to see Santa Ana Pérez, head of the local forces, who signed them up and equipped them with arms and a negligible rank. Did he suspect them of being spies?

On August 15 one attack column set off into the mountains, catching sight of Tomochic by September 2. With maybe sixty-eight men at his side, Cruz directed the defense. Most of the men, posted in five houses along the town's eastern boundary, were armed with excellent rifles. Cruz ordered them to carve openings in the thick walls so that they could direct their fire onto the narrow, pitted road that wound down into the valley from the Cordon de Lino hill. When they heard a piercing whistle, the right flank would make for the rear of the slope and climb to the summit, cutting off the enemy's only retreat. Then they were to descend on them to wipe them out or scatter remaining survivors.

All rifles were solemnly blessed.

It was rumored that Cruz drew his tall, rangy body to its full height—his chest massively armored by two crisscrossed belts of metal cartridges—and raised his arms above the men of Tomochic, who prostrated themselves before him and offered their rifles for his blessing. Then, it was said, he spoke the following words:

"My children! I, Cruz of Tomochic, high chief of all Chihuahua and Sonora, in the name of the power of almighty God, order you to slay only the commanders of these soldiers, sons of Satan. Blessed be the weapons that go into battle with the soldiers of hell. In the name of the Father, the Son, and the Holy Spirit, may the great power of God be with us!"

General Rangel divided his force into two contingents. One would go down the Cordon de Lino hill to attack the church; the other would descend the adjoining hill that formed a right angle to the first, its peak looming over the cemetery. This contingent would occupy the cemetery and then take the Medrano house situated at the edge of the main road.

While a few of the soldiers stood lookout, the rebels prayed with abject devotion. They were certain of victory since they were fighting in the name of "the great power of God."

The columns descended through the hills covered with pine trees and underbrush, and the soldiers divided into separate attack squadrons. At the foot of the mountains they encountered shots that hit their mark. A ferocious exchange of fire took place, and the battle had begun.

But at the Cordon de Lino hill, Santa Ana Pérez and his auxiliaries from Chihuahua did not open fire and were not fired on. Looking on from above, the general indignantly observed confusion and panic in the right wing of the second column, which eventually sought refuge in the cemetery.

Then, from behind, Cruz and his rear guard leaped like tigers, taking all men occupying the site prisoner. Lieutenant Colonel José M. Ramírez, who had been wounded in the arm, was among the captives.

Captain Vergara, Major Prieto, and Lieutenant Manzano fell dead, and Lieutenant Vespasiano Guerrero from the general staff was thrown from his horse as he was heading down the slope to deliver a message.

The defeat was massive, the catastrophe irremediable. The vanquished general retreated, weeping convulsively, and then in a bold move took refuge in one of the enemy's abandoned houses. Under cover of night and accompanied by only a few soldiers, he crossed the silent wilderness.

The victors, meanwhile, collected considerable booty but only used the horses, weapons, and munitions. The rest, including a small barrel of tequila and a few barrels of flour, was stashed away.

That same day the nurse Francisco Arellano, whose first duty was to his calling, entered Tomochic unarmed. Carrying only his first aid kit, he set about his humanitarian mission of ministering to the wounded, townsfolk and invaders alike.

Santa Ana Pérez had disappeared. Bernardo alone went to General Rangel in Guerrero, reporting that Pérez had been wounded in his leg and was fleeing toward the northern part of the state.

Later the federal government ordered a second expedition to Tomochic, commanded by General Felipe Cruz, and what occurred was almost beyond belief.

Shortly before arriving in Guerrero, the forces of the 5th Regiment, under the general's orders, fell upon a cornfield with sabers drawn. The destruction was fantastic. The slender stalks of corn were hacked to bits by the cutlass blades, covering the ground with waste.

In Guerrero a lieutenant from the 22nd Battalion was ordered to take another hill, the Cerro de la Generala, fifty-three miles from Tomochic, which he accomplished with no resistance.

The mountaintop was deserted and the commander, a leftover from a less disciplined time, telegraphed Mexico City that he had attacked the town and triumphed after a bloody battle, taking twenty-five prisoners.

The Tomochic hysteria, suppurating like an open sore, would be excised at last. Thus it happened that the capable hand of General Díaz, a veteran in these operations, found it was holding a dirty instrument, dull from lack of use. This complicated matters.

The army was overhauled with new chiefs and a worthy officer corps culled from the graduates of the Chapultepec military academy.

CHAPTER 11

The Dawn of the Idyll

Tentatively, the two lonely, ill-starred young people drew closer. Miguel was tenderly attracted to Julia. Her misfortune only enhanced his image of her, and he seriously contemplated abducting her from the ogre who held her hostage.

The aura of painful, almost fantastical mystery that smoldered in the dark eyes of the unusual girl from Tomochic was so compelling that Miguel contemplated setting her free.

Heroically, he would boldly drag her from the lair of the beast. Why not? She would accompany him from adventure to adventure. They would live out their passionate love affair alongside the 9th Battalion. The poet's soul lying dormant within Miguel Mercado seemed to revive.

The second lieutenant told Julia that he would come back, and he left money with her for his meal on the night of his return. He explained to her that in the town inn he received meager portions, and the servers frequently ignored him in favor of higher-ranking officers.

Bernardo welcomed the arrangement with evident pleasure and imperiously ordered a chicken killed in honor of his "chief." He asked Mercado to take him to see the cannon he had heard so much about, since the officer obviously had access to it. Bernardo was curious about it because, he declared to Miguel, he was on the verge of signing up, thereby cutting all connection with those fanatics.

Innocently Miguel instructed him to be at the Alameda at eleven o'clock in the morning, saying that he would take him to see it, albeit from a distance. The second lieutenant did not suspect that he was dealing with a Tomochic spy.

Silently he returned to his spot by the river, thinking about the accident of fortune that had thrown him so far off course, into terrible tumult. A day blessed with grace and love that could be the eve of his death.

He thought of his father, who had once been a liberal commander. After Tecoac, he worked as a humble scribe and spent the last years of his life making three of his clients rich, though each had abandoned him afterward. He thought of his beautiful widowed mother, who married a second time only to be vilely abused. Then came their scandalous separation and his departure from the military academy. He was destined to become nothing more than a second lieutenant, one who would shortly find himself in the hinterlands of the Chihuahua desert, 1,500 miles away from civilization and Mexico City.

What a hand fate had dealt him! And what a magnificent dawn was breaking on it all of a sudden.

He thought about his encounter, not with some idealized damsel out of a fairy tale nor a blond Margarita but with a despicably mistreated girl, the kept woman of an outlaw. She was a humble, candid creature who had gazed at him with her trusting black eyes as though pleading for his aid, offering him a love as genuine as her soul was pure. From the depths of his soul, Miguel pledged his protection—and even his love.

But what could he do for her? Only bring her more misfortune? Expose her beauty to his lascivious comrades? Make her live out the phrase "thrown to the wolves"?

And thus he pondered, seated on a large rock, while the scattered troops did their washing at the river's edge. There was a happy clamor of laughter and shouting, jokes and swear words, beneath a sun that shone brilliantly in a clear blue sky. The white burlap strung out to dry among the brambles sparkled. Officers gathered in small groups to smoke and chat, and bend an elbow behind a boulder or a tree while keeping their bottles out of the captain's sight.

The cold river water, slow moving and stained with soap, flowed on under Miguel's inward-looking gaze.

When he got back to camp, Mercado took up his rifle and joined the other officers for target practice, a drill that the general had ordered to familiarize his men with their new weapons. At twelve o'clock roll call, just as he was brushing the dust from the cape he had slept in, Mercado was informed that he had a visitor.

It was Bernardo. Miguel agreed to show him the cannon as promised, and they proceeded to the central hall of the house, which served as general headquarters. With a scornful, dim-witted gaze Don Bernardo contemplated the spanking new weapon of war, intended to raze Tomochic. Miguel took his leave of the old rascal as soon as he could but agreed to see him later at his house, where Bernardo had ordered a midday meal prepared "specially for the chief."

When Miguel was alone again he wondered whether he should go; it was stupid to eat some awful lunch in Don Bernardo's shack. And as for Julia, wouldn't it be better not to torment himself cruelly with the sight of the unfortunate girl?

Rescue her? he asked himself again. Romantic foolishness!

And so he made his way languidly toward the plaza, intending to eat at the inn. He met up with Castorena on his way out, who warned him that the officers had already finished off everything; there wasn't a scrap left. In revenge, he said, he intended to guzzle a half bottle of tequila and eat a pound of cheese—the only food he'd been able to find, other than thick flour tortillas.

As there was nothing left in the tavern, Miguel decided to eat at Julia's after all. He chatted a bit and drank a few tequilas with the poet, then took off in the direction of the river.

Julia had set a cozy table for him. There were two benches and an old plank covered by a bright white tablecloth with clumsy green figures on its borders; the only setting was a single pewter plate. In the fireplace, the chicken boiled in a black pot over a raging fire while golden pieces of chorizo sizzled in a sea of oil in an earthenware crock.

Julia was kneeling, head bent to her task, grinding the chili on the *metate* with the monotonous regularity and perfect unconsciousness of a beast of burden or a robot. Then, all of a sudden, she was up and bustling about, arranging, beautifying, illuminating all with her gracefulness and her lovely eyes.

Two skinny, strutting cocks tied up in the corner of the room squawked in turn, while a gaunt, yellow mongrel slept in a square of sunlight created by the open door.

When Miguel greeted Julia with a gentle squeeze of her hand, the blushing girl trembled. Her eyes moist, her throat constricted, she was, unable to utter a word. Finally she managed to control her feelings, saying that she was sorry the meal wasn't prepared yet; staring straight into his eyes, she added that she hoped he wasn't angry with her. "I'm such a ninny! But believe me, it won't happen again," she finished.

"Don Bernardo will be along in a moment, right?" said the officer affectionately, smiling at her innocence.

"Yes sir, any moment now. He always eats about now. You'll see how he scolds me because the food isn't ready. He's a harsh man, sir. So harsh!" When the young man heard the stricken tone in her voice, he was again overcome by boundless pity for her.

An extraordinary sweetness coursed through his being. Her frank glances captivated him. They were full of enchanting magic, somehow free of the sad mystery deep in her black eyes.

"How is it possible that you love him? Listen to me, Julia!"

"Quiet! Look out!" The poor girl could not go on. With a motion of her head she indicated old Mariana who, with her back turned, was pouring the ground chile into a crock.

The second lieutenant understood and fell silent. Then he said aloud that he would like to make Don Bernardo a gift of some canned sardines and good liquor.

"Doña Mariana, while I'm making the soup, would you go for them? And get more *masa* for the tortillas; this won't be enough," said Julia.

The taciturn Mariana lifted her head and focused her clouded eyes on the two young people. Then, wordlessly, she took a shawl from the green trunk and accepted the bill that Mercado held out to her with a look of horror and revulsion. The old woman set off like a sleepwalker, soundlessly, and without the slightest indication of having any will of her own.

Once they were alone, Miguel approached Julia, who, bowing her head, left off cutting a piece of cheese. "Look here, Julia, God is good and doesn't wish such things, won't tolerate them. You, so lovely, so young . . . with him . . . This is evil! It isn't good . . . No!"

Then, silence. He could not continue, and the poor girl, sensing everything with her budding feminine instinct, was equally unable to reply. After a few moments she managed to stammer, "I know that. But what can I do? Who would believe me? He would kill me if . . ." And she began to sob.

"Don't cry, you can't cry." The officer's voice grew warm, confident, and consoling.

"Don't cry, now . . . Do you want to be my wife? We'll go away from here, very far away, to Chihuahua, to the capital. You will be my wife. No, it makes no difference that you have lived with him. I know you don't care for him; I know that he is killing you, my sweet! Look here, I love you because you have suffered, because you know what it is to suffer, because you are intelligent, gentle and good . . . so good with your sad, dark, beautiful eyes!"

Enchanted yet fearful, the trembling Julia had stopped sobbing. She let herself be lulled by the music of Miguel's words, sinking into the warm current of his vehement, youthful tenderness. Her pain dissolved in a languid voluptuousness in which all thought, all action disappeared. Vibrating with an unknown ecstasy, she let herself be lulled, she let herself be swayed.

Haughtily shaking out their feathers, the cocks crowed one after the other. Flies buzzed in lazy circles above the dog sleeping in the sun. From far away the call of a bugle sounded in the warm air. Then a great silence, an infinite peace.

"Shall we, Julia? Tell me! Can you love me? Do you want to live with me? Do you want to go away together, just the two of us? Do you want that?"

Faintly, wistfully, she replied, "Just the two of us? Together? Why are you saying this? Why? It is evil of you. Oh, you are mean, sir." Once again she sobbed convulsively, holding nothing back, and then stared at him with wide, swollen eyes.

"Don't cry, for the love of God, please . . . I'm saying it because I love you, because you're going to be the woman I adore, don't you know that?"

"No, no! How can you say that? Don't you know? Haven't I told you I'm from Tomochic?"

A flash of haughty rage illuminated her moist eyes as she spoke the heroic name, but Miguel's pained expression, both submissive and fond, won her over again. Indeed, she grew calm and sweet again as a smile broke through her proud tears. "You don't know how much I want to leave here . . . but not like this! Do you understand?" And the divine smile that dawned on her fine, dark face made her lips even more alluring and the fire in her feverish eyes more splendid.

"If only I could go to Chihuahua or write to my godfather. It might be that I've already forgotten how to write . . . But no . . . no, leave me alone, go away! You see? You're the same as he is . . . No!"

Miguel tenderly put his arms around her waist and tried to kiss her forehead.

Taken aback by the officer's audacity, the trembling girl turned bright red with embarrassment; she lifted her arms into the void and withdrew to the back wall. Miguel followed and then brought his face close to hers and planted an innocent kiss on her cheek. It was a kiss devoid of passion, as if meant for a sister.

Julia sighed, covering her face with her kerchief, while a cowed Miguel contemplated her in melancholy silence.

"How I love you, Julia!" he said, calmer now. Then he brought his lips, still aflame from the kiss he had given her, close to her blushing face.

The youthful kiss, miraculously dissolving the anguish in the heart of the melancholy girl from the mountains, kindled a soft, voluptuous flame that burned for the first time in her eyes, her breasts, her belly.

Suddenly the yellow dog awoke, lifted its head and legs, and began to sniff the air and wag its tail.

"Here he comes. For the love of God, sit down!"

The impassioned young man nearly abandoned himself to his fury, but—as was not always the case—reason got the better of blind impulse. He controlled himself, sat down, and pretended to examine one of the cocks.

Don Bernardo, already drunk, stopped in the doorway to kick the dog as it came up to lick his hand. He squinted good-naturedly at the officer out of the corner of his eye, then slowly held out the bottle to him.

"Ah! Chief, you're a good man! Look at the fine tequila I've brought you. Hey, there—Julia! A glass. Right now, damn you to hell!"

Humbly, still dazed, she approached Miguel and held out the glass of tequila to him with a trembling hand. Miguel took it, squeezing the girl's hand. When she raised her head, her eyes gleamed with gratitude and love. Don Bernardo, stooped over against the wall, coughed long and hard, panting and spitting. A repugnant sight!

CHAPTER 12

Toasts on the Eve of Battle

That evening, sounds of a strange and joyous revelry pulsed through the camp on the Alameda. Previously a sad, deserted space, it had been transformed with new life and the vendors were having a field day. Lieutenant Torrea, the officer of guard, could hardly keep up. He was overseeing the registration of the *soldaderas*, and he couldn't keep order in the camp at the same time. Bustling around the cooking fires were more than sixty voluble women whose presence enlivened the rectangular space the troops inhabited, its periphery marked by pyramid-shaped stacks of rifles.

While the off-duty soldiers stretched out on their serapes[1] to rest from the exhausting march, the women collected kindling, stole chickens, and bought bread, cheese, and meat. Throughout the day thick plumes of smoke roiled upward, enveloping everything in a bluish haze, including the bayonets gleaming in their stockpiles. Groups of men and women stepped around pieces of baggage; hungry men circled the piles of kindling, blowing on them with bulging cheeks until the flames began to glow. Meanwhile, the officers strode back and forth, yelling out orders.

Some of the soldiers sang sad songs of the wilderness that lamented the plight of a savage brigand or the death of an unlucky bullfighter, their monotonous, plaintive voices sounding like brutish moaning.

> Rosa, Rosita
> Red, red rose
> Lino Samara has died . . .

The doomed resignation of a vanquished people seemed to throb in those songs.

The ragged, filthy *chimoleras*[2]—women vending cheap plates of food at two or three centavos—tended their enormous casseroles and black pots. With unkempt hair and bare arms, they pushed and shoved, yelling and gesticulating, and unleashed a barrage of obscenities as they argued with the *soldaderas*.

That night there was more reason for excitement than usual. The troops were relatively rested and had eaten well, since the women had rounded up some cheap meat and lard. Indeed, they could ask for no more.

In preparation for their departure the next day, men and women alike reinforced their huaraches with new soles. Renewed, they felt ready to march across the world, if so ordered. Although the poor devils were being led into the depths of the Sierras to die like sheep or to kill like beasts of prey, they were utterly calm; some even lounged like lords alongside their women.

A few steps away from the campsite was a house hidden in the darkness. Inside, two men paced back and forth in a room where a pool of reddish light was created by the open door. The men spoke urgently and then fell silent.

The men, Lieutenant Colonel Florencio Villedas and Captain Eduardo Molina, were reviewing their commander in chief's general plan and shaping their own in accordance with it.

While the two troop commanders continued their measured conversation, the camp grew livelier. In a spacious tavern behind the arches that circled the town plaza, the jovial officers grew animated and expansive as they drank and joked about their future, singing loudly of victory.

Just as on the preceding day, rounds of tequila were handed out in rapid-fire succession, accompanied by applause and toasts. A livid-faced Castorena, completely in his element, his tangled hair sticking up in disorderly tufts, sent couplets and quatrains flying left and right. "A verse from Castorena! Castorena, give us a toast!"

"Silence! The poet's going to speak . . . Pass him another round and let him toast," someone boomed.

"Now, Brains of Bronze! Who'd like some brains spiced with Castorena and washed down with tequila?"

"Bring him a keg so he can toast our health!"

"Let's have it, you feather brain!"

"Quiet! Let him speak."

The walls of the tavern vibrated with drunken hilarity.

Then, with a trembling hand, a beaming Castorena tried to lift his glass without spilling. Over the growing tumult of voices, he recited:

> I humbly beg your leave to speak
> Although the night is growing late:
> I toast to each and all who seek
> Tomorrow to annihilate
> The outlaw town of Tomochic!

"Bravo, bravo! Here's to the poet!" While thunderous applause rang out, outside a few impassive natives wrapped in thick red blankets gathered at the threshold of the door and observed the wild melee inside the smoke-filled tavern.

The enthusiasm verged on delirium; it was madness.

A captain forecast a brilliant future for the man who could compose such verses, and the bard began to prepare a new toast while the others continued talking in small groups. Then an uncouth man with long hair and a beard bellowed drunkenly. The officers' wild revelry was infectious, and Second Lieutenant Mercado began to drink too. Swept along in the drunken tide, his mind cloudy, Miguel vainly protested that this was the grossest stupidity, that poetry should be banished from a world where the most corrupt reality reigned. Thus he grimly soliloquized to himself amid the tumultuous din.

Once again alcohol had won, and he experienced an odd exultation, followed by a rush of bitter memories. In this melancholy moment, surrounded by the wild uproar, he tried to be philosophical. "Well, after all, what's so bad about a little drinking? Blots out the pain, doesn't it, Martínez? And I haven't drunk my share yet. Let me offer a toast, as well . . . A drink! Bring me a drink!" said Miguel.

"Friar Mercado wants a drink—a shot for the philosopher!" Castorena yelled out.

"The next round's on me," said Lieutenant Ramírez. "Let Mercado be the next to toast."

When the waiter set the drinks on the counter "in marching order," as Castorena put it, Ramírez, who had paid, served each man his glass. All the others, with their instinct for tactical formations, formed a circle around Miguel. The second lieutenant waited for silence before he began: "I'm not here to improvise quatrains like Castorena. I have no patience for verses, or for poetry either for that matter, because it's nothing but a lie, and all that is false is contemptible. Only truth has beauty, even when it kills.

"I am here, just as my comrades and superiors are, to live up to the worthiness of our mission. We are the sacrificial lambs needed to expunge society's errors. Our lives are offered up to destiny or chance in our mission as soldiers . . . Let us fulfill our duty, even if it costs our lives. I offer a toast . . . I want to offer a toast—to duty, and to the soldiers of Mexico!"

No one, not even Miguel, fully grasped this utterance, but it was applauded by all as elegantly expressed.

The glee continued unabated. As the officers gesticulated heatedly in the smoky atmosphere reeking of drink, the three lamps hanging from the ceiling bathed the sea of dingy twill uniforms in a sickly yellow light.

Castorena, who did guard duty from nine to eleven o'clock that night, yelled at Miguel as he made his exit: "Don't forget guard duty, Mercado. From eleven to one, it's your turn!"

CHAPTER 13

The Satyr's Trap

B ernardo was stretched out on a bench in a corner of the tavern, snoring with his mouth wide open, his head propped against the wall, and the short upturned brim of his old straw hat covering one side of his face. His dirty, tangled mane and grizzled beard made him look like a wild beast.

As Miguel downed another drink in a rage worthy of a madman, his gaze came to rest on the ogre who lived in the hut by the river. An idea flitted through his agitated brain that made him sit up and think.

Suddenly he bolted out of the tavern to cross the dark, lonely plaza. Taking infinite detours, tripping and falling down deserted side streets, at last he reached the river and was standing outside the low door to Julia's hut. He knocked and the dog began to bark, then was quickly silenced. The door opened soundlessly.

It was not yet ten o'clock, yet in the distant darkness the river's faint lapping could be heard, and the stars sparkled with uncommon clarity. At the river's edge, the north wind violently bent the dry shrubs.

The intense cold helped Miguel sober up, and when the door opened, he sprang inside. The lamp burning in a corner of the room went out, but not before he glimpsed an enchanting vision. Julia, shivering, having just risen from bed, stood barefoot in her nightdress that revealed her bare arms and breasts.

Then the maddening darkness snatched her away as she tried to retreat into the hut, alarmed at the vision of a man other than her master. "Julia, it's me. Where are you? Don't be afraid. It's me, Miguel. Come here! Come on, come on."

When she realized who it was, she stammered, "You, sir? How . . . Hush! But . . . for God's sake, where is Don Bernardo? Tell me. He'll be coming along . . . What do you want with me? What? Ah, no! No, I tell you, no . . ."

Miguel heard nothing, heeded nothing. In a fit of frustrated desire, he stumbled and groped for her in the darkness and then became increasingly agitated when he couldn't find her. In vain she tried to ask where Bernardo was. Under her breath she said, "I tell you, no, sir. You are so bad, so mean! Look, you'll wake up Doña Mariana!

The second lieutenant sensed her nearness from her heat, her smell, her frightened, pleading breathlessness as she evaded him in the dark. In the unfamiliar darkness, he couldn't see her though he sensed her proximity, but she was wary and agile, and eluded him again and again! Finally he resorted to tenderness—the lasso he would use to rope her in.

"Come here, my lovely one, I just came to tell you I love you, to tell you I love you and to give you a kiss, just one kiss . . . That's right, silly thing, one little kiss, just like this morning. One kiss. Give me one and I'll go. Come on, come closer, a hug and a kiss—please? Don't be mean. See, you're the mean one . . . Making me suffer, I who adore you, the only one who loves you so much I want to make you my wife in the church. Come now . . ."

"Quiet, I beg you, for the love of the Holy Virgin! Don't you see you'll wake up Doña Mariana, that Don Bernardo will come back? Go away. Don't say these things to me! Please don't. Go!"

"I love you, my word of honor. I swear by the almighty power of God. You are my wife now . . . God wills it!"

Hearing him invoke the divinity, Julia was shaken to the core. Then she sighed, dropped her arms, and did not resist. She let herself be taken.

Yes, she let herself be taken. The drunken second lieutenant crushed her and pressed her to him, fondling her, his eager hands and triumphant lips making their way down her fine throat to the small, erect nipples, then to her naked thighs. These sudden caresses unnerved the girl, yet an unknown delight surged through her at the same time.

Submissive, resigned, she let herself be taken. Resigned yet joyful, she abandoned herself. In the dark, on the brute's bed, she swooned in an ecstasy of sighs and kisses, in delicious agony.

CHAPTER 14

Forward . . . March

At half past noon on October 17 the buglers of the 9th Battalion sounded the "first marching order." The second lieutenant had eaten little and with a poor appetite. After mechanically arranging the administrative papers containing detailed company information, he left the others on the pretext he had received orders from general headquarters. Then he ran to Julia's house.

He found it closed up. Could they have left? He reflected for a moment, recalling the previous night's rites, remembering the madness that had driven him fearlessly to the ogre's den to steal his prey from him, had driven him to force himself on the vulnerable Julia. He called up the scene vividly in extraordinary detail, reliving in the plain light of day all that had happened in the dark.

He knocked on the door. When it opened, he saw, in a blinding flash, the nubile young woman from Tomochic, half clothed and shivering. Assault and eclipse. He flung himself forward in pursuit of the female body whose smell and warmth were just beyond his reach.

Then he relived the dialogue between them in the shadows as he ruthlessly pursued her, hunting her down with the fury and wanton desire of a drunken satyr.

Afterward the lasso, the trap of tenderness, oaths, his word of honor, and invocation of God Almighty, all to satisfy his appetite, to quench the thirst of his feverish blood!

God Almighty! God wills it! Those hallowed words that served fanatics and deceivers alike, the same for a people who will not bend to the yoke as for a woman who will not surrender! He remembered his prey fainting away in the dank closeness of that den: her sighs, tears, moans of love, the cry of pleasure at the height of ecstasy, the delicious agony of their bodies and souls. An unforgettable, shining, purifying union. Poor Julia.

He recalled that afterward she told him her sad story in a few short words: her life of servitude in Tomochic, the interlude of civilized life in Chihuahua, where she had learned to read and think, and then her abrupt return to days of slavery and nights spent passively, coldly, in the arms of the repulsive Bernardo.

"He is the cross I bear, God wills it . . . as you put it," she murmured as she ended her story.

44

After that she told him that she, Doña Mariana, and Don Bernardo would be leaving the next day at three o'clock in the morning for Tomochic. Directly ahead of the troops, they would travel along the most tortuous paths of the Sierra.

Then the two innocents, despite their shared misfortune, chatting like lifelong friends confident of the future, agreed to meet and make love again in Tomochic.

As he thought about the adventure that could have cost him his life— if, for instance, the old derelict had returned to his dungeon to find the second lieutenant embracing Julia, his favorite slave, in Bernardo's own bed—he continued looking at the closed door of the hut and the empty corral. Only a decrepit, sway-backed she-donkey, little more than skin and bones, wandered about the place forlornly.

Then he heard from far away the melancholy notes of the 9th Battalion bugles sounding the second call to march and rushed back to his post to face the rows of troops that were ready to file out.

Dressed in their blue wool uniforms, the soldiers had packed up all their gear. Meanwhile, the officers were attaching sun flaps to their kepis or packing supplies, knowing that as they passed through the sierras they would have only what they carried with them.

A few dragoons of the 5th Regiment led the 9th Battalion officers' withered, gloomy-looking horses out onto the Alameda. Then the officers began to load their baggage and rifles and girded themselves with their cartridge belts, a hundred cartridges in each.

At three o'clock in the afternoon, under a magnificent sun, the troops moved out. Their pant cuffs rolled, the first soldiers crossed the river and then turned left to await the three remaining columns to join them.

The first column included 2nd Company of the 9th Battalion and a unit of the Chihuahua state public security forces. The second comprised the 9th Battalion's 4th Company, plus a unit from the 11th Battalion, and the third counted with twenty horsemen from the 5th Regiment and a number of irregulars recruited from towns dotted throughout the region. Indeed, these adventurers were decked out like local ranchers, wide red ribbons tied jauntily around their hats.

The cannon traveled on mule back between the first and second columns. The entire force consisted of five hundred men.

Followed by the general staff, a few close friends, and some recently enlisted adventurers, General José María Rangel passed on horseback at the head of the forces as the men presented arms.

Then everyone waited for the arrival of Commander in Chief Rosendo Márquez, who was received with even greater solemnity, to the beat of marching drums. General Márquez, his face ruddy, his gestures imperious, restrained his rearing horse as he yelled out, "Sections! Right face!"

The second row of soldiers, facing south and spread out in march formation toward the Sierra, gave a "step back."

"Right!" yelled the general seconds later.

The troops immediately pivoted to the right while the even-numbered soldiers advanced to the right of the odd-numbered ones to form a long column, four men abreast.

"Forward! March!"

CHAPTER 15

Crossing the Sierra Madre

The slow ascent toward the west began with the troops clambering up the first foothills of the Sierra, leaving the village of Concepción, Guerrero, below. From above, the houses scattered along the banks of the twisting river paled in the dying light as the sun sank directly in front of the marching column.

It was a splendid afternoon, colored in autumn's ochre hues. Toward the east, the river appeared clad in shadows. At sunset the road spiraled upward through reddish terrain partly obscured by thick brush.

A tall cloud of purple dust enveloped the column while the endless woods of the Sierra Madre rose just ahead. On either side, ravines cut into the red earth of the mountain like bleeding wounds.

Miguel stood up in his stirrups and peered behind, where Julia's house was still visible.

As the Sierra began to curve, the valley below disappeared from view. Decked out in their splendid woodlands, the mountains revealed their austere majesty to the ascending troops. The first cold gusts of the oncoming night set the tall pine trees whispering.

The young second lieutenant was astounded was by the beauty of the strange mountain landscape. Ordered not to ride ahead of his position, he slackened the reins and let his horse stumble unguided up the rocky terrain.

The cool winds helped dispel his dark thoughts, and he gave himself over to the slow, voluptuous march of his fragmented column along the sheer mountain passes. He contemplated the dark undulations of the gullies from whose depths emerged swirls of snow, and his heart fairly surged when the brambles and thickets opened and he caught a glimpse of the violet sky. The enchantment of that powerful, untamed wilderness restored his ailing nerves. "This is astonishingly beautiful," he murmured from time to time.

When the men overheard Miguel talking to himself and saw him raise his arms to the skies, overcome with ecstasy and wonder, they tittered among themselves.

At nightfall the forces set up camp in a clearing surrounded by forest, called La Generala. The company was in a lively mood and fires were lit. The tall flames projected towering shadows onto the pines.

The troops started out quite late in the day on October 18, due to a curious incident. The horses of the 5th Regiment, sensing they weren't far from their stables in Guerrero, broke loose and stampeded back the way they had come. In wild disorder they galloped until they reached the outskirts of town, where they were stopped and brought back to camp.

The austere and robust life of the mountains appealed to the sensitive young officer; they spoke to him of pride and liberty and love.

Miguel abandoned himself to his solitary meditations. He looked toward his future and felt faith in existence. Why should he die so young, when he still had work to do? He might accomplish something useful, achieve an important undertaking, perhaps even know the joy of victory.

His momentary optimism belied a premonition that he would witness a terrible drama that would temper his soul. He felt he might experience epochal events, visions he would never forget. Possibly the memory would fortify him during crises and conflicts yet to come.

The prodigious spectacle of the Sierra Madre continued to unfold majestically before Miguel's contemplative eyes. The moment had come for the hazardous climb up the rocky paths and the vertigo of looking down into the black abyss on either side when, during the rest periods, the soldiers perched on sheer overhanging cliffs. Meanwhile, they marched in single file, one by one, along impossibly narrow passes or through great canyons above whose vertical walls, as though from the bottom of a black well, they could glimpse the brilliant sky far, far away.

Realizing the imminent peril, Miguel wondered why the enemy didn't polish them off right here, where ten men could destroy an army. Their adversaries knew these mountains like the back of their hand—why didn't they attack now, when the men were stretched over the steep, stony terrain at the bottom of the deepest canyons? Indeed, it wouldn't require much daring against so little resistance; however, certainly the brave rebels of Tomochic would prefer to wait until they were attacked on their home turf. They wouldn't want to leave their holy ground, where they knew they were invincible.

The general knew this all too well, so despite his painful past experiences, he was not overly cautious.

Sometimes the irregulars were deployed on the flanks of the columns, where they nimbly climbed on ahead to scrutinize the terrain. But it was evident to all that if an attack came they would serve as the doomed heralds of catastrophe.

At one o'clock in the afternoon the troops stopped to rest in the outpost of Peña Agujerada. A steer was slaughtered, and flour and meat handed out to the troops. This would be the extent of their rations for the day.

At four o'clock the troops resumed the march. They had to cross the river several times, which slowed them so much that they had to continue marching until eleven o'clock that night. That bold march in utter darkness had a negative affect on Miguel's mood.

They had to press blindly on, groping their way between pine trees and boulders that seemed twice their normal size in the blackness. Panting with fatigue, their feet leaving bloody trails in the crevices between the boulders, the troops pressed on silently. They stumbled, fell, and then rose only to stumble and fall again.

The laughter had long since died away, and with it the jokes, the happy chatter, and the singing that had transformed the harsh, tedious march across the hard rock into a festive occasion. Now, from the long, attenuated column came the painful sounds of labored breath, clomping footsteps, and rifles clanking against metal canteens.

"No lagging! No lagging!"

"Forward, forward!" yelled the officers mechanically to the stragglers; even on horseback, they felt as tired as the foot soldiers.

A few guides, paid in gold by the general, went ahead of the others.

The soldiers continued up and down tortuous, thicketed paths, sometimes leaping from rock to rock as they crossed the deep ravines, their feet, bloodied and sore, sinking deep into the glacial waters, an invisible lymph that rippled sinuously through the bottomless chasms.

Some of the soldiers threw themselves down to drink, impassively withstanding the furious blows of rifle butts as the sergeants tried to get them to their feet again.

The horses resisted going up and down the steep grades, their hooves striking sparks on the rocky ground. Sometimes they halted altogether, their eyes shining like huge phosphorescent orbs in the darkness, on the brink of exhaustion. Breathing noisily in the blackness of the trees on the vertiginous cliffs, they pricked up their great ears to the mystery of the night, as the stars sparkled icily in the black sky.

"Keep moving! No lagging!" the officers shouted again, hurling rude insults at the exhausted, terrified men dragging themselves through the rugged mountains to meet their death in battle.

"*Caramba!*[1] Why don't they cut us down right here? Those Tomochic devils must be imbeciles, with as many rocks in their heads as we've got underfoot, if they haven't thought of finishing us off in this place!" said Castorena to Miguel.

When he wasn't drinking, the poet was a pessimist. Having exhausted his bottle of tequila, he was beginning to feel a little frightened. "A few shots from the cliffs and there'd be nothing left of us. Can you imagine the rout?"

"I see it perfectly . . . it would be absolute panic, utter defeat," chimed in Miguel, alarmed by the fear that Castorena exhaled with each word. "They'd wolf us down too fast to even taste us!"

"So, we didn't even know the first thing about them!"

Miguel made no response. He knew the toll a nighttime raid in the Sierra would exact on the troops after their hard day's march. The soldiers would be desperately hungry and disoriented. They wouldn't know where they were being led or to what end, where the enemy was coming from, or how many there were.

The most tragic national catastrophes came to mind, maybe another fiasco like the one at Cerro del Borrego. There was enough cruel irony in the tragic name itself: the Hill of the Lamb. A few brave men had surprised the weary troops as they slept, half dead from exhaustion, and got the better of the Mexican military, a heroic army under strong leadership, yet set adrift like miserable beasts.

More than ever Miguel understood the difficult responsibilities of a commander, and how urgently Mexico needed a well-trained, disciplined officer corps.

A magnificent panorama took shape in his mind . . . From the depths of an endless valley walled in by high, blue mountains, the Chapultepec fort[2] rose out of a thick plot of leafy fronds. Chapultepec, with its presidential citadel and military academy; the classrooms where students acquired knowledge and strength and learned how to fight; the palace where the victorious were lodged.

Only from this modern, heroic Chapultepec could come the seeds of a Mexican army worthy of the bravery and patriotism of its men.

Suddenly the pensive officer's horse stopped dead in its tracks.

"Rio Verde! We've arrived. We've arrived. Finally!" scattered voices exclaimed.

It was nine o'clock at night. The day's march had come to an end.

CHAPTER 16

Recalling the Campaign against the Apaches

In anticipation of a surprise, two lines of advance guard posts were established in Rio Verde, with troops blocking all access points to the camp. Miguel, with ten trustworthy men from his company and two irregulars from Chihuahua, was delegated to the rear guard.

One of the Chihuahuans was an old man of seventy whose youthful eyes shone brilliantly out of his furrowed face. Tall, thin, strong, he was bursting with enthusiasm. Chatting like old friends, rifles in hand, the second lieutenant and the old man set out together through the thickets and brush that surrounded the guard posts.

On these rounds the old soldier recounted campaigns against the savage Indians, a triumphant entry into Chihuahua on a certain April morning, for one. The energetic old man evoked the scene with such vividness and color that in his mind's eye Miguel saw the poignant scene clear as day.

He could almost see the victorious procession of that heroic cavalcade: under the canopy of Chihuahua's lovely azure sky, a splendid sun warming the street below, which was suddenly bustling with excitement on that fine spring morning. He witnessed the brave men returning victorious from the ferocious campaign against the savage Apaches. Townspeople lined the sidewalks, families gazed from open windows, and storekeepers jumped over their counters to stand in their doorways while the large parish bells rang out through the clear air. The brave cavalry troops strode slowly in formation, four abreast. Broad hats covered faces darkened with the bushy growth of new beards. The troops sported gray shirts or leather jackets, yellow antelope-hide pants, and high boots; their makeshift saddles were made of deerskin and the hides of mountain animals.

The horses were small and thin but nimble and bursting with energy, as steadfast and brave as their riders. The long, sharp-tipped spears pierced the dazzling blue beyond. Those spears! For Miguel, they stood for the campaign itself, in all its savagery and glory.

Along the sturdy lances, from top to bottom, dangled long shocks of blood-spattered black hair: scalps ripped from the skulls of savage Indians to festoon the spears of the victors who had hacked them off in the desert. Each trophy represented a feat of selfless heroism. The long manes swayed in the wind as they hung vertically from the shafts. It was impossible to distinguish which locks hung from which spear. As they moved along, the clanking throng was transformed into a moving forest of black, bloody hair. On the horses' rumps rode tall bundles of sturdy riding pants once worn by comrades who met their death in the immense solitude of the Sierra or the arid plains of the north.

In turn, Apache chiefs decorated the empty skulls of fallen soldiers and used them in their orgies as vessels for corn liquor and sotol. Those chiefs, that is, whose hair was not hanging from the spears of the valiant Chihuahuans, thought Miguel.

Some years before, the Chihuahua state government had organized a campaign against the Apaches after they attacked settlements, sacking and looting with the invasive power of a natural disaster.

The government offered three hundred pesos for each Apache scalp recovered in battle. The leader of that particular campaign was none other than Colonel Terrazas, a wily veteran who was thoroughly familiar with the northern regions and the customs of the Indian inhabitants.

More than five hundred spirited mountain dwellers set out, hungry to avenge the death of loved ones, seeking only to wipe out the savage hordes who had brought fear and lamentation to the homes of hard-working, peace-loving people.

Such a long campaign . . . such unparalleled savagery!

No, it wasn't only the heroic combat—man to man, spear to spear, machete against machete, valor against valor; it was the hunger too that gnawed at the entrails, the feverish thirst that could drive men mad on those interminable days spent crossing the desert under an African sun.

And then the cruel winter, the nocturnal chill of the guard post, the shivering, and the hostile whiteness that blanketed the black crests. Those grimy winds off the Sierra brutally slicing at their faces with steely gusts; the fatigue, the insomnia, the hunger . . . the marches—climbing, tripping, slipping, always on your guard, wary eyes trained on every rock and tree, expecting at any moment an Apache arrow.

But what bliss when the enemy was cornered at the bottom of a ravine! The soldiers fell on them, spears in hand. With what terrible rage and superhuman effort they flung themselves into the fray!

In vain the painted Indians howled their frightening, malevolent war cries. Their burnished faces, painted in black and red, grimacing ferociously, they gestured menacingly as they leaped like tigers rattling their necklaces of human teeth. But it was all in vain. There was no escape, no way out, at the bottom of the ravine. They fell, pierced through by the spears of the valiant Chihuahua mountain men, who charged them as though defending their fathers or the family ranch.

At long last, the enemy was flushed from the territory and the battle came to an end. Indeed, the furious Terrazas had forced the savages back beyond the Rio Bravo. And one morning, a fine spring morning indeed, his horsemen entered Chihuahua.

Five hundred men had set out on the expedition; 115 returned. Nearly four hundred had been laid to rest in the deserted woodlands of the Sierra or on the vast, desolate plains. And now the savages who had escaped the soldiers' spears drank northern whiskey from their empty skulls.

But the sun-beaten survivors, with unkempt beards beneath their wide-brimmed hats, brought back the scalps they had won with the fallen heroes' garments, for which the government would compensate the widows and orphans.

As the people of Chihuahua reflected on this, watching the proud procession, the morning breeze stirred the locks of Apache hair. Long and black, horrid, matted with blood—a traveling jungle of hair.

At the same time a mournful symphony of wailing and crying arose. Because the women and children prisoners bore no blame for the savagery inflicted by the warriors, they would be taken in as servants in Chihuahua homes, bringing with them their nostalgia for the wild, nomadic mountain life.

CHAPTER 17

Tomochic! There It Is!

On the general's orders, the next day all local recruits and non-uniformed military men tied broad red ribbons around their hats to distinguish themselves in combat from the enemy. In addition, the officers were ordered to remove all stripes and insignia from their uniforms. In this way they attempted to avoid becoming the enemy's principal target. It was common knowledge that the Tomochic fighters stalked the commanders and officers, who were easily distinguishable from the enlisted troops.

On October 19, they would march for three hours from Rio Verde to Las Juntas, and from there it was only six miles to Tomochic, where the enemy was waiting.

The brief march proved treacherous. With no water and little food, they had to make the precipitous ascent on foot, exhausting them on the eve of the offensive. Despite their hunger and thirst and the crushing trek from mountaintop to mountaintop, they had a keen sense of satisfaction at approaching the mission's outcome, whatever it turned out to be.

Meat and flour from the lean provisions were distributed among the troops and officers at Las Juntas, a camp situated on a high plain that overlooked the area in all directions. Then a mute calm descended over the troops, masking the nervous excitement over the next day's offensive. Soon an anguished uncertainty reigned again. Voices were hushed and conversations few and far between as uneasy eyes peered at the rocky horizon, spotted with pine trees, out of pale, fatigued, hungry faces.

General Rangel, who was now first in command (before reaching La Generala, Márquez had returned to Guerrero), personally ordered and supervised all advance forays.

At eight o'clock that night the fires were extinguished and total silence reigned. Somewhere in the distance a bright lantern cast a ghostly, ruby-red luminescence and a continual faint murmur could be heard from the bivouac of general headquarters. "We know they're still eating supper and they even have something to drink," said Castorena. He sat crossed-legged with his rifle on his lap. Nearby several officers stretched out on the grassy field.

"You already ate. What you really want is a drink, you sot," retorted Lieutenant Torrea, who was trying to accommodate his head on a boulder.

"What I wouldn't give for a drink of water," added Miguel, who knew that water was scarce. Grilled beef, the only food he had eaten for two days, made him painfully thirsty.

"I'd give even more for a drink of sotol. I might even treat you to a poem," quipped Castorena.

"Oh boy . . . Let's see if the poet can work up a verse now," responded Torrea, stretched out at full length.

"Tomorrow we'll all be spouting rhymes when those Tomochic devils fry us."

An uncomfortable silence followed this exchange between the off-duty officers who had just finished their meager supper of grilled beef, a desultory meal without benefit of salt or water.

Now they were waiting to make evening rounds, to check on each sentinel post as well as ascertain general conditions in the main bivouac and quarters, while the off-duty troops slept.

"Well, what's it to be? How are we going in? What's the plan?" asked Miguel. "Will Colonel Torres come along or is he just here to share the glory?"

Captain Servín explained, "I think the first column will go down the Cordon de Lino hill while we take the main road, and Colonel Torres will lead the Sonoran troops to attack from the other side. First, the Hotchkiss is going to blow the church sky high, and then the women will come swarming out in a frenzy. At most, this'll take a couple of hours. A couple of hours, then we'll see . . . we'll see about this!"

"At last! We might be eating chicken by midday. A fine chicken à la Tomochic, grilled in the embers of the burning church!" said Castorena, licking his chops.

"Oh, who knows. Who can really say, boys? What if . . . ?"

"What if, captain? So what if they kill us . . . as long as we've eaten a proper meal!"

At that moment, wrapped in his cape, the first captain of the 2nd Company of the 9th Battalion stepped forward out of the darkness to greet them in a calm but stern voice. Just talking with them, he managed to lift their spirits; he reminded them that as officers trained at the military academy, they had to show that they could fight as well as they could study. "See you tomorrow, my good men. Take care. I'm going for a walk. Good work on your rounds—you're doing well!"

Off he went with measured steps, his small head held high as always. Paying scrupulous attention to every detail around him, the captain was always ready to impose discipline and restore order, to make the best of any situation.

Captain Eduardo Molina was liked for his good heart and readiness to come to the aid of his officers, whom he encouraged in any and all endeavors. True, he was exceedingly strict, and the men called him names behind his back. When he taught military theory to these same men at the military academy, he explained combat with firearms and bayonets so enthusiastically and that they called him "Little Napoleon." Captain "Little Napoleon" of the 9th Battalion happened to be diminutive in stature and, like Napoleon the Great, was in love with war. He was a slave to duty, but always a faithful friend.

"Tomorrow we'll see whose hide you can cut more straps from," said the poet. When nobody responded he got to his feet, restless and annoyed. Then he went off to try to convince some high-ranking officer to throw back a few drinks with him.

On the following day, October 20, at four o'clock in the morning, the troops were silently awakened. In the mountains at that time of year and hour of morning it is still darkest night, pitch black and intensely cold.

The troops passed back and forth like specters in the darkness. The first sergeants of the companies didn't bother to take roll call but counted the number of rows. The guards from the advance posts returned to their respective sections. Starlight showed the pallid faces, trembling chins, and dry lips under hoods pulled low over foreheads. The soldiers wore close-fitting capes, over which cartridge belts and combat packs stuffed full of cartridges were strapped. For a full half hour they stood shivering silently, waiting for the march to begin. During this half hour, full of cruel, cold anguish and the darkest of thoughts, there was not even a glimmer of dawn over the crests of the pines bordering the camp.

The general marched back and forth several times reviewing the columns, until at last the explorers of the advance guard—national and auxiliary troops—set off in the darkness.

An officer from the general staff had already informed the commanders which sections would lead the march, at which time the officers mounted their horses and took their positions. With a crescendo of sounds, voices, hooves clacking on rocks, and the sharp knocking of rifle butts, the columns began moving through the thick darkness, beneath a pitch-black sky constellated by magnificent stars sparkling like miracles through the tall branches and above the high mountain ridges.

In the beginning, the descent was terrifying. As though impelled by an invisible force, the troops pushed onward, believing that when they reached the bottom of the steep grade, Tomochic would be there and combat would begin in the dark of night.

The soldiers proceeded haltingly downward into a bottomless pit, stumbling on and on, to the accompaniment of the unique sound of metal hitting metal, as rifle barrels clanked against canteens. The officers' horses snorted, their hooves striking sparks against the hard rocks.

A deathly chill, a baleful, shadowy horror froze the blood, gripped the heart, tormented the empty gut, swamped the weakened brain with bloody nightmares.

The flock marched forward through the darkness and the cold, flung this way and that down rugged unknown precipices, slipping and tumbling through twisted black crevices, moving now at a trot, now a gallop, across the invisible stones. Sleep deprived, famished, and thirsty, they feared sudden annihilation by a burst of enemy fire.

Surely the Tomochic fighters were more than famTlar with the intricacies of these mountains. Couldn't they easily mount a dawn attack?

For the greater glory of their high chief or the girl saint of Cabora, couldn't those fierce mountain hunters, with perfect impunity, visit slaughter and panic on them at the bottom of some black ravine? The disheartening tales of the Tomochic fighters' unbelievable feats, recounted up and down the state of Chihuahua, revived bloody nightmares in weakened minds.

At last they reached a flat stretch and veered left. By the time the battalion had crossed a dry arroyo and started up the next hill, dawn had softened the sky and the stars had paled. As they reached the next summit, the splendid dawn abruptly rose orange and red beyond the black blade of the mountains they were leaving behind. Finally the officers dismounted and gave their horses to the soldiers of the public security forces.

When would they arrive? Where was Tomochic, anyway? After descending the second slope were they going to climb yet another mountain?

Suddenly the column stopped. Then they engaged in a move that amounted to a countermarch and the forces turned toward the right flank. As the rocks rose steeper and craggier here, they moved farther to the right and ascended the same slope they had just come down.

"Shit," yelled out Castorena. "Are we playing around or what?"

"We're going to outflank them."

"No, captain, they must have taken the wrong path."

The march continued as the sun began to warm the air. Some of the soldiers limped from exhaustion, for the terrain had become highly eroded and they were again marching on rock. There was no tree to be seen in this desolate landscape.

"Keep going! Keep going!" called out the officers time and again, even though they too were out of breath.

Marching along in the first column near a section from the 11th Battalion, Mercado was overcome by a hellish fatigue. Suddenly he saw the national troops running every which way and the advance guard retreating to the center. Silence and waiting.

At that moment, from far, far away beyond the mountains, the bugles sounded an alert, the password for Colonel Torres's column, which had come down the road from Pinos Altos. His forces and General Rangel's had come face-to-face with Tomochic.

Rapidly Miguel's column headed for the clearing on the mountaintop. Then came a strange explosive sound. "Colonel Torres is already in combat. Men, let's do our share!" yelled out an officer from the 11th Battalion.

The exchange of fire grew louder and louder. Some soldiers approached the edge of the rocky outcroppings, which now displayed a few pines and small bushes. Leaning over the crest of the craggy mountainside, they saw all the way to the bottom of the cliffs. In the remote distance lay an immense valley cradling the serpentine trail of a river. To one side of the valley, a misshapen, humpbacked mountain rose like a gigantic dromedary; on the other, gray and white houses centered around an old church: the town of Tomochic.

"Tomochic! There it is! That's Tomochic!" voices yelled.

Tomochic! Tomochic! That rough, heroic word echoed from the rocky mountain face down to the tight rows of troops, leaving in its wake an icy shudder.

CHAPTER 18

The Defeat of the First Column

The artillery troops unloaded the cannons from the backs of the mules, while Lieutenant Méndez descended the steep slope for a view of the entire valley. To estimate the valley's depth, he shot off a round from his rifle, causing a commotion. Once the cannon was mounted on the four-footed stand, the artillery officer took precise aim and fired. First came the sound of detonation; then the projectile described a great arc as it whistled into space. Within moments, the shell exploded with a terrific noise.

A wild roar ran through the columns as the first cannonball hit Tomochic. "Viva Mexico! Long live General Díaz," some yelled, certain that the cannon meant triumph and the town's defeat.

"Viva, viva! Long live General Díaz!"

"Back in line . . . positions!" shouted the officers when they saw the soldiers dispersing to watch the cannon fire.

Manned by the lieutenant, the cannon continued to fire while the columns awaited orders. At the same time the exchange of fire grew more intense from the mountains beyond Tomochic, where Colonel Torres was fighting, his bugles resounding through the distant tumult of gunfire and echoing interminably off the mountainsides every few minutes.

A luminous setting sun filtered down through the tall pine branches onto the loosely assembled crowd of nervous troops awaiting their attack orders, their anxiety bordering on fever. As the operation had been planned for level ground, the rough, uneven terrain prevented the columns from lining up correctly. In this formation, it was virtually impossible to maneuver while maintaining correct distances and intervals between columns.

And this is when Miguel Mercado, bringing up the rear of the first column of the second section in 2nd Company—overheated after the abrupt halt at the mountaintop—intuited how dangerous the situation was. Engaging the troops in the thick of the mountains, an enemy guerrilla force would have a clear advantage. What was more, the captains were as good as blind. They didn't know exactly where they were or what to do.

Meanwhile, the officers of high command, dressed like natives in wide-brimmed hats, red ribbons trailing, impatiently tried to bring the troops back to order. They were carrying orders from the commander in chief, who brought up the rear and was surrounded by nationals and soldiers from the 5th Regiment. Nearby the cannon fired off every three minutes or so.

"First column, advance!" yelled an adjutant to Lieutenant Colonel Gallardo at the head of the column. The column members loaded up and set forth, sending their first section ahead in broad attack formation.

Mercado shivered. He felt cold as ice. "Is my face pale?" the second lieutenant asked himself as he leaped down the rocky mountain path behind his section.

"Will the soldiers see me? Will I be afraid? I hope they kill me swiftly, with no time to feel anything . . . get it over with! What's going to happen? I just want to die . . . My stomach is in knots . . . is it fear? How cold it is! If they could only see me from the inside! What does life matter? You've got to pretend to be brave. Onward!"

With these dark visions swimming in his head, Miguel straightened up and refocused his eyes, although he saw nothing. Perhaps he was even blinder than his comrades.

They continued their slow descent in deadly silence. In the distance the detonations thundered, creating a continuous rumbling as if some enormous vehicle loaded with irons and chains was careening down the Sierra's sheer slopes, rolling, rolling over the rocky ground.

Meanwhile, the second section waited at the summit. Adhering strictly to plan, they sought to keep themselves at the regulation distance from the others.

Lieutenant Colonel Florencio Villedas deployed the second column to the left of the first. The third column remained on reserve as escort for the cannon, which at last had begun to fire regularly.

At the front of this force were the red-ribboned volunteers and the irregulars, who advanced cautiously, rifles cocked, to explore the craggy, overgrown terrain. The farther down they got, the harder the going was. And this was the most accessible path!

The *cordon*, or path, descending into Tomochic was empty, since here the troops were an easy target for the enemy. This was the famous Cordon de Lino hill where the defeat of September 2 had occurred.

Widely dispersed, the speechless soldiers, their ears trained and their pupils dilated, cast inquisitive glances through the trees and rocks, and advanced timorously. Meanwhile, the officers who were interspersed among the troops marched forward with resolve though they were as pale as ghosts. There was no shouting now, no speaking.

From the far side of the valley, the shooting could no longer be heard though the cannon fired regularly. All of a sudden came several nerve-rattling shots, crystal clear and fired with admirable precision. The volunteers came running back to the command posts of the first section, which had come to an abrupt halt. "They're coming, they're coming," the irregulars yelled out as they arrived.

At the head of the first section the shots multiplied while a whispered order passed from man to man. Dispersed over a wide area behind the pine trees and the bushes, the soldiers brought their rifle butts to their shoulders. "Take good aim and remain calm! Don't waste any shots on the trees!" yelled Captain Alcérreca.

A great uproar could be heard. Then both jumbled and seething, it rose to a menacing crescendo.

But so far no one had seen anything. Though the section was on alert, not a shot had been fired. They were on the defensive in foreign territory known only too well to the enemy, who would strike like lightning. Just then, it became possible to distinguish the distant hubbub. "Long live Almighty God! Long live the Holy Virgin!"

At last the section opened fire in the direction of all the noise, but still there was nothing to be seen. "So this is where the battle begins —in the middle of the woods, halfway up a hill!" thought Miguel, terrified, as he grasped the difficulty of their position, perhaps the imminence of extreme peril.

From down below the first enemy bullets began to whistle up through the trees. The fight had begun.

Trembling, the officer prepared his rifle and waited for a glimpse of the enemy. While they redoubled their firepower, the Tomochic fighters remained hidden from view. But their savage cries grew louder, sowing terror in the hearts of the men, who still couldn't see their adversaries. Forced to fight under the most unfavorable conditions, they could neither advance nor retreat.

Gradually the underbrush grew dense with white smoke and an acrid, bitter smell. The reports of fire penetrated the viscous fog of gunpowder with reddish bursts. With each passing moment, the yelling grew louder and enemy bullets whistled menacingly as they passed close to the tops of the men's heads.

"For Almighty God! For the Holy Trinity!" came the war cries—all too clearly at times—over the hail of bullets. Mortally wounded, a soldier fell to the ground, face down, his arms spread wide. He dropped his Remington and called out plaintively, "O Jesus." Then he fell forward, vomiting blood. He was the first victim.

A young corporal leaned over to pick him up and suddenly screamed in pain. Wounded in the knee, he too rolled to one side. The soldiers nearby stared aghast, but Lieutenant Torrea roused them with a sudden roar. Their courage restored, if furious and exasperated, they fired indiscriminately downward.

Through the thick air in the impenetrable brush Miguel made out the figure of a tall man with a long beard dressed in dark pants, a white shirt, and a straw hat from which floated a long white kerchief. The mountaineer lifted his rifle and cried out in a thick voice, and blindly opened fire. "Long live the Almighty. Death to the sons of Lucifer!"

"That one, over there, get him," a sergeant yelled.

To the second lieutenant's right, another soldier, who had been wounded in the hand, began to moan.

The entire section lost control; the soldiers couldn't even identify their own. Many took aim at the clearing where the Tomochic fighter, on his knees in senseless heroism, fired away. His shots hit a soldier's bugle, which bounced away over the rocks. A moment later the brave mountain fighter collapsed; he fell to one side, head resting on arm, the arm laid over his rifle, as though he might only be sleeping.

A heavy white cloud of gunpowder hung over everything. The smell was harsh but stimulating, like cheap liquor. Scattered gunfire, enemy war cries descending the hill, and snatches of the officers' commands could be heard. "Long live the Santa de Cabora! Death to Lucifer!" And a hearty round of shots accompanied these strange words.

Captain Molina rushed to and fro, attempting to rouse everyone, yelling hoarsely in an attempt to make a worthy response to the enemy's *vivas*: "Long live the federal government! Long live the Mexican Republic!"

"Onward, men! Onward! Long live the 9th Battalion!" the captains joined in.

A new wave of inspiration moved the sections steadfastly forward. Now they felt exhilarated, excited. "Yes, yes, onward—they'll see that the 9th Battalion can't lose! Long live General Díaz!"

Then a moment of calm descended. After the initial stupor had worn off, the men recovered their natural courage. Sweaty, breathless, crouching low, they started downhill again, stopping instinctively wherever there were clusters of trees or high boulders.

One soldier, just as he was about to fire from behind some tall shrubs, suddenly let his weapon drop and rolled away covered with blood.

An enemy bullet had hit the granite edge of a boulder, sending flying fragments of rock into his skull. The section continued its descent.

The gunfire from the mountain fighters let up, and the men found their first Tomochic corpse, deep wounds in head and stomach, and a gaping mouth that revealed strong white teeth.

"Long live the Ninth! Long live the government!" yelled a sergeant, exhilarated at the sight of the corpse. As he spoke, however, more soldiers fell to the ground wounded.

Enemy bullets took a terrible toll. The sections lost all semblance of order the farther down the craggy path they went. Now wildly dispersed, the marksmen lost sight of each other and operated in isolation. Officers tried to regroup for another advance, but they had no idea where they were going or which paths to follow. Consequently their efforts only led to further disorder.

Worse still, shots were heard from behind. This was enough to sow cold terror in every heart. What was happening? They were being overtaken from behind! But how? The government soldiers were surrounded, caught in a crossfire. Just then a soldier caught a bullet in the chest and fell dead.

There was a terrible moment of hesitation in the smoke-darkened thicket, before they tried to retreat. But the enemy was behind them! Which way should they fire?

The lieutenants at first managed to contain the pandemonium, but the panic eventually got to them too. Meanwhile, a few soldiers began to throw off their gear.

"Don't run! Don't run! Cowards, where do you think you're going!" they yelled to the first retreating soldiers, who had begun to run back up the mountain. Behind them, the gunfire intensified and the bravest men turned to answer fire with fire. Suddenly Castorena came hurtling down the mountainface and yelled, "Don't shoot to the rear! Hold your fire! They're our men! It's 2nd Company, and they don't know where we are. I tell you, don't fire!"

In the helter-skelter of gunfire and clamoring voices only a handful of men actually heard Castorena, and none paid the least attention. As though gripped by a sudden madness, they began to fire every which way, battling an invisible enemy in a jungle of ghosts.

What was most frightening about this terrible situation—even more so than the uncertainty over the enemy's whereabouts, firepower, and numbers—was their disorientation and the lack of orders from above.

Stunned and abandoned to their fate, the lower-ranking officers were paralyzed by indecision at that treacherous juncture. When they heard the shots at their back again, what little morale they had managed to retain soon dissipated. Now panic reigned.

The smoke from the gunpowder, the thunderous reports, the whistling bullets, and the enemy's fierce cries surrounded them, turning their area of the mountainside into a disaster zone.

In a moment of lucidity, Second Lieutenant Mercado thought, The first column is going down to defeat!

CHAPTER 19

Worse Than Defeat

Miguel was astounded by the bizarre turn of events. In fact, he felt he had lost his reason altogether. As comrade after comrade was cut down, the soldiers, bullets whistling by their heads, began to fire indiscriminately thinking that the enemy could be anywhere, everywhere. Since they were helplessly lost in the labyrinthine mountains, there was no place to run.

Then the enemy resurfaced in front of them, raising their eerie, hair-raising war cries to the heavens: "Long live the almighty power of God. The power of God is with us!"

Crouching low in the bush, a recruit—just eighteen—suddenly shot out from his hiding place and matched the incantation with furious hero-ism: "Long live the 9th Battalion. Our Lady of Guadalupe protects us!"

Hidden in the pine groves, the Tomochic fighters advanced slowly, with superhuman litheness, bounding from rock to rock, tree to tree. Then suddenly they sprang like tigers into the very midst of the hail of bullets that toppled branches and splintered rocks.

When they caught a glimpse of them, the soldiers saw that their adversaries were tall and shaggy haired, wearing rolled-up pants and white shirts. Cartridge belts crisscrossed their chests, and strips of white linen adorned with red crosses dangled from their hats.

They flew from place to place. Sometimes only the steel barrels of their guns were visible as they poked out between the branches and enveloped the trees in billows of gunpowder.

The intrepid young soldier who had invoked the Virgin of the Republic fired at a man only eight paces away, but the Tomochic fighter landed right in front of him in a single bound and fired his rifle point-blank into the soldier's chest.

The fierce youth fell backward. Meanwhile, a bullet struck his adversary's knee, and he fell at the young soldier's side. Pulling himself up to a seated position, the enemy relaxed his hold on his rifle. But when the Tomochic fighter realized the dying boy was pointing his rifle at him—although he was too weak to fire—the Tomochic fighter shot him again just as the boy managed to squeeze the trigger.

The two shots rang out as one, and a single plume of smoke rose to the heavens. The two heroes were cut down at the same instant and now lay side by side. Similar scenes were played out behind every boulder and tree, in every crack and fissure of the mountain.

If the federal troops had continued their advance, they would have held the advantage in hand-to-hand combat due to their numbers, but it was too late: chaos reigned. The three muddled sections of the first column had no front or flanks, and they were spread willy-nilly over a wide area. Only a few of the coolest heads even heard the orders when they were shouted out.

Even though the outnumbered enemy could have been obliterated in a single all-out attack, it was impossible for the soldiers to go forward amid the chaos. The men's spirits and energy were dangerously low, but most demoralizing of all were the whistling bullets raining down on the rearguard sections.

Just as a breathless, red-faced Captain Molina took charge and began shouting orders—his voice so full of rage it was barely intelligible —a tearful sergeant informed him that Commander Pablo Yépés of the first section had been mortally wounded.

As luck would have it, at that moment Lieutenant Delgadillo was retreating from the fray when a bullet passed through his right leg. At the site where he lay wounded, the corpse of his second sergeant at his side, the courageous officer heroically continued to command his section.

Meanwhile, a rabid Castorena ran this way and that amid the havoc, seeming to be everywhere at once, trying to force the soldiers back to their posts. The nobility of his rage had transformed him. "Damn those louts, why don't they stop shooting us!"

"We're shooting at ourselves! How can this be happening?" Miguel replied, admiring Castorena's surprising bravery.

From one calamity to the next, the terror and panic had become even more pronounced, and clearly a catastrophe was imminent. The gunfire from the rear increased, the wounded and the dead kept falling, and no one was following orders anymore.

The soldiers had dispersed now that all hope of order was lost, and they continued to retreat, scattering their gear as they went. The retreat turned into a wild rout. It was every man for himself!

The loss of morale infected the hardiest fighters, causing even the bravest to take off running in no particular direction. Shaken and trembling, many huddled together, as far away as from the crossfire as they could get.

CHAPTER 20

Defeat of the Second Column

M iguel felt a surge of indignation and wrath deep in his soul at the spectacle of such out and out chaos. So this was the way battles were lost and slaughter prevailed! This wasn't the war he had imagined when he read about the great campaigns in his history books.

Yet the contagion of fear had infected him too, and he was forced to retreat along with the others. The section that had been shooting at them from above was also making a muddled retreat and had finally stopped firing.

Standing on top of a boulder like a madman, bareheaded, his hundred cartridges recklessly spent, Castorena was brandishing his rifle and promising to break the neck of anyone who fled. No one paid the slightest attention. Morale and discipline had been cast to the winds in the delirium of defeat.

"Don't run! Don't run! About face, assault them, men! Long live the Ninth!"

Huddled behind the big rock that served as Castorena's pedestal, an emotional, deflated Miguel called out to his demented comrade and tried to convince him that audacity was useless now. But Castorena refused to listen, weeping with rage: "Come out! Come out into the open, you cowards! Cowards!" he cried again and again, his voice hoarse with impotent fury.

What a sight that indomitable boy was, drawn up to his full height on the boulder, dust covered and heartbroken! With his head exposed, cape in shreds, red hair bristling and tears in his eyes, he was swinging his rifle around by the barrel like a windmill in the dense cloud of gunpowder. A sight indeed!

Captain Molina gathered a few brave men from the retreating masses, and behind a copse of thick bushes they formed a nucleus of defense, a fortress for those who had the heroic will to keep fighting. "Hey, Castorena, Mercado, over here! Get down, take cover!" he yelled.

One behind the other, rifles in their right hands, the pair ran from bush to bush back up the hill, the savage calls of "Long live our Lord Jesus Christ!" and "Long live the Blessed Virgin!" ringing in their ears. From their dugout, this handful of men put up a strong resistance. Nearby lay three Tomochic corpses.

The men's kepis and rifle barrels could be glimpsed between the rocks and boulders or clustered around the trunks of the pine trees. The rifles gleamed in the filtered light as the sun's rays penetrated the high branches and leaves floated down in pieces, blown to bits in the hail of metal.

The two officers reached the spot and Miguel, on his last legs, threw himself to the ground. They could kill him where he lay, but he had to rest. The heat was hellish and sweat streamed from his body. He would have given his life for one sip of water. It was eleven o'clock in the morning.

There on their knees or face down on the ground, some twenty soldiers—four officers and the captain—continued to fire at the enemy. But either their adversaries had retreated or they were attacking the second column on another flank of the mountain, because heavy gunfire could be heard coming from that direction.

A group of these men passed by in the distance, running for cover between the trees as an officer at their head yelled out *vivas* that managed to penetrate the din. "Where are you going, soldier?" the captain asked Miguel, running over to cut off his passage.

"To take up a better position in the rear, sir, because . . ."

"Go to your post immediately!"

Shamed into silence, the officer slowly turned back, crouching down between the trees until he reached the others. This was the same officer who in the morning had lamented not "getting his share" of the fighting.

So the second column moved out, leaving ample space between itself and the first; then both veered left. The second column received orders for its first section to fan out; the other two sections remained on the mountaintop while the first section spread out to guard against an attack from the side. Indeed, while the first column was attacked from the front, the second was beset from the left. Clearly these Tomochic fighters knew something about strategy.

On the same precipitous terrain, the combat looked exactly like what was taking place to the right. The brave men of the mountains uttered their terrible cries and delivered mortal blows with prodigious accuracy. "Death to the soldiers! Long live the Virgin Mary!" they yelled.

The first two columns intended to make their way down the mountainside into Tomochic side by side and take possession of the first houses in the town while the third column remained on alert. All would be protected by cannon fire.

The lieutenant colonel of each column issued orders from the rear guard after receiving orders from the commander in chief through the federal troops.

But the space between the first two columns was so wide that a handful of bold Tomochic fighters wedged in between them and opened fire on both sides. They captured the rear guard of the first section, which responded by attacking desperately on three fronts. In their hopeless situation in the middle of the forest, they could only answer fire with fire.

Then, as a storm of bullets broke over them through the fog, the rear sections broke ranks in total disorder and began firing downhill indiscriminately, devastating their own forward sections. It was mortal chaos in a valley of despair. Not a single voice from the high command could be heard; no one could be understood. The soldiers fired like madmen. It was a moment in hell.

As the Tomochic bullets crossed those from federal rifles, they wove a web of death beneath the dense fog of gunpowder. There were men wounded in the back, dead men shot straight through the temples, corpses with their heads crushed to nothing.

The confusion was terrible as the men rolled between the rocks, blinded by the gunpowder. And all the while their invisible mountain adversaries fired again and again, not even raising their rifles to their shoulders but simply gripping them under their arms.

Heading the first section of the second column was Emilio Servín, a slim, gaunt-faced young man with a chestnut-colored mustache and small, brilliant eyes. He was literally crazed with rage. Seeing his men running in all directions with no notion of where the enemy was, he began to howl and curse, striking those who dared to flee with his rifle. "Get back, you cowards! Long live the government! Don't run away, you swine," he shouted, red with rage, his eyes starting out of their sockets. "Follow me, don't be cowards!"

Rashly, impelled by unspeakable despair, he rushed forward into the brush where not a single man dared to follow. He reached a wide clearing on the mountainside and fired at an enemy fighter who was headed up the mountain.

The shot went astray. Barely taking aim, his adversary felled him with a single bullet through the chest. It was said that when the Tomochic fighters walked past the dying young man and heard him curse, they shot him again from point-blank range.

From their hiding place behind the rocks and trees, a few men saw the young captain raise his rifle and try to lift himself up to fire. But he collapsed face down, his gaping, foam-flecked mouth biting the pebbles of the Sierra beneath him, which he seemed to embrace with arms spread wide.

Macabre coincidence: Domingo Alcérreca, second captain of the first column, swept up in the storm of chaos that now ravaged his column as well, had just reached the spot where Servín had fallen when he was blasted by three bullets to the head and fell next to his ill-fated comrade.

Lieutenant colonels Gallardo and Villedas were wounded at almost the same time but at different spots, the former attacked at dangerously close range and brought to safety by his adjutant, while the latter was shot in the head.

The rout was inevitable then, even in the second column. Each man ran off helter-skelter with no destination or direction in mind, jumping over corpses and abandoning the wounded where they lay in their piteous postures, flailing their arms and trying to rise.

Between enormous boulders and tall pines, the mountainside was strewn with weapons, corpses, wounded men, and gear. A red banner lying near the corporal who had been carrying it appeared to be a great pool of scarlet blood, in contrast to the pale face of the corpse. The man's mouth gaped, eyes staring fixedly at a splendid morning sky from which all the smoke had evaporated.

The tumultuous sound of gunfire had died away. Only isolated shots were heard now and then echoing off the sides of the mountains, or the intermittent report of the cannon, which continued to spit projectiles into the town.

The combat was over.

CHAPTER 21

Tomochic Prepares Itself

When Miguel left Julia on the night of October 16, giving her one last kiss, he promised that they would see each other in Tomochic. After he left, she flung herself down on the broad bed, covered herself from head to toe and lay trembling with fear as she waited for Bernardo to arrive.

She could still feel the burning imprint of Miguel's embraces. It had all been a delicious dream, an hour of high delight that awakened her senses. For Julia, these were the first inklings of love. Even the anticipation of her departure for the city of her sufferings couldn't dull the ecstatic memory of those moments of paradise. Now she shifted about in bed feverishly, nervously springing up at the distant sounds of barking dogs. Auguries of doom.

Afterward, when the girl tried to think about all the problems in her life, being of an unschooled though resourceful mind, she alternately fantasized a future based on pleasant images of love and happiness and then plunged into panoramas painted with the bleakest of colors, tragic scenes, and pictures of death. With all her young and virginal heart, Julia loved the young man who had spoken to her of love and tenderness. Indeed, he was nothing short of her life's greatest dream come true, nothing less than a splendid ray of hope in the night of her misfortune.

Of course . . . that was why she was so afraid of following her father, Bernardo, and Cruz to Tomochic. They would fight against him. Surely, she thought, they would kill him; perhaps she would see his bloody corpse on the threshold of the door to her house. His eyes would be slightly open as though his last wish was to glimpse his adored Julia, whom he had promised to wed in church in the name of the great power of God.

In vain she tried to sleep. Feverish thoughts assailed her. The same whirl of images that were either delicious, heavenly, protected by the archangels of glory or the Virgin herself, or hellish kept turning over and over in her mind. The evil specters showed her nothing but corpses. Satan appeared holding her beloved in his terrible claws condemning him to burn in the flames of hell.

At two o'clock in the morning, Bernardo roughly pushed the door open. His earlier drunkenness had dissipated and he was ready to prepare for the trip home. Tomochic had to be warned of the troops' arrival a day ahead; Bernardo knew that they wouldn't be leaving until afternoon. "Wake up, little friend. Just when do you think we're leaving?"

"Right away, sir. At your orders."

Julia sat up immediately. Shivering in the bitter cold, she pulled on her slip and dress. Then she helped pack up the clothing while the old man went to the corral for the animals and tied up the hens and roosters, which were beginning to show signs of nervousness.

The taciturn Mariana took care of the most difficult tasks. Candle in hand, she came and went, lugging boxes and gunny sacks.

Everything was ready. The two donkeys had been laden with clothes, pots, packages of roasted coffee, a few bottles of sotol, hens tied by the feet, and a few other odds and ends. Then Bernardo ordered Mariana to build a fire using an old plank, and the three of them downed their boiling coffee with a few slugs of sotol.

At four o'clock in the morning they set out. Bernardo took the mule, and the two women rode on strong donkeys. Julia was anxious and worried but remained silent because it was her nature to be submissive, a resigned victim to fate.

Bernardo, a veteran of the Sierra's twisting roads, boldly set out to cross the mountains. Taking barely navigable shortcuts that bordered the precipices, he rode along silently on his mule. Openly mocking the military surveillance in the area, he sat back every fifteen minutes or so to tip his bottle of sotol to his mouth. Not once did he look back at the women who followed him on donkeys, majestically clicking along on their hooves of steel through those wild mountain ranges.

Sitting easily in her saddle, the unhappy Julia was wrapped in a thick American poncho for protection from the glacial winds of the Sierras. She sighed from time to time, and fat tears sprang from her wide, un-focused black eyes. Julia, with her natural vigor and her exquisite sensibility, her fine intelligence! How could she have been born among these barely civilized people engaging in their mad conflicts? The only traits she shared with them were her unequaled heroism and uncanny bravery for nobly bearing up under adversity. But for all their sad heroism, all they knew how to do was die.

The three arrived in Tomochic on October 19 at three o'clock in the afternoon, a day ahead of the forces that would mount an attack the following day. The town was prepared to defend itself. The houses at each end, as well as the ancient tower, had been outfitted with openings for rifles. At the foot of Cerro de Cueva hill, which loomed over the whole valley, the old tower rose into the sky.

Tomochic, although sparsely populated, covered a fairly large area. The scattered dwellings were linked by footpaths, which twisted and turned through the cornfields and cattle pastures. A few days before, fifteen to twenty families headed for other mountain towns along with the few men who refused to take up arms. Cruz Chávez's house was an impenetrable fortress. Fully barricaded, it was outfitted like a blockhouse with its three rows of rifle openings.

Cruz's brothers José and Manuel also lived in the house with their wives and four children. A circle of wood posts reinforced with barbed wire enclosed two large, solid adobe sheds. An oven stood in the center, and nearby on a bleached pedestal stood a tall wooden cross adorned with white ribbons dangling from both arms.

One of the sheds housed fifty-one prisoners taken in combat on September 2. The other—larger and more solid than the first—consisted of the living quarters, or three linked rooms. A single door opened to the central room, which gave access to the other rooms.

The families of the three brothers lived in the main room; one served as a warehouse and storeroom for munitions, and the other was the chapel and inner sanctum of the new pontiff of the desert. Only a select few were granted admission. It served as the commander's camp and the bedroom for the head of household.

Bernardo told Cruz all he knew about the attack on the town sched-uled to occur the following morning: the troops would come down the road by the cemetery or attempt to take Cerro de Cueva hill, which dominated the valley. Sitting by the fireplace in front of a large pot of boiling coffee, Cruz bent his hairy head to think about what had just been said. When he looked up again, his mouth curled in a half smile as he said, "Who cares? The soldiers of Jesus Christ never lose. We'll beat them again. Look here, six more came in from Yopomare; count-ing the boys, that's 103. I've put five guerrilla forces together and I've ordered Reyes Domínguez to kill his only cow . . . the women are already cooking up the chickens and corn. God protect us and grant us his blessing!"

Then the two started down the path that led to the church, whose walled courtyard was filled with men waiting for Cruz. All rifles were prepared and cartridge belts full.

The men sitting on the steps that led to the great cross in the cen-ter rose respectfully when the chief arrived. More than ninety moun-tain fighters were waiting in the courtyard paved with funeral slabs and a few small crosses. They were decked out in white or blue shirts, cot-ton or leather pants, and knee-high boots. Belts loaded with cartridges were crossed on their stocky chests, while others circled their waists. Kerchiefs against the sun were attached to the tied-up brims of their palm hats covering the mops of hair and shading hirsute faces, out of which dark, gleaming eyes peered.

Cruz was strikingly tall with broad shoulders and a thick, curling black beard. Despite the hair falling over his broad forehead, he had a regal bearing, imposing and wild. As he went by, groups of men made way for him to pass. He entered the old church without removing his hat and walked directly to the altar. Turning his back to the imposing crucifix on the altar, he waited for his faithful to enter. Once everyone was assembled, rifle butts resting on the stone floor, Chávez began to speak in a clear, resonant voice: "Brothers, children of Jesus Christ and of Our Holy Mother. Prepare yourselves for tomorrow. Give your infinite trust to the almighty power of God. He will destroy and send those impious sons of Satan to hell. Those who seek to govern us according to their laws deprive us of our liberty!

"They treat us like animals. They take away our saints. They take our money and their government sends soldiers to kill us. But we are fighting for the kingdom of God . . . Blessed Mary protect and keep us.

"We will not die because the bearers of the cross cannot die. If we are hurt in battle and seem dead, we will rise up again on the third day just as our Lord Jesus Christ did, to finish with His enemies once and for all. With our sovereign cry, Long live the great power of God, we will prevail."

Then Cruz took a packet of yellowed papers from his shirt pocket. Unfolding them, he continued in a confidential tone of voice. "I have put together five guerrilla columns. The first will be in my charge and will remain here in the church. The second will be in Manuel's hands. Here is the list," he said, giving a piece of paper to his brother standing to his left. "They'll go to the cemetery with the third and fourth units, which will be commanded by you two." He pointed to Carlos and Victor Medrano, and handed them the lists. "Pedro Chaparro will take charge of the fifth, and you," he pointed at Bernardo, "will proceed to Cerro de Cueva hill. And now, down on your knees."

All knelt and lowered their heads while Cruz stood tall, with his left hand on his hip. With a slight shrug of the shoulders his red-and-black plaid poncho slipped from his back to fall around his feet. He looked out over the crowd with the piercing, steely gaze that characterized so many of history's great military men.

How imposing he was! His demeanor suggested both conqueror and pontiff as he inspired his people to fight in the name of God and his saints. His splendor dazzled them. What heroic fanaticism his people would display, their Winchester rifles blazing as terrible instruments of war! Meanwhile, Bernardo remained standing, a sly smile on his face. Cruz stared at Bernardo with a steely gaze until at last, visibly paler, Bernardo kneeled with bowed head. Then the caudillo[1] raised his right arm to bless them in the name of God and the Holy Trinity.

The crowd dispersed to carry out final preparations. Cruz stayed behind with his top officers to explain his strategy and give them their orders. The plan made skillful use of tactics, which were informed by an intuition as keen as a mountain hunter's.

The terrain dictated that they divide into guerrilla cells. Cruz knew that the enemy, in an attempt to vanquish them at the cemetery, would enter Tomochic by way of Cordon de Lino hill. The other alternative was to take the key positions of Cerro de Cueva hill, from which they would dominate the church and the main cluster of houses that surrounded Cruz's residence, which served as armory and warehouse as well. In the event of a disaster, these last would allow them to hold out.

The Tomochic chief decided to protect the cemetery with three guerrilla units. A few alert men would be deployed toward the hill to be on the lookout for the enemy, whose long line of combat-ready men would come down the mountain through thick underbrush. The fifth guerrilla column, commanded by Pedro Chaparro on Cerro de Cueva hill, left of Cordon de Lino hill, would attack the aggressors on one flank while they were engaged in battle at the front.

The first guerrilla column, composed of twenty-four men, was split into two divisions. One took up quarters in the Cruz house and the other in the tower, where Cruz could observe the fighting and communicate his orders to a general staff of fifteen or twenty men who were as astute as they were valiant and agile, qualities needed for running and clambering through the mountains.

Cruz, intuitively grasping the art of modern warfare, planned to take the offensive as the enemy descended the treacherous slopes of Cordon de Lino hill. He could annihilate the enemy forces as they picked their way through the bushes and rocks of the mountainside. Cruz reiterated the need to eliminate the officers and commanders; they could be identified by their pale skin and dominant attitude.

The women were given the rigorous work of punching and digging the rifle holes in the adobe walls, hammering posts, digging trenches, stringing up barbed wire, grinding the corn, drying strips of meat, and preparing bandages for the wounded. In addition, in the hour of combat they were to pray for their men.

At six o'clock in the afternoon the Tomochic rebels gathered in the courtyard of Cruz Chávez's fenced-in house, where the chief called roll with grave decorum. He made sure that everyone was ready, well supplied with arms and provisions of *pinole*,[2] or ground corn, thick tortillas, and jerky. With equal precision, he noted the number of scapulars and images of the Saint of Cabora and then reviewed the ammunition and rifles. Afterward, the guerrilla commanders took up their positions with their respective columns.

Then the women, a few children, and seven sickly elders entered the church where they were to spend the night in prayer. Only the immediate family members and half of a guerrilla column remained in headquarters—once Cruz's home.

Following the briefing, Cruz visited the federal soldiers who had been taken prisoner and chose five of them who expressed a wish to take up arms to defend "the cause of the great power of God." The rest were supplied with meat, flour, and water.

Finally Cruz returned home and took his seat near the fireplace, where his wife sat silently stoking the blazing fire. She was thoughtful and never once looked directly at the keen, worried face of her husband, Tomochic's high chief.

Sitting on the edge of their bed, her sisters-in-law looked at her sadly.

"It's three minutes to eight," said Cruz suddenly, removing the old silver watch from his shirt pocket and staring at it. "Let's say a rosary." They knelt before a dirty paper image tacked to the wall and then murmured the strange prayer Cruz had composed.

When it was over, the taciturn Cruz retired to his room, closing the door behind him, leaving the inert, pensive women blankly contemplating the crackling fire. Outside, the black valley of Tomochic was muffled in a silent, funereal cold—that seemed to fall from the heavens above.

CHAPTER 22

The Sad Retreat

After spending a day on the rough roads of the Sierras, Julia sat down on an improvised seat covered in hide near the fire in Cruz's house. She reflected on her experiences of the past few days.

Thinner and paler than ever, her long dark face and beautiful black eyes reflecting the tawny brilliance of the fire, Julia slumped abjectly and frowned, hands hanging limply by her sides. Mariana dozed, curled up in a corner on a deerskin, while the other four women—the Chávez brothers' wives and Cruz's daughter—sat two to a bed, bravely attempting to fight back their anguished sobs.

A profound silence reigned, one of those silences that precedes great catastrophes and prepares the way for tragedy. Not even the dogs were barking; all nocturnal movement had ceased. The silence of the tomb.

"You're tired, daughter, lie down and sleep," Cruz's wife said to Julia, moved to compassion by the girl's obvious pain.

But Julia answered energetically, "No, Señora, we have to stay awake, as the Good Lord wishes." After a long sigh, she added, "I have so much to pray to the Virgin for." Her full eyes gazed upward as though pleading for compassion from the heavens. Once again the silence weighed heavily, black and cold, over the bitter truths gathered in that room.

Suddenly they heard murmurings, ferocious barking and other garbled sounds, along with detonations, echoing through the mountains. Then it all ceased, and after a few minutes someone knocked at the door. Assuming her usual servile attitude, Julia opened it to a man wrapped in a heavy red blanket. "The power of God be with us! Is Cruz here?" the man asked, removing his outer layer of clothing. The polished barrel of his rifle flickered in the shadows cast by the fire.

Then Cruz looked out of his bedroom and greeted his newly arrived guest: "Come on in, Pablo." Pablo Calderón had just arrived from Pinos Altos, where he had been reviewing a division of the 11th Battalion garrisoned near the Sonoran border, and he was here to communicate somber news.

A column of more than five hundred men commanded by Colonel Torres was on its way to Tomochic. The division included more than two hundred men from Guaymas and Navojoas, joined by many brutal Tarahumara Indians, and more from the daring and feared Opata tribes. Additionally, there was a section from the 12th Battalion, another from the 24th, and a detachment from the 11th garrisoned at the Pinos Altos mine.

They were scheduled to attack the town of Tomochic at seven o'clock in the morning on October 20. They would descend by way of the Pinos Altos road.

But the most alarming news of all was that St. Joseph had been captured and perhaps executed. After Pablo had debriefed Cruz, the latter told him to keep the information under wraps.

Cruz already knew some of the details. What he didn't know was that Torres was planning to attack that very day. Understanding now that the assault would come from many fronts at once, Cruz changed strategy. Girding himself with his cartridge belt, rifle in hand—and Calderón at his heels—he followed the serpentine path toward the cemetery at the other end of town with the wary steps of a wolf. As they traversed the town, the dogs woke and began to bark. In the silence of the night, the barking echoed with an unbearable sadness through the rocky hollows of the distant Sierras.

Cruz ordered his brother Manuel and Jesus Medrano, with their respective guerrilla columns, to guard the enclave of houses next to the river—which at this time of year was shallow and narrow—that passed west of Tomochic. When his orders were carried out, one guerrilla column remained at the bottom of Cordon de Lino hill.

On the other bank of the river were another two columns that would prevent Torres and his forces, coming in from the west, from crossing it. At the first hint of dawn the two guerrilla columns, both out of sight in the dry cornfields, occupied the entire length of the riverbank facing the northern and northeastern hills. Cruz and the first guerrilla column brought up the rear as reserve units. He would decide all further actions depending on how the fighting went.

The men positioned in the cemetery deployed themselves along the base of Cordon de Lino Hill, while Pedro Chaparro's men fanned out right and left along the base of Cerro de Cueva hill, ready to confront General Rangel on the right and Colonel Torres on the left.

Meanwhile, at six o'clock in the morning a few men from the Pinos Altos columns could be distinguished occupying the western hills. There they would wait until receiving the signal to the Guerrero columns marching in from the east. Because the signal had not yet arrived, Colonel Torres commanded his bugler to play the same passwords repeatedly. From the other end of the valley the same mocking drill echoed over and over again.

Intuitively Cruz understood the advantage he would have were the battle to begin immediately. Thus he reviewed his long line of men spread along the riverbank in the cornfields and hiding behind a large hill. He ordered them to advance, and when they reached a height of two thousand feet, they were to fire deliberately on the hills occupied by the enemy, forcing them down the slopes, where they could be wiped out on the ragged terrain of fields and stubble or, alternately, when they attempted to cross the river.

A desultory exchange of fire was initiated, and a half hour later the Sonoran columns, having almost reached the foothills, answered the Tomochic fire. In the front lines, on the foothills of Cerro de la Cruz hill, stood the mad Pimas of Sonora, armed with Remingtons. They could barely contain themselves when they heard the Tomochic fighters hooting and yelling as they challenged them with a lazy round of fire.

The Sonoran Indians had a well-earned reputation for brutality. Tall and bold, they were accustomed to mountain life, hunting, and endless raids through the rocky Sierras. Dressed in blue shirts and pants and heavy yellow shoes, they screamed ferociously and fired from behind the rocks and the trees. The Tomochic fighters, understanding that the Pimas were their most fearsome enemies, invited these worthy adversaries to confront them down on the plain. They yelled out, "Send the Pimas down! Send those brave Sonorans down here! We're waiting for you. Long live the power of God! Death to the government! Death to Lucifer!"

Cruz had ordered his men not to draw the enemy into an attack on the town until the Chihuahuan forces responded. To the despair of Colonel Torres, who had been on time, those forces still hadn't arrived.

Now the detachment from the 11th Battalion, commanded by Captain Castro, initiated combat on the left, ferociously attacking the mountain fighters at point-blank range. In this group was Sergeant Zavala, the same officer, who, along with the captain, had defeated the then irresolute and weak mountain fighters the year before. The federal troops answered those screams of defiance with fire and their own inspirational cries: "Long live the federal government! Long live the 11th Battalion!"

In the first lull came the feeble sounds of the elusive password from the far side of the mountain. Rapidly covering ground, the 24th and 11th Battalion columns and the Pima Indians advanced, while the 12th ascended Cerro de Medrano hill, whose high summit, like that of Cerro de Cueva hill, dominated the entire valley.

The Tomochic fighters, whose strategy was to creep along, spread far apart and low to the ground while maintaining intense fire, slowly retreated while keeping their aggressors at bay. Only the infamous Sonoran Indians went forward brashly, anxious to pit themselves against an enemy known for its ferocity. But the Pimas' positioning worked against them. Unprotected at the top of the barren hills, they were cut down by gunmen aiming from the church tower, the cornfields, and the outlying houses at the outskirts of town.

Once they had retreated inside the houses, the Tomochic fighters fired from the openings they had prepared and kept the aggressors contained. After crossing the river, the soldiers saw that there was greater danger in retreat than in throwing themselves headlong into the fray. Continuing their advance while kneeling down at times to take aim, breaking through the cornstalks, jumping over rocks, they were blown to bits by well-aimed shots coming from dwellings that had been transformed into virtual blockhouses.

A first sergeant of the Eleventh received a bullet in the face and fell to the ground fatally wounded. He had been on his knees aiming at what appeared to be a head jutting out from behind a distant boulder. But the strangest thing was how he remained frozen in that same position, his weapon between both hands as though he were taking aim, his eye sockets empty, the barrel of his rifle spattered with brains.

The fighting had spread down the line. Now it began to look like battle. The smoke from the gunpowder acted as further provocation, and everyone grew hoarse from yelling; their shouts rang out louder than the noise of gunfire itself. And it was then that the about-turn sounded from Colonel Torres's general headquarters, and they had to retreat after the heroic attack.

Second Captain Francisco Corona of the 12th Battalion, with the graying mustache of the longtime veteran, bellowed out encouragement to his troops as they neared the houses. "Farther in, my boys. Go on, boys! Way in. Whoever dies, so be it! We're not the ones who die in childbirth, are we? Long live Colonel Torres! Long live the 12th Battalion!"

"Long live the great power of God. Long live the Holy Trinity," replied the mountain fighters from inside the adobe huts. Enemy bullets ricocheted off their stone-hard walls into showers of splinters.

Followed by a crowd of men ready to carry out his commands, Cruz ran to and fro, bent low to the ground, yelling out orders to his men. He seemed to be everywhere at once, bolstering the flagging vigor of his men.

At dawn, his explorers had warned Cruz that the Chihuahuan forces were on their way. His guerrilla columns were on standby at the foot of Cordon de Lino hill, waiting to attack as soon as the soldiers attempted their descent. Meanwhile, to the south, Pedro Chaparro blocked the valley at Cueva hill, ready to attack the enemy's flank from the underbrush.

The Tomochic fighters who had originally engaged the Sonoran forces retreated to the safety of their dwellings where they maintained steady fire, causing serious damage to enemy lines. Moreover, the men stationed at the top of the church tower didn't miss a single shot. It was the worst of all possible triumphs. The Tomochic fighters serenely chose their victims from behind thick adobe walls.

The section of the 12th Battalion that attempted to get as far as the church—Tomochic's military fort—had scattered. Leaping like deer, the Pimas advanced more cautiously. They waged frightful hand-to-hand battle with the Tomochic fighters they encountered, roaring savage war cries that mingled with the din of crackling gunfire that echoed from all sides of the western part of the valley.

On the slopes of Cerro de Cueva hill, Colonel Torres stood observing the disastrous battle with his campaign telescope, trembling with rage at the prodigiously strong resistance from the Tomochic fighters. It was all over, and he ordered another about-turn to be sounded. The pathetic retreat was initiated, which ended up costing more lives than the battle itself.

They left behind a trail of wounded men and corpses. Unable to grasp the sad reality, the Sonoran veterans just followed orders. First Captain Tellez fell down dead. A few moments later Captain Corona was wounded in the arm and within moments was hit in the foot as well. A second lieutenant was captured while a corporal who had been running to help him caught three bullets in the chest. Lieutenant Cota had vanished with an entire section of the front guard.

A second sergeant, weeping with rage, crazed and furious, held his rifle by the barrel between both hands and bawled like a baby. No one even paid attention to him; the few gray hairs in his beard trembled as he called out, "Long live the 12th Battalion. Viva Colonel Torres and General Rocha! Those of us in the Bufa don't run. Long live the federal government!" A bullet pierced his leg and the second sergeant fell to his knees next to the corpse of a bugler who had been shot four times in the chest and stomach. Running to catch up with the others crossing the river under a rain of lead, two brave soldiers tried to take him with them. But the second sergeant, intoxicated with fury, slammed the butt of his rifle into the head of one of them and screamed out hoarsely, "Cowards! Those of us in the Bufa don't run. Long live General Ro . . ."

Before he could finish, he fell onto his back, his head pierced through with a bullet, which must have originated in the church tower.

Meanwhile, after announcing the retreat, Colonel Torres's bugler continued to sound the alert. Finally from the eastern mountain range came the response. General Rangel was arriving just as the decimated Sonoran forces were on the retreat.

Then from far away, over the Cordon de Lino hill, came the sound of the furious detonations of the Hotchkiss cannon aimed at Tomochic. Off toward the mountains in the east could be heard a vigorous exchange of fire, which became progressively louder.

They were beginning to fight on the other side of the valley, while on this side everything was coming to a close. Combat ended with the sounds of the sad retreat: a sonata of defeat, withdrawal, blackest night. This requiem to the delirious enthusiasm of war, both touching and tragic, echoed like a sob through the souls of the brave fighters. About-turn! The sad retreat.

CHAPTER 23

An Extraordinary Surprise

The group of brave fighters headed by Captain Molina, including Miguel, picked up more men as they moved—those who had earlier dropped from exhaustion beneath a tree, faces flushed and breathing labored.

Walking in two rows, the stunned men mutely exchanged desultory glances, as though they were shipwrecked sailors knocking haphazardly against each other. They had been swept away in a sea of misfortune, and as survivors of the same catastrophe could at least console one another.

Great effort and perseverance went into training a good battalion. And for what? One wrong command could result in a half hour of futile bravery where blood was liberally spilled, quantities of gunpowder consumed. All that remained of the well-disciplined battalion was a shapeless, bloody tatter.

So this was war? Idiotic, blind, and savage, shameless, and rife with banal evil, an atrocious, almost inconceivable tragedy. Who should be blamed? Who was responsible for this crushing defeat? A few ignorant sons of Chihuahua's stony terrain had blown one of the army's finest brigades to bits.

These were Miguel's thoughts as he mechanically marched along the rocky paths that skirted the hills east of Tomochic heading toward general headquarters, which had been established above the main road to Guerrero. Situated in a large clearing on a high mesa, the new head-quarters was a comfortable camp.

Meanwhile, the muted cannon stood by and a field hospital was erected.

Surrounded by national troops, General Rangel anxiously surveyed the scene, his telescope held up to his right eye. He watched silently as groups of beaten, speechless soldiers arrived in no discernible order and flung themselves on the ground next to their comrades.

Now a brave hero from the Twelfth arrived with twenty men. He and his unit, their retreat cut off by the enemy, had nearly been forced to cross the town. By some miracle the brave Lieutenant Cota lived to tell the story. Of the original twenty-five men in his section, only seven remained. The others had been cut down.

While the wounded officers had arrived earlier, several irregulars left camp to bring in the moaning, bleeding soldiers who had managed to get close enough to the camp to advertise their presence. The major, who was also a surgeon in charge of the expeditionary corps, stepped gingerly among the shipwreck survivors in that far-off port of call. When he yelled out his orders, the wounded groaned. The atmosphere radiated deepest gloom.

Overwhelmed, Miguel threw himself to the ground. He lay with his perspiring head on a tree trunk. He had not awaited orders to do so and he could have fallen fast asleep. However, he was obsessed with one thing—a single, even filthy, drop of water, yes, just one sip! A delirium of flames lashed him; his tongue was dry and his face purple. Oh, how he was suffering. He had a high fever and a mute rage over-took him as he clenched his fists. He remained like this for an inter-minable hour of anguish. He saw nothing, thought nothing. Finally he slept. He had barely closed his eyes when he felt them shaking him.

"Hey, Mercado, wake up. We're going to take roll call. Up!" He woke with a start, returning to the pathetic reality all around him. Fewer than half his company remained: two disorderly rows of tattered soldiers with emaciated faces, their sunken eyes staring vacantly at the ground.

Shame, exhaustion, ravenous hunger! And yet every single one of them had fulfilled his duty.

Miguel took in the enormity of this disaster. Supporting himself on his rifle, which he hadn't abandoned for a moment, Miguel took notes as the first sergeant called roll. He noted all the missing but couldn't be certain whether the missing men were dead, wounded, lost, or if they had deserted. There could be no search until the enemy deserted the field.

Armed escorts with stretchers had been able to rescue only a few of the wounded, those found close to general headquarters. When they tried to approach the battlefield, the brave men were stopped by intense gunfire. Out of pride, they answered fired with fire but were forced to withdraw.

Only two of those rescued were from the enemy camp. One, who had been shot through the stomach, refused to utter a single word. The other man died on the road.

Meanwhile, the *soldaderas* had been allowed into the camp. The women rushed flour tortillas, broiled meat, and canteens of water to their men. A clamor rose. Cries of happiness and pain, whimpering, swearing, and quarreling . . . and all for a sip of water!

Water! Water! At his first glimpse of the precious liquid, Miguel made a beeline for the unkempt woman trying to hold back a group of soldiers begging her for one drop, just a single drop. Some begged while others threatened.

What happiness! She had a full canteen! Flinging himself into their midst, Miguel cried out impulsively, "Make way, make way. What's all the fuss about? I'm offering one peso for the canteen! Look, here it is," and he showed her his four bills of one peseta each.

"Oh, lieutenant, sir, it's for my man, he's really bad! Leave this one for me, I'll bring you some later." Miguel didn't pay the least attention and snatched it away, tossing bills at her. Then he released his rifle from his grasp, and with the barrel against his legs and the butt against a rock, he grabbed the canteen with trembling hands, threw his head back, and guzzled. And he would have drunk it all except that an imperious hand snatched the canteen out of his hands.

"Hey, Mercado, leave me some, will you! It's not good for you to drink so much all at once!" It could only be Castorena. His thirst sated, Miguel felt ecstatic. He handed over the water, which Castorena downed in an enormous gulp. By this time the woman had disappeared, and they were being called to attention. Miguel threw the canteen and it ricocheted noisily among the rocks.

The remaining men of the Ninth received instructions to set up an advance observation post on the main road to Tomochic. A lookout was set up, and pairs of soldiers were assigned to surround the camp, protecting it from possible night surprises. The off-duty soldiers were given one-hour watches at the nighttime rounds beginning at six o'clock in the evening. A number of soldiers were stationed to guard the Hotchkiss while several stood sentry outside the compound. Meanwhile, the national troops slaughtered a cow and distributed flour. It was about time, too. Twenty-four hours had passed since their last meal.

Miguel, who was to be second in charge on the advance along the road, ordered that a large piece of meat be grilled. While he waited, he visited the wounded officers who were gathered in a large tent at the center of camp. Laid out on serapes, the men moaned with pain.

Miguel tearfully saluted Lieutenant Colonel Villedas, whose head wound alone could have cost him his life. His hands were mangled and bloody from his subsequent fall onto the rocks. Then he spoke with Lieutenant Pablo Yépez and Second Lieutenant Pedro Delgadillo about the two captains who had gone side by side to their deaths. Abruptly the wounded men stopped talking and fell into a semiconscious state between exhaustion and terror.

He observed them for a while and then turned to leave. Then he noticed the general angrily interrogating several soldiers from the Chihuahua public security forces who had recently arrived at camp. What had happened was this: an officer belonging to the second column of the corps had commanded his forces to do an about-turn, away from the theater of combat, where they eventually abandoned the terrain. What he had done constituted an act of desertion during combat and in the face of the enemy. This is nothing but poor military preparation, lack of discipline, and inadequate training, the young second lieutenant reflected to himself.

Miguel left the general's tent for his meat ration, which he devoured ravenously though it was unsalted and almost raw. He held the piece of meat with both hands and chewed noisily like a savage, while the blood oozed from the sides of his mouth. He would have been capable of biting anyone who tried to take it away.

Then an acute thirst overcame him again, but there was nothing to drink. Next he went to check on the forces that would protect the guard post. With Lieutenant José Soberanes at the head of the advance squad, they marched down the main road until they came to a place where the road descended abruptly.

Off to one side stood a wooden cross on a pile of rocks. Here three sentinels stood guard over the wide road. It was already getting dark and bitterly cold after a sad afternoon, which had skipped dusk and turned into night. There, high on the mountaintop in the clearing where the camp lay, the fires burning in general headquarters were visible. They blazed like rose-tinted stars while in front of him rose the hills, like stationary clouds, covered with rocks and pine trees.

They crossed the rocky escarpment, passing by the cross erected on its pedestal of stone. There, in the half-light of the dying day, they looked down into the vast depths of the Tomochic valley. Not one light, not one sound—not even the barking of a dog—could be made out in the evil town that lay barely visible at the bottom of the valley. Nothing indicated there was any life in that hole, that colossal eagle's nest in the middle of the Sierra Madre mountains.

Exhausted by the day's terrible labors, the melancholy lieutenant sat down next to a tree and, despite all efforts to keep his eyes open, was soon nodding sleepily. Miguel leaned his head against the trunk of an enormous pine and let his rifle fall between his aching legs. He unbuckled his cartridge belt and, crossing his arms, reflected on what he had learned, his eyes very wide in the darkness.

After suffering a bloody defeat, they would now confront the enemy lost in the mountains, far from home. As usual, his grand schemes had reaped bitter rewards. All his lofty ideals had vanished. He couldn't say he had any faith left in the grand poetry of war! War as he had once understood it, as he had read about it—great, ennobling, heroic, epic.

What had occurred wasn't even a shadow of the great classic combats of an earlier day—Europe's legendary battles—that had once inspired him. Not even a parody of them—indeed, not even comparable to the recent revolutionary struggles that had bloodied the country. Yet something about the tragic barbarism of this catastrophe seemed all too familiar. The horror of the massacre had been just as vile as the defeat.

Vile, just like defeat.

Defeat. The dark essence of that word, full of shame, sullied by mud . . . it didn't even glimmer in the inferno of his mind. His meditations skirted the shore of that sea of darkness, the town of nightmare, Tomochic.

Defeat. No, it wasn't shame that he felt. Not for himself, nor for his comrades. He didn't even feel shame on behalf of his beloved 9th Battalion or the Mexican army. Others were responsible for the defeat. The military academy's crème de la crème, its youthful officers, had shown their mettle, leaving petals of their own blood to stain the rocky road to Tomochic.

Those green officers defended their honor in the thick underbrush amid the dense red and white cloud of combat. They had been shoved into the fray with no clear objectives in mind. No one had shown them the way. And the troops, even more than the officers, were the tragic victims of chance.

The number of dead and wounded was enormous. He thought of the soldiers who had been shamelessly abandoned to their fate out in the silent wilds: their thrashing, screams, curses in the half-light, insane thirst, and dying eyes contemplating the stars that sparkled in the cold sky. Fear clutched him as he tried to clear his consciousness of the vision of all those unhappy souls. Overwrought from weakness and fatigue, his fevered brain conjured up bloody scenes horrific as nightmares—only he was awake.

With his mind on fire, a lump in his throat, and an ache in his stomach, he experienced a morbid fear. Fear of shadows, nightfall, the odd sounds that drifted down from the camp, even his own thoughts, his consciousness; fear of his very being! Fear of everything! It was the beginning of dementia. An invincible fear gripped his weakened organism, like a delirium tremens.

It was an hour of crushing grief. In the end, his fatigue won out. Despite the danger, he slept a few moments. He was awakened by the sounds of indistinct voices: a lieutenant and a corporal on watch were speaking excitedly.

"Are you absolutely sure? It may be your nerves."

"No, listen carefully, lieutenant, sir. Don't you hear that?"

The lieutenant fell silent. Then, pricking up his ears to make out a vague sound in the distance, he heard something and said to Miguel, "Look here, Mercado, accompany the corporal. Right over there next to the guard . . . See if you can make anything out . . . You know what to do, right? Shoot on the spot. No 'who goes there?'!"

The officer followed the corporal, tripping over rocks all the way. He couldn't see farther than the shadows of the rocks and trees just ahead of him. When he came to where the guard was posted, he attempted to survey the terrain by sight. He held his breath in order to hear better. With a shudder of terror, he thought he heard the mingled sounds of voices and footsteps.

For nearly ten minutes, he stood there, his eyes peering blindly into the darkness. He began to tremble when he realized the sounds were getting louder and more distinct. There was no doubt about it; people were moving in—the enemy.

He went to report his findings and his chief immediately woke the sleeping soldiers and ordered them to load their weapons and form a line across the road. He situated himself on the right flank and ordered

Miguel to take the left; then he told the three advance guards that at the first sight of the enemy they should rejoin the company.

Everybody was upright now, trembling, waiting anxiously for the enemy to attack boldly in the pitch-black night. Still, all eyes were cast behind as though to keep the road of retreat in full view.

Suddenly the noise of the approaching party became recognizable: coughing, laughing and talking. This was unheard of! They didn't even do them the honor of making a silent approach. They were so sure of their triumph that they could laugh and chat as though they were out for a jaunt. "Aim carefully! Here they come! Here they come!" the lieutenant mouthed silently.

The men were on edge. They aimed nervously, unable to see a thing. Then a few shadows appeared on the lower part of the road. The lieutenant yelled "Fire!" and the squad group opened fire. The thunderous clap of bullets echoed ominously through the night's deep silence.

A clamor of frightened voices rose up from the advancing group, who immediately began to retreat: "Don't shoot . . . don't shoot! We're from Guaymas! We're with Colonel Torres." they yelled.

"Let Colonel Torres come forward or we'll open fire again!" the lieutenant shouted back.

"Sir, he's way back at the rear of the column," a voice replied.

At that moment all heard the column's password, and the newly arrived troops were allowed to advance.

CHAPTER 24

Lyricism: The Virgin and the Hero

With his forces decimated following the bungled attack on Tomochic, Colonel Torres decided to put his troops under the command of Colonel Rangel. There was little sense in maintaining his position on the other side of the valley.

That very night he undertook a dangerous enterprise that involved possibly exposing himself to enemy fire in the surrounding hills. And this would mean risking all-out slaughter in the Sierra foothills.

As fate would have it, either the general's communiqué, which had been sent that afternoon, hadn't arrived or the general had failed to inform the advance guard of their proximity. But as the battered troops from Sonora advanced, they were received with gunfire from the advance post guarding the road.

In the ensuing panic everyone shot upright and yelled back and forth in a confusion bordering on pandemonium. "Come to order! Order! In formation! Put out the fires!" The fires were extinguished instantly.

With ashen faces, the wounded lifted themselves upright. An officer of the Eleventh—the one with the imposing mustache who had boasted that the battle would be over in a couple of hours—was trembling so fiercely he could barely get on his feet. Still, he cocked his pistol, ready for anything. "It's a dawn raid, comrades, prepare your weapons! Tomochic sons of pigs!" he hissed.

Castorena grabbed a bottle of maguey liquor and took a generous swig. As he started to prepare his rifle, however, a captain arrived with the following orders: "Everyone back to your posts. It's Colonel Torres's column."

Fortunately no blood was shed, and the Sonoran troops advanced into camp. There were only a couple of hundred men, since the Twenty-fourth and the Eleventh had suffered devastating losses in the combat against Tomochic.

When calm was restored, Miguel returned to his thoughts. Reclining against a tree, the lieutenant had exhausted all means of keeping himself awake, so he had decided to take guard duty half the night and leave Colonel Torres with the other half. While his chief slept, Miguel walked and his mind returned to its dark brooding.

Why was I spared? Miguel asked himself, as he pondered the heroic death of the young Captain Servín. "This was an indispensable man, a worthy son of the military academy, who would have become a worthy leader of the Mexican military's next generation. Yet here I am, alive but good for nothing, a pathetic, vacillating creature, with a brain made less for thought than for anxiety, oversensitive and useless. Yes, I'm capable of suffering, of showing strength, but to no effect. My soul is prematurely old from grief and bad living. It's a rudderless soul . . . no, an honorable, proud soul, generous and sad, but solitary and given to wavering. Why go on living like this? Alone, alone!"

Tears of woe surged in Miguel's dry, burning eyes. Then suddenly the image of Julia appeared. She smiled at him sadly from the depths of his desolation. Julia! And he thought of the kind, melancholy girl from Tomochic, that sweet, intelligent, and oh so unfortunate girl of the mountains. And Julia's clear voice, as she halfheartedly resisted him, resonated again in the bottomless night, the night of Tomochic and the dark night of his soul. "Oh, you are bad, so bad!"

He was bad? Poor creature! Giving in to his instincts, he was irresistibly drawn to the fresh, almost virginal body of the girl from Tomochic. But Miguel didn't feel he was "bad." After their encounter he felt an even greater love for his sad, lovely betrothed, whom he had vanquished using her own innocent phrase "God wills it!"

Then a delightful fantasy opened in Miguel's mind: how she filled his existence with her strange love at once wild and proud, sweet, pious, rare, and mystical. That flower of the Tomochic mountains! The daughter of St. Joseph of the Sierras, prey for an old ogre, a sylvan mountain lily prematurely plucked. A cloud of gunpowder, a puddle of blood revealed in the conflagration's blinding light. How ennobling was his exotic love affair! How his ordinary second lieutenant's life had been transformed by the profound and lyrical passion of the girl who had given herself to him at the threshold of the sacred mountains, on the eve of the catastrophe, murmuring all the while in her plaintive martyr's voice: "Have me, take your pleasure. It is God's will."

The officer caught his breath at the intimate nature of this memory, and a smile passed over his emaciated face. In his imagination, Miguel combined past and future events, composing one long, luxurious poem of love, incense, and blood, in which the nuptials of the Virgin of Tomochic and the Hero Miguel shone resplendent and victorious.

CHAPTER 25

In Pursuit

The wounded were ready to be transported to Guerrero on the morning of October 21 along with a small entourage from the 5th Regiment and two day's worth of provisions. Miguel bade an emotional farewell to his friends. He witnessed Captain Molina and Lieutenant Colonel Villedas silently shaking hands. Molina had given Villedas his gold watch and a packet of bank notes to be delivered to his wife in the event of his death.

Afterward they conversed for a few moments. They lamented the fate of the battalion, ill prepared for battle and decimated in the chaos of the unforeseen defeat. After graduating from the military academy, Captain Molina had made his humble career in this battalion. A soldier by vocation, he was deeply pained by the unexpected disaster. "Sir, what worries me is how desperate the colonel will feel when he finds out . . . he's going to find out one way or the other."

"No," Villedas answered him. "This is all I'm putting in the telegram: 'Engaged on the twentieth with the enemy, many dead, many wounded,' and nothing more."

A wave of tenderness came over the second lieutenant as he considered the love the 9th Battalion's officer corps had for the old colonel. He came from a tradition of ancient austerity and honorable nobility. His chivalrous customs had originated with the Spanish Guard, whose sabers were always clean and elegant.

What's more, underneath the rigid frown, beyond his harsh expression and his brittle, commanding voice, what sweet, warm affection he had for the young officers he hoped to transform into the flower of martial nobility! How dear to him were the "boys" in the troops!

Colonel Miguel Vela was a conservative through and through, and not only in name. He was naively true to the mystical chivalry of Religion and Right. The commander of the 9th Battalion was a patriarch of war, not due to his hard implacability but because of his sweetness.

He selected his officers from the young military academy graduates who hoped to move directly into the ranks of the army. He poured into those young souls something of the ancient and chivalric military tradition that had shaped his own. And so it was that in the garrison of the Plaza de Mexico the soldiers of the Ninth provided a rare example of the infantry officer whose conduct is as clean as his uniform.

How would that veteran feel when he learned the fate of his own battalion? This thought, added to the sight of the miserable wounded and the presence of Captain Molina, the sad "Little Napoleon of the Ninth," made Miguel's vibrant spirit swell with a wave of tenderness that brought tears to his melancholy eyes and a lump to the back of his throat.

The general had modified his plan of attack. He decided to bivouac his troops on Cerro de Medrano hill, which rose almost straight up into the sky to the right of the town. From the very top of the hill he could harass the enemy with impunity. Besides, this was the perfect place for the little Hotchkiss cannon.

The only problem was that Cerro de Medrano hill was set apart from the other hills, which circled the valley. The only way to get to it was by going down, crossing the plain, then going up again. If the Tomochic fighters noticed their movements, they could easily defeat the plan.

The various groups lined up with their respective officers. Because they had suffered severe attrition, the two companies of the Ninth were combined. The Pimas and Navojoas made up the front guard. Then came the Ninth and the Eleventh, then what was left of the Twelfth, and finally the Twenty-fourth. The National Guard of Chihuahua, more nuisance than anything else, brought up the rear, along with a few horsemen from the Fifth regiment and the Chihuahua irregulars. As usual, the glorious cannon traveled in the center escorted by members of the Ninth. The food and ammunition traveling with another escort from the same division closed the column, which set off by way of the hills on the right until Tomochic was no longer visible from behind Cerro de Medrano hill. Then they descended toward flat ground with marksmen guarding the front lines and flanks.

Fortunately the enemy ranks, barricaded in their houses, could not or did not wish to mount an opposition. The soldiers continued up the far side of Medrano hill, and they set up camp at the summit. Here they were safe from attack and completely invisible to the Tomochic fighters.

It was like an unassailable fortress where all of Tomochic could be observed from less than two thousand feet away. The soldiers lay face down or stood behind trees and boulders, taking careful aim at any Tomochicans who dared to come out of the houses or show themselves in the church tower.

This system reaped better results than an outright attack. All day long, without letup, a slow but unnerving gunfire pinned the Tomochic fighters down in their houses. So steely was their resolve that they would convert those houses into their own tombs. Over by the church tower, Cruz's guerrilla forces answered the fire from time to time, trying to conserve ammunition.

A number of projectiles were launched from Cerro de Cueva hill half a mile away on the other side of the valley, in front and to the left of Medrano hill. The missiles whistled and described a great arc in the sky before descending on the camp.

The cannon had been set up advantageously at the highest point of the hill behind a natural parapet that protected the artillerymen. It saluted the enemy politely before sending them a few mortar shells, which exploded outside the houses and raised flurries of dust.

A few cows belonging to the people of Tomochic wandered the plain and lower hills of the mountainside. The irregulars chased a few of them down and then distributed generous portions of meat to the troops. Flour and raw, unsalted meat were the rations given out that day. The officers ordered the soldiers' women to make tortillas. In fact, the *soldaderas* had never been so valuable for they brought them firewood and water.

Water continued to be rare and precious. Selflessly, the hapless women made their way down the right side of the hill. No peak or escarpment was too sheer for them. Their feet bled through the worn soles of their huaraches as they grabbed on to the shrubs in order not to fall, chattering incessantly, mixing crude obscenities with devout invocations to the saints.

At the risk of being hunted down by the Tomochic fighters in the houses at the far edge of town or by the guerrillas in the tower, the women pressed on, reaching the plain and then the banks of the river, where they filled canteens by the dozens.

While some of the women stocked up on water, others got down on their knees and faced Tomochic. They lifted their outstretched arms as though in prayer, believing that the Tomochic fighters wouldn't dare fire on them in that sacred posture. In fact, the highly acclaimed marksmen never opened fire on the women who provided fresh, clean water to "the sons of Lucifer." The chivalrous sons of the mountains didn't kill women.

The eagle-eyed sons of Tomochic must have been able to see the women quite clearly on the riverbank, but they nobly respected their lives.

Then the women would turn and ascend the mountain again, stopping now and again to catch their breath, clambering over the rugged, undulating back of the monstrous cyclops that swarmed with the dread pursuers of the Lion of Tomochic.

What a commotion broke out when the water arrived, so fresh, so delicious! Coins and dirty bills rained into the women's dripping hands. The soldiers yelled out, "water, water" from between the arms stockpiles, and the camp became animated with a fresh, crystalline joy; it was as though a warm jolt of energy passed through the sadness of fatigue and thirst.

And the soldiers drank. They quaffed long and deeply until the water dripped off their dusty, torn blue jackets. Once their thirst was satisfied, they flung themselves down to wait for their white flour tortillas and bloody pieces of smoking meat.

After eating and resting, gathered around the tents of general headquarters, under the open sky, on their peak towering over the silent immobility of Tomochic, the defeated troops recovered their confidence. Once again they felt capable of fighting, ready for death, as long as they were under skilled command.

As the afternoon waned, the officers of the Ninth gathered to eat, while the two remaining captains, Tagle and Molina, presided. The latter, as usual, was trying to enliven the conversation and encourage the soldiers' hopes for success and sweet revenge. The junior officers listened attentively as they devoured their broiled meat and white tortillas. When they were sated, the conversation turned to events of the previous day.

It was rumored that the general was indignant about the 9th Battalion's performance. He had not expected them to retreat the way they did. In fact, Castorena claimed that he happened to overhear a nighttime conversation between the general and Colonel Torres, in which the general said, "Listen, Colonel, they didn't just run like sheep, they ran like ewes! The officers of the military academy, nothing but inexperienced boys. Like raw recruits! Baaa!"

Hearing this, Captain Molina, frowning and trembling with rage, replied, "We have to show them what we're worth, guys. We'll soon see. It may have been someone's fault, but it sure wasn't ours . . . The blame lies . . ." Then realizing that he was straying into the area that regulations called "questioning orders," he held his tongue.

A suddenly thoughtful lieutenant spoke up: "What's really hurting us is the number of deserters. This is very serious."

Miguel interrupted the conversation to pompously interject: "What's really happening here? Those the general calls deserters are only scattered, which is a big difference. Either way, deserters or scattered, in reality, there aren't that many. More of them are dead—and do we really know how many died? Only the ones we've seen with our own eyes, or at least someone has seen, show up on the list. But can we say how many are dead, how many wounded, how many scattered or deserted, until we've thoroughly combed the field? I'm sure that they put things down in the reports that were completely false.

At that moment the general's bugle rang out the honor roll to convene the officers. Nighttime rounds were assigned. Duty consisted of checking up on the sentinels and the guards paired in the advance posts.

In the dispatch order, which was read out to the men at six o'clock each evening after the change of guard, the duties of night rounds were spelled out in detail. From nine o'clock to ten o'clock it was Miguel's duty to check up pair by pair on the line of sentinels and guards surrounding the camp; at each step he would trip on the rugged slope. Mistakenly overhearing a few words of conversation in the Pima camp, he learned that an old Tomochic fighter who had been brought to the camp as a prisoner from Pinos Altos had been sent before the firing squad.

"Commander, if what those Tomochic fighters say is true, we're damned to hell or gonna be struck down by lightning! We just executed the famous St. Joseph. He died like a man, all right . . ." said one of the Pimas.

The officer turned away. He didn't want to hear any more. Then it dawned on him—they had executed Julia's father! That poor old fool drunk on the delirium of Tomochic! Poor Julia!

In the immense peace of the cold, black night, standing near the group of brave boys from Sonora, Miguel shivered and drew his cape tightly around him. The troops were talking about the heroic death of an obstinate old fool, a pitiable, credulous hero who thought he had been sent from God. Standing amid the rocks, Miguel's heart throbbed with love and pain as he thought of Julia.

CHAPTER 26

After the Looting, the Fires

October 22 came and went with nothing to report. Early in the morning the marksmen began to open a desultory fire on the town to prevent flight.

Every once in a while the cannon shot a round that hit Tomochic, opening up large craters in the hard adobe walls of the houses and raising clouds of dust. Both the brigade doctor and the general who ordered the cannon fire were passionate aficionados of target practice. After the cannon's resounding boom, profound silence again reigned over the desolate valley. When the two had detonated several true hits, they would celebrate with a glass of cognac to the great distress of Castorena, who couldn't buy himself a sip of sotol for all the money in the world.

By now it was generally known that the proud Tomochic fighters would not go cheap even though they had suffered significant losses, were acting strictly on the defensive, and were waiting to be attacked in their own homes. Meanwhile, the hours passed in a thick, heavy daze that became denser over time.

There were occasional outbursts of rage in which the peak of Cerro de Medrano hill would be pelted with bullets. After the cannon blasts, the Tomochic fighters targeted the troops who manned the Hotchkiss cannon.

Federal forces found many advantages in that high peak. The ample mesa was protected by natural flanges that served as useful parapets. Behind the high mesa, the soaring mountains offered their protection to the camp.

The highest crest overlooked the entire valley where Tomochic's scattered dwellings could be seen from the foothills. At the southernmost end of village rose the mighty church tower, which was crowned with sudden sparks as it pelted the federal camp with lead. Watched over by a guard of twenty men, the cannon projected out over the town. Then came the 12th, 24th, and 11th Battalion camps.

The 9th Battalion occupied the most vulnerable spot, situated at the center of the mesa close to the only accessible part of the hill. Since leaving Guerrero, the companies of the Ninth had been assigned the most dangerous tasks, which they tackled with uncommon spirit, precision, and discipline, whether it put them in the good graces of the troops and officers of other contingents or not.

The picturesque, comfortable camp of the Pimas and the Tarahumaras lay behind the Ninth's camp. How their attitude of defiant freedom lifted spirits! Then came the camp of the Chihuahua nationals. The series of camps ended with the Chihuahua National Guard, a disorganized mass of poorly armed men.

The detachment from the 5th Regiment had undertaken the march to Guerrero. They were providing safe conduct to the wounded officers and soldiers who, by their presence, would constitute an eloquent, if silent, report to General Márquez about the events of October 20.

On October 23 General Rangel discovered that the Tomochic fighters had pulled back into the church and dwellings that surrounded the little barracks (the soldiers' name for the Cruz Chávez house) and had abandoned the ones farther out. He ordered a few corps from the 12th, the 11th, and the 24th Battalions to go down and set them on fire. They would try to corral the enemy bit by bit, until hunger and fire vanquished them.

Following orders, they encountered no resistance. The soldiers entered the abandoned dwellings, robbed what they could, and then doused them with gasoline and set them ablaze. After the looting, the fires.

The more isolated dwellings at the far side of the valley began to burn at once. Black smoke stained the limpid blue sky with dirty smudges peppered with sparks. The soldiers returned to camp laden with swine, chickens, clothes, and musical instruments. They even retrieved the saddles taken from the 5th Regiment on September 2, in addition to old weapons, paintings of saints, hides, cartridge belts, and even tin pots and pewter plates. The looting lasted all day; by nightfall the flaming Tomochic dwellings threw plumes of smoke into the gloomy darkness.

In the afternoon, the marksmen posted to the mountaintop watched awestruck as a man burst out of the Cruz house and darted toward the mountains. At first they fired on him without wounding him. He hid in the underbrush and then reappeared carrying a long white pole with a white cloth dangling from it. The men held their fire, thinking he might be an emissary offering to surrender. But when he reached the foot of the mountains he was fired on from the tower. When he finally disappeared behind a grouping of rocks, everyone was perplexed. Finally the man arrived at camp. An old, exhausted Indian, he was sweating profusely from his narrow escape. Thin, barefoot, and hatless, he wore a torn shirt and old rolled-up pants, and to the surprise of all, he spoke with great resolve.

He had accompanied General Rangel on September 2 and had been taken prisoner. On October 19, Cruz proposed that he take up arms. He accepted with the hope of eventually escaping, which he had just risked his life to accomplish. After the general interrogated the old Indian at length, the news he brought spread among officers and soldiers alike. Among all the details—both insignificant and blown way out of proportion—there was a single piece of important news: Cruz Chávez was demoralized and his provisions were scarce.

The men's spirits lifted, and they believed that the very next day "they would be eating chicken" in the town of Tomochic, whose outermost dwellings were burning to the ground. The officers strolled through the camp in small groups of three or four, happily smoking and commenting on what the fugitive had related.

That night Castorena cadged a drink of tequila from Dr. Arellano in exchange for an improvised poem, and then he let Miguel know about the enemy's situation. The Medranos had died. So had the Calderóns. Manuel Chávez was seriously wounded, as well as four or five of the Mendías who were recovering in the Chávez "barracks." If they were lucky, there wasn't a single healthy Tomochican left!

Pedro Chaparro's forces were the only ones left. Holed up on Cerro de Cueva hill, they were more ferocious than ever. This was important because Chaparro dominated access to the nearby church, the town being located to Chaparro's left. In fact, this was the Tomochic fighters' only avenue of retreat. Understanding this, Cruz had Cerro de Cueva hill solidly protected.

Around twenty men guarded the church where the families were holed up. There were other men in the so-called barracks, or Cruz's house, where the families of his brothers, the Medranos, and Bernardo were staying.

Meanwhile, provisions were running out. Besieged as they were, however, the men weren't willing to risk their lives to gather the corn, beans, potatoes, or grains from their abundant crops. They knew they would be hunted down and slaughtered like animals. Their cattle roamed freely, wandering through the valley along with the pigs and chickens. The dogs were jumpy, nervous. They howled through the day and barked viciously all night.

The cannon's detonations had little effect on the Tomochicans. The minimal explosives could only dent the walls of the empty dwellings. Sometimes an exploded mortar shell killed a chicken or two and sent the other chickens clucking off in panic, running this way and that in the black clouds of dust and gunpowder.

Cruz Chávez ordered a few women to go out under cover of night-fall to bring in the dead. They were buried with elaborate ceremonies inside the dwellings. Tomochic was being converted into an immense graveyard. And despite everything, they kept the hope of victory alive by making their people believe that the day of retribution was near, since "the dead, just like our Lord Jesus Christ, will be resuscitated on the third day and will once again take up their rifles."

Every night Cruz visited the prisoners. He brought them water and toasted corn, and after making them pray, heads bowed, he left them "in the peace of the Lord." He was as forgiving as he was implacable, and he spared their lives: "Because it is a sin and a crime to wound the defenseless, even though they are children of Satan, just as it is the high-est good to kill them like dogs in the hour of combat."

He also consoled the women who were crying in desperation. Though they understood little of the upheaval, they hated the myste-rious enemy that dared besiege their holy territory. In addition, he spoke to the children about bravery, manliness, and the sacred loathing of the sons of Satan, the ungodly soldiers.

Both officers were seated before a bonfire where a corporal was cook-ing their meat rations for them while Castorena recounted the refugee's tale. Mercado contemplated the distant smoke that bled reddish in the gloom, and he thought of Julia. The tale told by the fugitive from the inferno had inflamed Miguel's lively imagination. The vivid scenes he saw were painful, atrocious. Their tragic colors only highlighted the gracious aura of that sad adolescent girl.

He saw her on her knees in the church beneath the battered dome, praying before a terrifying crucifix surrounded by clouds of gunpowder and ominous sparks. The smoke from the Tomochic guns and the smoke from the fires were visible whenever the high winds gusted in from the mountains which still echoed with the chaotic sounds of the looting. He could see her, right from where he stood planted thinking of her; from a chink in the tower she was aiming straight at him, her black eyes hostile and flashing. Those beautiful eyes, aflame with the insan-ity of her savage pride, as they were the day she said to him, "I am from Tomochic!" How she had pronounced that barbarous, heroic name!

CHAPTER 27

The Capture of Cerro de Cueva Hill

At the break of dawn on October 24 the cannon aimed at the Tomochic church made a "routine call" on the town while bugles from the various companies began to play a strange symphonic reveille. Resonating with the sound of victory, it sang out to the miserable little town of Tomochic, echoing with a grim irony from the top of the hill to the distant rosy reaches of the valley below and reverberating through the sprawling, smoking cemetery. Repeated by all the buglers and trumpeters of the defeated sections, it rang out forlornly in that agonizing dawn

"What a pathetic reveille! Thoroughly pathetic," said an officer behind General Rangel, summing up the poignancy and shame of their circumstances. The general turned away, making out only black hoods, spectral silhouettes, he restrained his wrath and said nothing.

Later, all contingents except the 9th Battalion descended as far as the outskirts of Tomochic to occupy all dwellings. Before setting them afire, they thoroughly ransacked them whereupon the noisy, victorious bunch returned to camp laden with booty.

Miguel's responsibility that day was to keep guard from the highest point of the hilltop over the cannon. From behind the parapet he surveyed the terrible spectacle of the fire below. Indeed, the enemy must be contemplating the same destruction, but they waited silently at their posts to be attacked.

Miguel could hear the few bullets fired from Cerro de Cueva hill, where the red flag flew in the air, whistle fatefully over his head. Later that night he heard that the general had decided to take Cerro de Cueva hill and had assigned the job to Fuentevilla, an adjutant in the Twenty-fourth. But in the end the risky undertaking went to Captain Francisco Manzano of the Eleventh, who stealthily departed from the camp in the still of the night with seventy men on a surprise mission to take the designated checkpoints.

But whether he didn't comprehend his orders or was unable to carry them out, Manzano went marching down the wrong road. Making a sweeping circle, he attempted to approach the enemy from behind. The irate general ordered the captain to return: the buglers played the passwords, which rang out in the night and woke the troops. The officers on their rounds had to warn the pairs guarding the farthest reaches of camp not to open fire on the forces of the Eleventh as they trailed back in from the failed mission.

Captain Molina, who was on guard duty, observed the men's arrival. Once they were all back in he queried a second lieutenant of the Eleventh. "Hey, what happened, comrade? Why did they bring you back in?

"The general was asking for the impossible. You can't take that hill, not even with a thousand men. See here, if they had discovered us, they would have torn us to pieces. It was impossible, captain!"

"Where's the general, comrade?" asked the captain.

"We just left him. He and his doctor are still up there. He hasn't gone to bed yet. It's already past twelve."

It was late, and the general had slept little and was out of sorts. Gathered in the general's tent, Lieutenant Márquez from the general staff, the doctor, and the general were speaking about the issues involved in launching an all-out attack on Tomochic.

The captain came in briefly then hurried out again. "There's no news, captain," an officer offered as he passed by on his rounds.

"Thanks, comrade, keep a close watch on the sentinels," he answered before disappearing among the sleeping soldiers.

After reveille played the following day, the troops of the Ninth came to attention, with all arms intact and only seventy-eight men. Thirty of its troops had been instructed to guard the ammunitions depot. The captain thoroughly reviewed the arms and ammunition, replacing anything that was missing and making sure all was ready for use. He divided the battalion into three squadrons and then took off down the rocky mountainside without saying another word.

The sun had not yet appeared over the hazy horizon, but the highest mountain peaks were crowned with fire, while a fresh breeze swept away the tufts of fog floating above the river toward the valley. The dirty, unkempt soldiers descended in silence, their weapons hanging by the rifle straps on their shoulders. Without their greatcoats, the men shivered in the cold morning air.

Miguel bounded down the rocky slope, happy to stretch his legs after four days of immobility. Although he had no idea where they were heading, he was confident that it had to be a better place than where they had been.

When they reached the plains and started to cross them, the captain ordered them to stop. "Company, fall in!" When the three sections were lined up one behind the other, and with the regulation distance between them, he commanded sternly, "Combat formation! March!"

The first section advanced straight ahead, fanning out into a crescent of marksmen while the others remained at the rear, following the movement of the first. Then the captain commanded, "Hit the dirt!" And everyone fell to the ground.

Straight ahead, from the distant top of Cerro de Cueva hill, a shot sounded and a bullet whistled above their heads. Only then did they understood what was happening.

The captain was standing with his head held high, and his left hand on the barrel of his rifle. He pointed his right index finger at the looming shadow of Cerro de Cueva hill and said, "We're going to take that hill, then each and every last one of them will see how the Ninth fights. We'll get up there any way we can. Don't let me catch anybody turning around, because I'll kill anyone who turns back. Listen very carefully, my good sirs. I'm authorizing you to kill anyone who does an about-turn. Even if it's me! Attention, weapons!"

The sharp sound of steel on steel was heard as bayonets were clipped onto rifle barrels, and then stillness. As more bullets whistled by, the captain adjusted the rim of his kepi and yelled, "First section. Hold firm. Straight ahead, on the double. Forward!"

Aligned in formation, the marksmen lunged forward at top speed, their weapons poised, their eyes glued to the summit of the hill. Within moments it was crowned with smoke from a tremendous volley of fire. The other sections followed the first "at a trot." You had to see it to believe it. They were evenly lined up as they charged, coming under fire from a terrific hail of lead from the front and from the right. At the moment, within sight of the Tomochic tower, they were conserving their ammunition. Breathing hard but not slackening their pace, the aggressors advanced into the middle of the plain across a plowed field, which tired them, but not a single soldier lagged behind. They were in perfect harmony, a single soul full of courage, inspired by the captain's words and his miraculous will. Then a soldier on the left flank fell backward, his chest pierced. Another was shot in the leg but managed to keep going, hopping on one leg and howling in pain.

Miguel looked straight ahead and saw nothing in the extraordinary white cloud that blinded him. What's more, a terrible thunder deafened him though he could discern quite clearly the penetrating sound of the bullets, which whistled perilously close to him. But they no longer produced that icy terror, that pain deep in his gut. Now what he heard and felt egged him on, intoxicated him with rage, hatred, and a ferocious pride as he listened to the strident cries of his captain.

"Onward, boys! Long live the 9th Battalion!"

The furious turmoil continued—the running, the leaping, the jumping in and out of unexpected ditches, impeded by dried clods of earth and sharp yellow stalks. Before them loomed Cerro de Cueva hill, its dark summit studded with white clouds. His legs grew weak, and an oppressive weight on his chest took his breath away. He was going to faint, to die. Just one moment's rest, but no. Then he heard the voice of the captain yelling, "Onward, onward! Whoever falls behind dies." He went relentlessly on, as though carried forward by some supernatural power. Then he heard a cry of agony at his side and a soldier lying on the ground blocked his passage. He jumped clear over the soldier's sprawling form without seeing it and continued his dizzying run.

Soon enough the tower disappeared behind the first few summits of Cerro de Cueva hill, and at last they were beyond the tower's line of fire. Then Miguel heard the loud command: "Drop to the ground!"

The time had come. Finally, to be able to rest. He would sink into a dark death and feel himself ripped open. Miguel flung himself down. There was one moment in which he heard nothing, saw, felt, thought nothing. Then he flung his rifle aside and breathed in with all the force left in his lungs. After a few moments, the captain commanded, "On your feet! Load weapons!"

Then he added, "Onward! Long live the 9th Battalion! Upward and onward!" The soldiers took cartridges from their combat pouches and loaded their rifles, ready to fire, anxious to charge up the hill, to fling themselves into the fray.

Now the combat entered a new phase. From behind the shrubs and boulders that dotted the mountainside came a heavy fire that decimated the first group of soldiers to arrive, momentarily paralyzing the line of marksmen.

It was evident now that the troops would have to proceed with the utmost caution. The enemy had come down from the heights to fight them in the foothills. In fact, they maintained a vast advantage, and from that moment on the battalion's advance was necessarily much slower going. The front guard had to take cover, moving stealthily from tree to tree and boulder to boulder. Now the officers and the brave captain had to transfer their energy to the troops, whose first surge of energy was dying away. The men began to waver, fearing that the invisible enemy would annihilate them in one fell swoop.

"Keep going, forward march! Onward, upward! Let's get them," yelled the hoarse officers while Captain Molina marshaled his inner forces to instill the troops with resolve and carry forward the attack.

"Long live the 9th Battalion! The 11th is watching us! Onward, boys!" Captain Molina ordered the bugle to sound the attack. Its clear, resonant notes vibrated amid the heavier din of the detonations. Drunk with enthusiasm now that he had managed to lift the men's spirits, the captain yelled over and over again: "One more push and we'll be on them with our bayonets! Upward, boys!"

Holding his rifle splendidly aloft, Molina flung himself into the fray, setting an example to those who followed in his footsteps. Now there was no fatigue, no vacillation. The flush of bravery that had accompanied them in the beginning returned.

Finally they began to glimpse the fearful Tomochic fighters, firing from behind the trees as they fled in the direction of the summit. At last they were witnessing the retreat of the invincible sons of Tomochic.

Then, once again, they heard the strange and ferocious war cries: "May the great power of God endure! Long live Holy Mary! Death to Lucifer," they screeched from behind the trees. Their shirts and cartridge belts were barely distinguishable in the smoke of the gunpowder, which wrapped the high caps of the pine trees and the craggy mountain peaks in white clouds.

"Onward, men! Upward!" The officers called out, their cheeks aflame and eyes blazing. Some soldiers fell, spattering the rocks with their blood, leaving behind a kepi here and a rifle there. Their comrades did not aid them; in fact, they didn't notice them at all. What's more, they had lost their formation; the sections bringing up the rear had blended in with the first sections. So they marched upward in a single undulating line, following the mounds and hollows of the terrain.

Marching on the left flank, Miguel managed to recover his breath and was firing his rifle at a man whose red serape made a good target in the distance. But his attention was drawn to a thin, childlike voice screaming out through the dense fog: "Long live Holy Mary! Death to the sons of Lucifer."

The enemy fire diminished as the Ninth continued clambering up the slope.

The defenders of the hill were riddled with bullets as soon as they came into view on that rugged, perilous terrain. Then the enemy fire ceased altogether. On the left flank, however, Miguel heard several shots that came even closer but once again that tender child's voice calling, "The great power of God is within us. Long live the Holy Mother!"

Then, pointing toward a craggy peak, a soldier called out, "There he is. Everyone aim and shoot." The soldier aimed, but before he could fire, the rifle fell from his hand. A bullet tore through both his hands and ripped open his jacket as well. He howled with pain. A few comrades nearby fired. Then another man fell down dead. From behind the rocks came the screeching victorious voice of the indomitable adversary, whose rifle was peeking out from between the crevices of the far-off rocks. "All power to God! Death to the soldiers!"

"Fire on them! Run them through. Let's get up there!" yelled Castorena.

Breathlessly, Miguel arrived on the scene, his rifle cocked. Four or five soldiers had stopped to examine a cadaver that lay with its mouth open, its head and chest covered in blood, eyes open and fists clenched. It was the corpse of a young teenage boy, a red cross and a serape lying by his side.

His smooth dark face betrayed a calm, almost ecstatic look. Red spittle flowed between two rows of brilliant white teeth, and he almost seemed to be laughing. In his right hand he clutched a rosary, and in the left his black rifle.

Combat had ended. They had reached the summit of the hill.

CHAPTER 28

The Death of a Hero

From the tower, errant bullets shot directly to the right of federal troops. Most of the soldiers had flung themselves to the ground, tired as dogs, while others examined corpses and retrieved their weapons. Then, from the direction of the Medrano camp, a distant bugle faintly intoned the general's order: "Cease fire."

The soldier Captain Molina commanded to play the bugle was the one who had been wounded and abandoned at the foot of the mountain along with his instrument. The bellicose notes of the reveille resounded amid the dry cracks of the last gunshots. The weary soldiers, their breathing labored in the thick, sulfurous air, shouted out long and hard, full of enthusiasm. "This reveille means something!" an officer called out.

The red flag, which could be seen waving at the top of a gigantic pine in the Medrano camp, was an affront and had to come down. Crouching low, several soldiers rapidly advanced. Then came the sound of a sharp report close to the ground, and a rifle barrel peeked through the smoke. "There's another one! Get him! Kill him!" a corporal yelled.

A sergeant opened violent fire on the head, which emerged behind the weapon. Then came a cry of pain. A few men rushed over, their bayonets ready. But when more screams, even more horrible than the last, emerged from the foxhole, Captain Molina came forward: "Watch out . . . He's wounded . . . Leave him alone!

Then the huge, hairy head emerged again. The rifle followed, another bang, then the captain raised his arms and fell onto his back . . . dead.

Those who understood what had happened stopped in their tracks, stunned senseless. Then in a collective impulse, they threw themselves at the foxhole and, as though they were digging a hole with their bayonets, they cut the enemy corpse to pieces.

Miguel witnessed all of it. He was about to deliver a communiqué to the captain: A soldier from the 11th Battalion was on his way with an order from General Rangel. Astounded, Miguel saw the captain throw his arms up and collapse onto his back without uttering a single cry. Overcome by the strength of his emotions and rigid with horror, he stood staring at the scene of the troops' revenge as they hacked the body of the captain's killer to pieces.

The dreadful news spread in all directions. "Captain Molina is dead! They've killed the captain," said the stunned soldiers in grief-stricken surprise.

Finally the young officer approached the corpse, leaned over, and kneeled on the ground. Miguel, who was not a believer and had not prayed in a long time, prayed now. He prayed under his breath, but with the faith of a woman and the tears of a child.

The diminutive body of the captain was wrapped in his blue great-coat with his cartridge belt cinched around his waist. His brown face was contracted into a horrible grimace, and his small black eyes seemed to gaze one last time at the sky. His arms were stretched out on either side, and from his neck flowed a gutter of blood that formed a great red puddle on the slick rock. Yet his left hand kept a firm grip on his rifle.

The air was still thick with gunpowder and in the distance a few shots could be heard as the general's orders were issued on the bugle, though they were indistinct and seemed to come from far away. Arriving on the scene, Castorena grabbed a sergeant's serape and covered the corpse's face.

Captain Tagle, the only survivor among the four 9th Battalion captains, ordered the remaining forces to gather; his bugler played "fall in" and the officers and sergeants of the Ninth began to convene their men. Of the Tomochic fighters, only corpses were left. The disorder was extreme. Soldiers were scattered through the hills, laid out in attitudes of mortal fatigue among the pine trees. A few of the abandoned wounded cried openly.

"Fall in!" the sergeants yelled at the soldiers, prodding them with the butts of their rifles. The unhappy victors lifted themselves up painfully. Some rose with excruciating slowness; others limped along supporting themselves on their rifles.

Mercado and Castorena stood as honor guards by the dead captain's side. The officers finally left him in the care of a wounded corporal and started up the hill to the designated meeting place. All of a sudden Castorena shook Miguel violently by the arm: "Look at that, will you!" A few steps away from them was a stinking black pile of arms, legs, rags, and hair sunk in blood, shit, and bits of human guts.

Miguel's hair stood on end. He shivered with cold and felt sick to his stomach. He was about to turn away but his friend clenched his fist and shook him again, saying: "Don't look away, man! That's the man . . . the captain was going to spare him and he shot him down. Bastard! Look at him!

When Miguel took another look at the corpse, his mouth fell open. All of a sudden his mind cleared and his rifle dropped from his hands and rebounded against the rocks. Among the bloody body parts, those tatters of flesh and bone, he recognized the wild beard and repulsive nose of Don Bernardo, the old rogue.

"Lieutenant, sir, the captain wants to speak to you," a soldier addressed the officer. Miguel was alone now, since Castorena, thinking his comrade had taken leave of his senses, had abandoned him there in his stupor before the pile of muck.

The sleepwalker returned to reality. With his brain functioning again, he managed to pick up his weapon. As he proceeded to the meeting place, he repeated to himself over and over again, "Bernardo! The ogre in the house by the river, that bandit, Julia's rapist, dead, cut into pieces!"

It was he who had murdered Captain Molina!

The officers and a first sergeant called roll to the troops divided into two rows on the summit. Off to one side, another sergeant counted the guns, rifles, cartridge holders, and ammunition belts collected from the enemy camp while others carried the wounded.

Farther away lay the red flag, spreading out like a bloody stain on the rocks, the one that had waved in the air at the top of a pine tree. In his trench, Bernardo had defended his flag and in so doing had killed Captain Molina.

All of a sudden a faraway commotion could be heard and fierce cries of "Long live General Rangel! Long live the federal government. Death to the Tomochic fighters! Death to the bandits." The epithets were hurled by a noisy bunch of irregulars, rowdy farmers who had been recruited from Guerrero. They managed to expose the front line soldiers of the Ninth in their blind advance on the Cerro de Lino hill on October 20. These were the famous nationals who advanced easily on the hill, when the Ninth had already fought hard to sweep the area of enemy forces.

The brave soldiers on the front lines witnessed how the wild horde of "nationals," enriched by the loot they had sacked from the dwellings on the outskirts of Tomochic, climbed the hill triumphantly. Perhaps they believed themselves to hold the keys to the town as sole victors of the position atop those lofty heights!

"Long live the government of Chihuahua! Death to the Tomochic fighters!" Reaching the summit first, a soldier passionately grabbed the red flag, which had been the standard of the defeated Ninth on the slopes of Cordon de Lino hill, and yelled at the top of his lungs, "Death to the Tomochic fighters!" He repeated himself in tremolo.

"Okay, brother, that's enough yelling from you. The poor devils are already dead, and we're the ones who killed them!" shouted Castorena, furious that the riffraff should take the glory of the day for themselves.

Later, one of the general's adjutants communicated several orders to the single surviving captain. Mercado was instructed to occupy an edge of the summit, on a precipice as sheer as a razor's edge.

The officer led ten men to the top of the steep crest and ordered them to take their places as marksmen at every crevice. It seemed to Miguel that the high peak where he was stationed lay atop the highest tower in a medieval fortress.

From the heights of that pinnacle the entire valley could be taken in, as it overlooked the nucleus of scattered dwellings of that miserable, deserted town. Through this terrain the curving river flowed, sometimes black and sometimes glimmering in the sunlight. The surrounding fields crept in abrupt, uneven steps, zigzagging up the distant hillsides. There lay the immense amphitheater, the extinct volcanic crater, where one distant night the wild eagles of the mountain decided to nest and brood their mad pride and fanaticism.

Beyond, on the other side of the scattered town, lay Cerro de Cueva hill, mirroring the mighty Cerro de Medrano hill that sat on its hind legs like a gigantic dromedary, on whose great humps bivouacked the sentinels.

Miguel looked down on the blackened, scored, pocked tower, next to the sturdy main house that must have served as convent and granary. Every once in a while a hail of lead flew toward Medrano and Cueva hills as though to prove that the tower had not seen its last Tomochic fighter.

The second lieutenant lay back, so exhausted and downcast that he inspired pity in one of the nationals, who offered him a few flour tortillas and a piece of cheese.

"Go ahead, chief. It's Tomochic cheese, made with lion's milk. A little hard, but nothing a little sotol won't soften up. Take it," the soldier said to him.

After Miguel had devoured the cheese and guzzled the sotol like water, without taking a single breath, he felt fully revitalized. "Thank you, my friend, thank you. You'll never know the good this has done me."

Never had Miguel spoken a truer word, even though he was by nature both ingenuous and effusive. When he spoke from his heart, he knew how to communicate the restless nobility of his sensitive, childlike soul—despite his vices, despite the emotional pain that was his eternal element. Having come back to life, his stomach sated, now he could think again. He had the energy to go on suffering.

The last scenes of the fight for Cerro de Cueva hill put everything that had happened previously into perspective. Of all the terror, of all the many corpses and heroic deeds that he had seen that morning, one event towered above all others, one body, one deed: it was Captain Molina falling backward in front of the hidden enemy he had sought to save.

How could it be that the miserable devourer of young flesh, that infamous bandit who had spirited the poor Julia away to his lair . . . that it was *he* who was the assassin of Captain Molina!

CHAPTER 29

The Tomochic Sun

A scream interrupted Miguel's thoughts as a tragic event unfolded before his eyes.

This is what happened. Sitting against a pine tree protected by a natural parapet, a corporal and a soldier lit a fire, creating a thick plume of smoke, and were about to broil their rations of meat. The corporal was on his feet cutting dry pine branches and the soldier was on the verge of standing up to reach for the meat, when a well-aimed bullet fired from the tower pierced the chest of the first and lodged in the skull of the second. Then a double scream trilled in the air, and two corpses rolled onto the rocks of the crest.

At one o'clock in the afternoon, the company that had taken the enemy's position abandoned it. At the rear a work crew lifted the wounded onto improvised stretchers. To avoid becoming targets for the gunmen holed up in the tower, they decided not to take the same route they had followed during the offensive. Instead they went the long way around, zigzagging around the foothills of the mountains that circumscribed the Tomochic valley.

When the company arrived at the summit of Cerro de Medrano hill at three o'clock in the afternoon, the men were beyond exhaustion. They had not eaten all day. Their comrades from the other corps lavished wild praise on them for their triumph.

Miguel discovered that the general, standing at the highest point in the camp, was unable to contain his enthusiasm. Witnessing the marksmen advancing rapidly over open ground, attacked by two converging lines of fire, with their heroic captain on the right flank, he had thrown his cap down, yelling: "Bravo! The 9th Battalion has vindicated itself. Now October 20 can be forgotten."

When the makeshift stretcher arrived carrying the hero of the day, the general ordered that the serape draping his face be removed. There lay the rigid body of the captain, a gaping wound in his neck, his face bruised, his eyes obstinately open. The bullet had passed through his neck and shattered his spine. When that veteran of such tragic, repellant events—who had witnessed so many wasted acts of heroism in his long military career—saw this, he was so shaken that he nervously ordered the corpse covered again. "Cover him, cover him! Take him away, and name a sentinel to watch over him."

A second sergeant spontaneously asked to be included in the guard. Meanwhile, a single sentinel stood guard at the foot of the corpse, which had been laid out in a crevice in the rocky escarpment on the left side of the hill. In addition, a few disheveled *soldaderas* approached the site and, arranging themselves in a pious group, settled down to pray for the hero's soul.

With Cerro de Cueva hill under army control, now the enemy had only the church and Cruz's house. Because these two strongholds housed the women—mostly widows and orphans by now—it was understandable if their morale was broken and their bodies more so. The looting, sacking, and burning of the town continued mercilessly. Only its center was still intact.

Throughout the day large black clouds could be seen rising from the bottom of the valley, spiraling slowly upward until they finally dissipated, staining the bright blue sky a dirty shade of gray. Every hour a cannon shell broke the solemn silence of Tomochic, which now sheltered more corpses than people. At the highest point of the hill, the marksmen were poised to cut down any Tomochic fighter who emerged from the church or the Cruz house.

At five o'clock in the afternoon, the bugler from general headquarters sounded the call to duty. Major Bligh, chief of the general staff, read out the orders and named the officers responsible for nighttime rounds. And as the rules of active duty dictate, he set the time for relief at six o'clock in the evening.

At night the houses burned brighter than in daylight. The flames tinted the dark sky with yellow bursts of light that shone brilliantly, died down, then flared again into a bright red color against the inky black horizon like stains of pale, luminous blood. Below, in the solitude of those raging fires, the only sounds to be heard were the monotonous barking of the dogs, their doleful howls, and occasionally a plaintive faraway voice.

At dawn on October 26, the Ninth's remaining men accompanied their captain's body to burial in the town cemetery. After the previous night's fighting, it was important that it lay outside the enemy's range of fire.

The rectangular cemetery was enclosed by a low wall of stones and contained only humble graves, the majority of which were unmarked, while the town's more illustrious citizens were interred in the church courtyard.

The cortege stopped at the entrance to the cemetery, and only the officers, a second sergeant, and six soldiers carrying the stretcher with the body went inside. The rest of the company—which now resembled a section—remained outside in open order, their rifles held at a diagonal over their shoulders. The body was solemnly placed on the ground next to a shallow grave, which had been dug with several pickaxes found lying nearby.

Afterward, when Captain Tagle gave the sign, the sergeant loaded his rifle and shot three rounds into the air. Then the corpse, with a greatcoat serving as shroud and a serape as coffin, was placed into the earth. A handful of dirt was thrown on the corpse, and then a few stones.

And nothing more.

Once the funeral ceremony was over, the company members returned to camp. Thus ended the funeral of the hero of Cerro de Cueva hill.

The officers marched silently, shivering with cold, on either side of the column. The sun still hadn't risen. Miguel felt sadder than ever as he jumped over the rocks and ditches of the crudely plowed fields, a terrain that closely resembled the site where the assault occurred.

"Poor Captain Molina," thought Miguel. He had been full of integrity, an enthusiastic, lyrical, ingenuous spirit. Not only could he hold forth passionately about Napoleonic battles, he had also explained the "sun of Austerlitz"[1] and Mexico's patriotic military buildup . . . to die like that, unsung, ingloriously, in some remote corner deep in the mountains, his heroism invisibly and anonymously celebrated.

To spill blood for the good of the country . . . to idealistically sacrifice oneself . . . to immolate oneself for liberty and honor. Surely that was enough for immortality, for lowly death to be converted into eternal life. But to be brave, good, to always prevail in a country's unhappy campaign, waging war against absolute fanatics! He was young, recently married. In Guerrero City he had just received word of his child's birth. He was soon to be promoted to major . . . then to die in obscurity, in that unhappy war waged against heroic Mexicans. They were all good, faithful men. Finally to fall beneath the perverse, wicked bullet of a dying bandit!

He watched his captain being lowered into a shallow grave in a forgotten cemetery at the foot of the Sierras. When the miserable Tomochic was destroyed once and for all, the wild animals would come to feed on the remains of their hero. Not even his bones would remain. Would they even be able to recognize the place where he had lain —maybe for a single day or an entire night. Poor captain! That poor, brave man.

Only those few simple words to encompass all of Miguel's feelings of pity and regret.

It was seven o'clock. Toward the east, from behind the Cordon de Lino hill, an enormous red sun emerged in an explosion of pale gold light illuminating the summit, turning the lilac sky white and sweeping away the wisps of fog. The steel of the rifle barrels sparkled.

"The sun of Tomochic! Poor captain!" Miguel said to his comrades. They didn't understand him, and he continued his funeral oratory in silence. A few soldiers began to sing energetically. Light, perhaps warmth! The sun was coming up, the sun of Tomochic.

Poor captain!

CHAPTER 30

Sotol and Kerosene

While the Ninth was burying a captain in the valley, a lavish event was under way in the camp hidden in the rolling hills.

A convoy stock full of provisions arrived from Guerrero City. An entire squadron of men from the 5th Regiment escorted a drove of strong mules into camp weighed down with sacks of flour, cans of gasoline, and barrels of sotol.

In addition, the head of the escort guard brought sealed orders from General Márquez addressed to General Rangel. The latter was remaining in Guerrero to see how events unfolded.

Taking advantage of the convoy, others sent several mules packed with barrels of sotol, cigarettes, bread, cheese, sausage, salt, sugar, and coffee. Since leaving Guerrero the troops had continued to receive their pay and, as there was nothing to spend it on, they were fat with cash. It wasn't strange, then, that the camp was pervaded by a sense of jubilation, a pulsing explosion of noise, with everyone bustling about in the fresh, clear atmosphere of morning.

After the captain's funeral, the Ninth arrived at camp and established its corner. Meanwhile, an officer ordered the arms stockpiles to be stacked.

Then the flour and meat rations were divided and wages were passed out by roll call—a wad of dirty bank notes issued on the banks in Chihuahua.

A few men were placed on guard duty, but the majority were given permission to break ranks. Soldiers and officers alike gave a hearty hurrah, and off they went.

As the sotol began to circulate, the men's faces went from somber and exhausted to radiant. The screaming and shouting became fiercer as well. Soldiers from all battalions, their women, locals, and Sonora and Chihuahua irregulars in blue, gray, or white pants, and sporting the characteristic hats tied with red ribbons, came and went, gesturing wildly.

In a clearing between the three stunted pine trees next to the general's tent (the only one in camp), the goods that had arrived in the morning were put up for sale. With a couple of old planks and tree trunks the men improvised a broad countertop behind which the adventurers—poor devils who accompanied the troops like a retinue of the general's servants—tried to keep up with the tightly packed mass of soldiers as they advanced on the barrels of delicious sotol.

Indeed, the soldiers elbowed and pushed their way to the front, uttering the crudest of imprecations. The strongest and the quickest managed to get to the front where they carried off the booty: bottles, canteens, demijohns, and jugs. After a week of abstinence, they were eager for a drink.

Meanwhile, the barrels of sotol emptied as though the bottoms had been pierced through. While scores of filthy fingers handed over the blue and green bills in a virtual rain of money, the piles of cigarettes as well as the bags of ground coffee disappeared, and the sausage links were unceremoniously torn apart.

Everything was being sold at outrageously high prices. A single pack of cigarettes cost a real, as did each sausage, and for seven reales you could buy a half liter of sotol. Still, in the flurry to buy up all the goods, the soldiers felt incredibly rich. Never before had they possessed so much money at one time. They had suffered so much and then found themselves suddenly able to forget, to enjoy, to live! *Viva el sotol!*

"Hey, let me through, goddammit!" yelled Castorena, delivering kicks left and right as he pushed through the troops. "Hey, Mercado, my good lieutenant, straight ahead, push!"

Castorena, Mercado, and Lieutenant Torrea reached the makeshift counter where a group of soldiers politely let them pass. The poet was carrying a large jug. The three officers had agreed they would be lunching today on a chicken they had bought from a *soldadera*, and meat with potatoes, beans, chili, thick flour tortillas, and coffee with sotol. "A true banquet," commented Castorena.

Pointing to the barrels of sotol, Miguel retorted, "That says it all, as a modern philosopher would put it."

As they filled their decanters with *aguardiente* (pure, undistilled alcohol) they saw a picturesque group of Pimas returning from looting Tomochic dwellings and then setting them on fire. They were carrying effigies and sculptures of saints, pantaloons, petticoats, accordions, saddles, hides, and kitchenware—with a few donkeys and horses in tow as well. With all the shouting and excitement the animals were getting edgy and breaking into a trot. "The Tomochic prisoners," exclaimed one joker. "The only ones who've let themselves be taken alive."

For just four reales, Castorena purchased a magnificent accordion. With their jug of sotol and their musical instrument, the three comrades went in the direction of their chicken simmering in a gigantic black pot, thanks to a certain corporal.

It was ten o'clock in the morning. Throughout the camp the mood was tumultuous, noisy, and gay beneath a clear sky and an already hot sun. The commotion here was more intense and animated than in the Guerrero camps. Cash, jewelry, dice, assorted Tomochic baubles, alcohol, nearly fresh meat, and women all circulated freely.

The *soldaderas* were not as numerous as they once were and they enjoyed an elevated status. Being fewer, richer, and in heavy demand for their fried goods and physical intimacies, they reigned as sovereigns over many a chaotic coterie. Ridiculously coquettish, many traipsed about in clean clothes, rare petticoats made of the finest cloth, and woolen shawls draped over their shoulders. These were real woolen shawls—not musty old rebozos—with patterns of red and black squares. Presumably they escaped the fires down below.

The air vibrated, as though the camp had been transformed into a tumultuous county fair, dense with men of different ranks, sporting distinct uniforms. There were infantry soldiers, cavalry soldiers, even members of the artillery, or the cannon guard, public security forces, Tarahumara Indians and Pimas. Also present were the Chihuahua irregulars and gaudily decked out locals, and the common soldiers who had arrived that same morning from Guerrero trailing an acrid odor of burning—but not fear—and the glory of having been in Tomochic behind them.

Those who hadn't eaten yet took to drinking and playing dice in small groups. The rest of the men played cards under the benign shade of a boulder or shrub.

Here and there columns of blue smoke—this was not the thick black smoke emanating from the fires below—rose as fires were stoked for the midday meal. A cerulean cloud hovered over the camp, with the circle of bayonets, tied together in stockpiles and lying on their ends, sparkling resplendently in the sunlight like a great bouquet of exotic steel lilies.

Add to this potent mix the strident yelling and high-pitched voices of the women, the peals of laughter, wild bragging, commanding voices, whistling, joking, songs, strumming guitars, and accordion laments. Replenished with food and drink, the troops felt refreshed, calm, and rested while down below Tomochic burned slowly to the ground.

Bands of voracious soldiers surrounded the *soldaderas'* stalls. The women fried pork in large casseroles; it crackled in a boiling sea of grease and saturated the air with an appetizing aroma. Waiting for their food, the men spat impatiently and soothed themselves with long quaffs of sotol.

It was a magnificent spectacle. At that moment each and every man felt like a hero. All were happily eating, drinking, singing or conversing. Gallivanting merrily, they were prepared for anything.

In the abandonment of the moment, no one remembered those left behind in the hills. By now they were surely corpses. Black and terrible to behold, they would languish for all eternity isolated in the mountains—if they were not devoured by wild animals. No, at that moment of furious, intense jubilation, of unbridled frenzy, nobody remembered the victims of Duty.

After the bountiful meal the three officers consumed in the shade of the bushes, even Miguel felt a measure of contentment. They sat crossed-legged on their greatcoats and leaned back languidly as if enjoying a day in the country. The bottle of sotol passed from hand to hand, and they chatted about happy things, taking the sadness in their stride, joking it away. As the women offered casseroles of refried beans, the men enjoyed the female banter. Out of the blue, Torres asked a woman named Mazzantini, "Look here. Wasn't Corporal Trujano your man?"

"Yes . . . yes indeed, lieutenant, sir. May God pardon him and take him home." Mazzantini gingerly crossed herself.

"What about now?"

"I've gone over to the Eleventh, out of respect for my man. He died in battle. So as not to go with somebody else in the Ninth. It's a good idea don't you think, chief? Now I'm with Sergeant Guadalupe Riva of the Eleventh. My girlfriend Pánfila did the same thing. She used to be with Gregorio Moncada. Do you remember him, Lieutenant Mercado, sir?"

"Of course I do . . . Gregorio Moncada, the bugler of my company who died at Cueva screaming out vivas to General Díaz. He was a seasoned and brave soldier."

"My girlfriend Pánfila is arranging for three masses to be said for him in town. What can *we* do? It's all for the love of God . . . going off with the boys from the Eleventh, we won't be offending the Ninth, right?"

Miguel's face registered his dark thoughts. How could the soldiers' consorts calmly take up with others the day after their men died? They were so calm, so devoted as they commended the souls of the dead to God. Then, unashamed and unrepentant, they abruptly found new masters to serve.

"What a bunch of sluts," Castorena exclaimed crudely.

"Whoa, hold on a minute, lieutenant, sir . . . just tell me. What are we supposed to do all alone? We belong to the troops; we go wherever they go. When it's our turn to go we'll die on the road somewhere, laid out like dogs, not like good Christians. God help us."

Touched to the quick, Miguel felt a profound pity for these miserable women who belonged to the troops, the sad flesh of the barracks.

C H A P T E R   3 1

The Dogs of Tomochic

It was one of those cold dusks that fall suddenly in the mountains. Soon the immense valley was shrouded in a melancholy shadow that seemed to glitter in the bitter cold. The crests of the mountaintops were visible against the sky's tenuous, golden hues—as though to create a majestic amphitheater—until only a deep, dark blue remained, spattered with tremulous drops of light above a sea of black ink.

Sometimes gritty, biting gusts of wind blew in from the forest depths, howling mercilessly, desolately. And as they passed over the sunken depths of the valley, the gusts carried vague, lonely sounds, the breath of the wilds. The ancient trees creaking in the night cold sounded like a painful sigh expelled by the savage mountains.

As the shadows deepened, the icy sigh of the winds intensified. Finally, when there was nothing but darkness and more darkness all around, a symphony of brash nocturnal sounds reverberated throughout the valley. At the farthest reaches of the abyss, Cerro de Medrano hill rose like an enormous sleeping dromedary, the river lapping at its right side. Straight ahead was the valley of Tomochic; farther away, Cerro de Cueva hill rose steeply into the sky, aggressive and sullen, gazing jealously down like a tiger poised on its hindquarters.

On the summit, a parapet dominating the deep valley protected the main lookout where the great steel snout of the Hotchkiss advanced ominously into the emptiness. It peeked out between the rocks and bush, stalking its prey in the dim light, aiming toward death.

At night in the camp those on guard duty obeyed the order to maintain strict silence, and the happy sounds emanating from the troops' revelries ceased. Along the attenuated Z that zigzagged across the mountain peaks, where only moments before the joyous din of the soldiers' good humor prevailed, now the winds carried only a vague rumor of hushed voices, a far-away laugh here, a cough there. Occasionally there would be a single strident voice, a command given in ironic irritation, or maybe the sharp sound of rifles hitting stone or a sad Mexican song intoned with savage inflections. Whistles crossed from one end of the valley to the other. Then there was utter silence. It all disappeared, all that variegated, quivering richness of sound. It just disappeared. The order of silence was definitive.

Sometimes winds from the distant forests were saturated with fragrance as they passed through the treetops with their melancholy sighs, the mountains' exhalations. From the dark eternal pines a chorus rang in epic grandeur, a hymn to the American cyclops. From the depths of Tomochic other sounds were detected . . . different, tragic.

From the highest point of Cerro de Medrano hill, Tomochic valley, like a wide deep gash through the night, was terrible to contemplate. Standing behind the natural parapet that protected their positions, Miguel stared for a moment at that black sea. Red dots or scarlet stains wavering like ghostly phantasms emerged from the blackness, and engorged drops of luminous blood appeared to spread out on a vast expanse of dark velvet, like islands of fire.

Islands, dots, drops, stains of light and blood. They disappeared, then appeared again in the inky black, grew pale, only to be eclipsed again. Strange, tragic disappearances.

Mournful complaints: far-off whinnying and howling, which seemed to make the shadows shiver, burst forth from that dark cavity, constellated by tragic sparks of fire and blood. In the darkness, Tomochic slowly burned. Spread out from one end to the other, the remaining deserted dwellings—a few huddled in the center close to the church— had been set on fire and sputtered away in the shadows. The desolate town burned. These were its last few moments, its dying breath.

In the depths of his poetic, lyrical soul, Miguel meditated. The home to that fanatical tribe blazed in spectacular flames. How arrogant they had been in their boundless, savage ignorance. The rabid sons of the mountains faced extinction. The barbaric pride and capricious obstinacy of the colossal eagles high in their impregnable nests! They had challenged death with epic disdain. Their tragic smiles became heroic and sublime in the last few moments before annihilation. O Tomochic! O barbaric, superhuman Tomochic. O annihilated town once inhabited by mountain hawks, solitary young eagles protected by a fortress fashioned of the highest peaks of the mountains . . . the incomparable vigor of your delirious, childlike dream. In your immense empire of forest and mountain you treasured above all your absurd, savage liberty and faith in the arrogant high chief, Cruz of Tomochic. This is your blood that flows, and the generous blood of your brothers, the blood that will flow until the last one of you dies. This marks you as something infinitely rare, exquisite, sad!

"The day went well, wouldn't you say?" Mercado asked of a sergeant who had just returned to his post after reviewing the sentinels.

"This time, yes, it was good, sir!" replied the old Oaxacan soldier, a man whose pedigree made him a candidate for long, hard sacrifice, tempered in unceasing toil. He had a round, bronzed face, an obstinate forehead, prominent cheekbones, and a sparse white beard. His neck was tense, while his body was short, stocky, and agile. Hale, hearty, and full of goodwill, he faced the second lieutenant. Poor sergeant! Who could say if he would ever see his beloved southern lands again?

Below them the luminous islands of blood spread out on a dark sea. The beasts of the valley raised their pitiable chorus, howling desperately. Then the sergeant, who had spent the day incinerating the latest victims of the combat, began to recount the day's events to Second Lieutenant Mercado. The poor devil burst forth with a torrent of words that Second Lieutenant Mercado would never forget.

"Sir, sir! The dogs . . . the dogs of Tomochic! I've never seen anything like it in all my life. How terrible, how brave they were, what good, sweet dogs. They were wonderful, beautiful. I'll confess to you. I cried . . . They're still barking . . . Don't you hear them? They're barking but they're crying . . . they're crying near their fallen masters . . . They watch over their bodies. They cry. They don't leave their sides for a moment. Those dogs are better than any Christian. They watch over their loved ones. Hear that, lieutenant, sir? They're not barking out of anger, make no mistake, they're crying, wailing. I'm not lying to you. When we were piling up the dead bodies, the animals rushed at us, baring their teeth, their fangs . . . We had to kill many, hitting them with our rifle butts . . . and some of the really big ones, we had to go at them with our bayonets . . . and, I'm not lying to you, when they were still alive . . . I swear by the Holy Virgin, they lay down by their fallen masters again and again, or they followed them up to the piles of bodies we were burning. They would lick the blood from their beloved dead with their parched tongues . . . Oh, those poor animals. So you see, sir, why we love our dogs . . . The troops, the common soldiers, are not comfortable without their dogs . . . We had to kill them . . . they were bothering us, biting us. We killed them, then we threw them onto the pile. They got mixed in with the Tomochic fighters, and with our own dead. They all went in together. We had to throw in plenty of kindling and dry grass, just so they would burn up good. From over the plain, other howling, sad dogs came running. It made my hair stand on end like when you're really, really cold. And my stomach hurt. Poor devils. It's just that they were looking for their masters . . . They went uphill and down, returned to the river, threw themselves into the water, came out shaking themselves off, and took off running, running between huts and stubble and ruins, jumping over the corpses of our dead or over the Tomochic dead, oblivious, running and running, barking and barking because they couldn't find their own . . . and they continued like this, driving themselves crazy, running around and around . . . And do you know what else happened near the houses by the river? Can you see over there, that red smoke? Where they burned the barns, or who knows what. Well over there I was on work detail with my section. Pheew! The pigs had made it as far as that . . . what pigs, I swear to God! I piled up . . . It was almost a pleasure to see them there, so fat . . . but those pigs were hungry . . . the nasty swine wanted to eat the dead bodies of Tomochic. I think . . . I think . . . they smelled all that blood, and they went wild. Full of mud, the pigs rushed the pile of corpses . . . and then I saw them fight!"

The sergeant was silent a moment, overwhelmed by his dreadful memories, then he continued: "When the dogs saw the pigs running toward them, they flung themselves at the pigs . . . and that turned out to be another battle waged on the piles of dead. The swine grunted with hunger, the ever faithful dogs barked furiously . . . and all of them wrapped together in utter turmoil, the pigs and the dogs, frightful pig grunts and the howling of the dogs, half dead with hunger, still guarding their masters . . . That made my skin crawl; I turned all cold, but what I really wanted to do was cry . . . the poor things . . . Listen to them, listen to them, sir. Right now the pigs must be fighting over the bodies, and the dogs are still defending their masters . . . Do you hear?"

The sergeant's hoarse voice went silent as though disappearing in a whimper of pity and terror. Miguel shuddered, and when he tuned his ears to the dark depths of the valley, he detected terrifying howls in the darkness. The mountains returned the desolate, muffled echoes.

The northeast winds sometimes made the tragic sounds of that animal scuffle more vivid: the sounds of dogs and pigs fighting over a human body in the eerie gray solitude of Tomochic.

CHAPTER 32

The Burning of the Church

The next day, a boisterous racket again filled the camp on the hill. Then suddenly word spread that the 11th Battalion was preparing to launch an attack on the church. The news stopped every off-duty soldier and officer in his tracks.

General Rangel already commanded Cerro de Cueva hill, and thus access to the Tomochic church had been secured. In addition, Sonoran troops at the bottom of the hill were already directing a steady stream of fire at the church tower.

Armed with knowledge of the enemy's untenable situation, the general ordered a company from the 11th Battalion to assault the church that morning. First, they were to occupy the dwellings immediately in front of the church. Then they were to organize work details and secure plenty of combustibles, cans of fuel, kindling of dry branches and straw. Finally they were to proceed rapidly to the courtyard gates, covered by federal fire from both hills and from the dwellings, and scatter their materiel at the church door. The church was constructed principally of wood, and the fire would ignite immediately, obliging the Tomochic fighters inside to flee. As they tried to escape the engulfing flames, federal troops would open fire as soon as the enemy was visible.

Captain Francisco Manzano led the forty-man unit that aimed to take positions in several dwellings until the cannon opened the way for them with its mighty blast. Describing a full circle, crossing cornfields and treacherous ground, the troops of the Eleventh were forced to cross the river one by one. If the Ninth's bravery and precision in taking Cerro de Cueva hill had inspired troops and officers of other divisions, the Eleventh was no less heroic.

Walking single file, rifles held high, carrying bundles of kindling or cans of gasoline on their backs, their pants hitched up to midthigh, the soldiers of the Eleventh waded into the river. And as soon as they entered the Tomochic line of fire from the tower, however, they fell one by one, wounded or dead.

But they didn't retreat. Their officers, the rims of their kepis jammed down onto their heads, their pistols cocked to fire at anyone who tried to retreat, yelled loudly, "Long live the 11th Battalion, long live General Díaz! Don't fall behind!"

The critical situation lasted only a few moments. Meanwhile, the survivors reached the other side of the river. Once hidden in the outcroppings and hollows of that treacherous terrain, the advance could continue safely. Still in single file, they proceeded rapidly through the brush toward dwellings near the church. Though they had been abandoned earlier, these dwellings were oddly untouched by looting or fire.

With the dwellings now occupied, the national troops on Cerro de Cueva hill were preparing to assault the tower. At eleven o'clock in the morning the general's bugler played "fire." The cannon thundered. Simultaneously, thick gusts of gunpowder smothered the dwelling entrances and the summit of Cerro de Cueva hill in smoke. The bundles of flaming materiel, rolls of smoking hay, and sacks of straw began to rain down in dense, incandescent clouds. Occasionally cans of fuel, serving as hand grenades, were thrown from Cerro de Cueva hill into the church atrium.

Meanwhile, all the general's buglers, as well as those in the dwellings near the church, sounded the attack. Assault columns were priming to move in on the crumbling church that had become the last stronghold of a bunch of dying outlaws.

Twisting columns of smoke rose from a dwelling with thick mud walls adjacent to the church. Apparently several cans of fuel that had fallen and burst on its patio exploded. Now even the winds turned against what remained of Tomochic: burning wicks of dry grasses, cyclones of splinters, ruby red rags of flaming smoke went flying in the direction of the burning tower.

"Long live the Blessed Virgin of Tomochic. Long live Santa Teresa of Cabora . . . long live Santa María of Tomochic," yelled the besieged from behind their chinks in the walls. Then, in an avalanche of armed men, the entire 11th Battalion flung itself forward toward the courtyard, leaving a trail of blood.

It was over before it began. The soldiers, drunk on enthusiasm and sotol, flung their load of fuel and explosives at the churchyard gates. The powder ignited instantly, and flames shot up as the attackers retreated behind the graves in the courtyard, hiding their long twisted torches dipped in black tar.

"Long live Father Cruz . . . long live Our Lord. Death to the sons of hell!" the voices from above howled.

"Long live the government. Long live a united nation," screamed the officers furiously, crazed with fervor, as they sought to break down the church door and enter its inner sanctum, their pistols cocked.

Despite the gravity of their situation, the Tomochic fighters were conserving ammunition. They took precise aim to avoid wasting a single bullet. Sometimes their fire ceased altogether.

The flames surrounding the church door rose higher. Soon the entire church was hidden in a thick, black cloud of smoke, which revealed the yellow lightning shooting from the Tomochic rifles. At the very top of the tower thunderous voices competed with the piercing sound of gunfire.

"Long live the power of God. Long live the Holy Mary. Long live Santa Cabora!"

"Long live the federal government. Long live the 11th Battalion," came the reply from below. To avoid the hail of bullets, the soldiers regrouped close to the church wall.

Suddenly the burning church door flew open, and a few soot-blackened, almost naked men emerged, rifles in hand, bounding with extraordinary agility through the raging fire. The soldiers retreated in fright. Without taking aim, the men fired their weapons at the stunned soldiers and then took furiously to their heels and were swallowed up by the cornfields.

With other specters emerging, a terrifying sound was heard as the ancient door hinges gave way. Falling at an angle across the entrance, like a burning wall, the door panel cut off all possibility of escape. Neither entry nor exit was possible. Waiting for the inevitable, the aggressors remained rooted to the spot. Now it was only a question of time. Then the forces waiting in the Medrano camp descended into the valley and entered the town, occupying the dwellings next to the Cruz Chávez house, which had a lovely tricolor flag waving from the roof.

The 7th Company, general headquarters, and the cannon were relocated inside the Medrano house on the main road next to the foot of the mountain. There had once been a shop in that ancient house, the largest in the area. The day before, fire had left a number of rooms and a section of the inner doorway intact. Now the soldiers cut openings in the back wall, which gave onto the center of town, so they could keep watch over the "little barracks" (Cruz's house) and the church that was now burning out of control.

Miguel observed the spectacle from an opening in the wall. The flames had to have reached the church's interior because smoke was escaping through the windows and tower arches. The worst news of all was that most Tomochic women had taken refuge in the church.

Then Miguel witnessed a tragic event. At the top of the tower, an old woman appeared behind the handrail, gave herself a mighty push, and flung herself toward the abyss. The spectacle was too much to endure. Feeling both pity and horror, the general ordered his bugler to sound the cease-fire. But it was too late. Great red plumes of smoke rose above the church, and soon the whole structure collapsed. There was a tremendous shuddering and then a dull, prolonged roar, as the roof caved in. Successive creakings could be heard, and the major part of the tower came tumbling down in a shower of sparks and soaring flames.

Everything was over. Only Cruz's house, with its three rows of openings cut into the wall and its arrogant tricolor pavilion waving on high, defied the triumphant forces. In the opinion of the general, taking the house was risky and required strict defensive measures.

Clearly the troops were up to the task, but the bloodshed would have been overwhelming. The general had been given the strictest orders to avoid that. He preferred to test the men's ennui and endurance, rather than chance the loss of more men.

Cruz's dwelling was constructed of adobe so thick that cannon fire launched from three hundred feet away didn't even make a dent in it, and the door had been bricked up with stone and mud. Since not even the faintest glimmer of hope remained for the besieged inside, they would be defending themselves to the death. Nor would they let themselves go cheaply.

What's more, the last stronghold, dominating all roads and surrounding fields, was located at the dead center of the besieged town. All paths converged there. Men from the Sonoran and Chihuahuan "national troops," the public security troops, and the 12th Battalion took advance positions, occupying the dwellings that surrounded the "little barracks" to form an invincible ring.

From the ruins of the church and dwellings, thick spirals of smoke from smoldering fires continued to unfurl into the blue sky. At night the black horizon was stained with bloody reflections even more intensely beautiful and abundant than on previous nights, illuminating with even more tragic ceremony a valley overflowing with savage graves.

CHAPTER 33

Prisoners of War

The dawn broke in despair, with mist and smoke indistinguishable. The valley was deathly quiet as Tomochic languished in ruins. The only signs of life were in the Medrano dwelling occupied by general staff and what remained of the 9th and 11th Battalions. A number of other buildings housed squadrons of the Twelfth and a few Sonoran national troops, but the silence was terrible.

At general headquarters, three or four marksmen, who were relieved every hour, stood in wait outside the patio walls. Meanwhile, the implacable, stationary Hotchkiss cannon on its four-footed stand stretched its neck through an opening in the wall.

At nine o'clock in the morning, when the rations of meat and flour were being divided among the remaining troops, an emaciated man ran out of Cruz's house. He was a prisoner who had been locked in the shed in the courtyard of the "little barracks." The prisoners had managed to crack open the shed door, but none wanted to be the first to flee for fear of being shot by one side or the other.

Colonel Torres, second in command, interrogated the fugitive and then ordered that he receive whole food very gradually, as he had subsisted on nothing but raw corn. Shortly thereafter, astonished marksmen surrounding Cruz's home watched as a woman materialized on the threshold of his door. Advancing slowly, she jumped over scattered pieces of wood from the destroyed dwelling. Then the woman began to wander through the fields, a stunned expression on her face. Nothing if not a ghostly apparition, filthy, dressed in rags and with disheveled hair, the woman waved her arms wildly and repeatedly crossed herself.

Finally she wandered meekly in the direction of the Medrano dwelling, and the general ordered that she be treated humanely. When a Pima took her arm to escort her inside, all turned to stare, horrified at the sight of her frail, stooped body with its gloomy halo of ash-gray, unkempt locks that seemed to float around her head. Her eyes glassy and bloodshot, she was wearing a threadbare blue petticoat and old rawhide boots. She was unable to utter a single word.

"Well, well, if it isn't the negotiator to officially hand over the keys to the city!" joked Castorena when he caught sight of the unlucky woman, who was fixing her dumb gaze on the general.

"They're surrendering, at last, those devils are finally surrendering!" came the voices of those who believed that Cruz had sent an emissary to dialogue with them. Soon the soldiers learned that the old woman, half crazy over the death of her grandchildren, had decided to search for their corpses and return with food for the wounded, many of whom were her children and grandchildren.

After finishing the bowl of soup the general offered her, she stuttered out her story. At first Cruz had forbidden her to leave, but as she was the oldest female in all of Tomochic and had engendered the most fighters in the cause of Our Lord, ultimately Cruz felt he had no choice but to set her free. As he did so, he entrusted her soul to the Holy Virgin. Some say Colonel Torres asked her, "What are people doing in there?"

"They pray and pray," replied the old woman.

"And Cruz, what does he do?"

"He prays and prays."

Then General Rangel and Colonel Torres attempted to convince the woman to communicate the hopelessness of their position to the enemy and advise them to surrender. Even, they stressed, if their reason for surrendering was nothing but compassion for the women, old people, and children dying of starvation in that hellhole. If they weren't dying of starvation, then surely they were at risk of disease from the corpses decomposing in the courtyard. The corpses, they continued, must provide a spectacularly frightening vision of death to the huddled families, piles of rotting flesh left against walls supported by nothing but obstinacy and fanaticism. The horror!

The old woman's stunned ambivalence betrayed her fear of the chief. He had forbidden her to communicate with the "heretical sons of Lucifer." Finally she returned with a communiqué signed by General Rangel demanding the unconditional surrender of Cruz's people. He warned that were his orders rebuffed, every shred of resistance would be squelched to the last drop of blood, although he would spare the lives of the women, children, and elders who left the house.

A half hour later the old woman came back with the Tomochic chief's reply. He responded unequivocally that he would not surrender and had no intention of releasing the last families, since he had no reason to believe that the general would keep his word and ensure their safety.

The attackers were offended that they could not even be trusted with the lives of the women and children. The general insisted that it was heresy for them to continue suffering in that inferno. Finally Cruz conceded by releasing the relatives of the mortally wounded.

To the astonishment of the soldiers and officers who stood and watched the fantastic procession, a motley group of women straggled through the low doors of headquarters, dressed in dirty petticoats and tattered clothing that barely covered skin and bones. A low buzz of moans, groans, coughs, and whimpers came from the children who followed after them.

The scene paralyzed all who saw it. The soldiers and thick-skinned Sonoran Indians felt great pity for this group of shipwrecked victims, a handful of wretched beings who traipsed by bleeding, Tomochic's last dying drops. Some of the officers grew pale, while the *soldaderas* were speechless. Miguel couldn't remember reading anything so utterly painful or pathetic in any novel or play.

Looking on in awe, all made room for the tragic parade of victims.

Leading the group was a hunchback with long white hair who supported himself on the shoulders of an emaciated girl. A bullet had pierced one of her hands, and a large black stain seeped through the dirty bandage covering the wound. Next came an ancient woman who was moaning piteously, her face smeared with blood from a gaping head wound.

Then came a tall woman with big black eyes. Standing very erect, she cradled a month-old baby in her arms. The men guessed that several of the young women were very beautiful, draped in their colorful mantillas or red-and-black checked shawls. As a six-year-old boy limped by, his knees dripping blood, his two eyes brimmed with tears though he did his best to force them back.

Next a blur of stick-thin bodies paraded past with pale, withered faces and fevered black eyes. Bringing up the rear of this procession—this flock of widows and orphans, this pile of human misery—came the ancient emissary, that stammering woman who had supplied high chief Cruz with so many of his martyrs.

These disaster victims and pariahs didn't even make up the entire group. A few women whose husbands and sons were still alive obstinately remained in Cruz's house.

Miguel thought of Julia. Was she one of those unhappy souls parading past? Could she be among the living? He observed, as closely as he could, the faces of all the women as grief oppressed his soul. He feared that he might see his long lost love, his melancholy bride.

But most of the women covered their heads with coats or tattered shawls, and soon they disappeared behind an old gate. Visible behind it was a rundown shed that had served the Medranos in better times. They passed into the shed and were swallowed by the shadows.

Miguel saw tears in the general's eyes as he mutely gestured for Dr. Arellano, who was at his side, to attend to the wounded. Flour, meat, and potatoes were brought to the prisoners, and the medicine cabinet was opened so the first patients could be attended to. Gathered in small groups, the soldiers silently contemplated the ruckus emerging from the storeroom. Sounds of groaning and wailing competed with the despondent cries of children and coughing of the elderly. A guard was posted at the entrance with orders to bar entrance to all, even the officers. These were prisoners of war.

Now there was little to keep federal troops from annihilating the headstrong enemy who remained holed up in their last stronghold having decided to die on their feet, proud and unvanquished, defying the troops who dared not launch the final assault.

The only sign of life in that stronghold was the flag waving in the wind whose three colors lent a happy countenance to the bleak panorama: The irony of the heroic, tricolored Mexican flag floating above the ruins of a veritable tomb! They had stopped firing from the openings in the walls and had stopped yelling too. A morbid calm spread through the isolated valley.

The abandoned cattle had wandered into the Sierras, leaving behind the flustered pigs and dogs. The pigs picked their way through the rubble, chasing the chickens and hungrily devouring corpses. The dogs howled pitifully, piercing the dead silence of the countryside.

The general knew that the besieged would have to venture out at night to forage for the corn, potatoes, and beans growing in the fields, and to fetch fresh supplies of water from the river. To prohibit the stealthy movements of the enemy under cover of nightfall, he ordered all forces to split into guerrilla units and to surround the Cruz Chavez home or inhabit the next dwellings over.

Each unit, under the command of an officer, had its own bugler so passwords could be answered when headquarters gave the signal. To avoid confusion with the Sonoran or Chihuahuan national troops, they were to remain dispersed and march rapidly in whatever direction they were commanded to go. To make sure they were recognized as they approached their posts, they were to respond with the appropriate password.

After sunset, at six in the evening, the guerrilla units took off for their designated sites disguised in the dimness of oncoming night. Out of formation, they crouched behind the slopes of uneven ground, taking extraordinary precautions not to be seen by the eerily silent enemy holed up in a tiny fortress that could hardly be seen among shadows lit by a single sliver of moon that shed white, icy light in the cold sky.

Shattering the silence in the depths of the valley with its penetrating notes, the bugle call sounded at eight o'clock that night. As soon as the last vibration had died away, the call was repeated at the far end of Cerro de Medrano hill and again on Cerro de Cueva hill.

Simultaneously from all positions throughout the valley reveille rang out, producing a strange litany as it echoed through the mountains repeating and multiplying in a vague, melancholy decrescendo, finally expiring in the mysterious depths.

It was intensely cold. Posted behind the adobe bricks of a partially razed home, Miguel stood wrapped in his greatcoat, peering straight ahead at the black walls of the Cruz dwelling, some 150 feet away. A slice of moon illuminated the horizon with pale light and enveloped the landscape in a nightmarish veil. Miguel felt infinite sadness reawaken in his soul. The image of his disgraced mother came to mind. Her life would end without her ever savoring one moment of pleasure, without faith or love. Then he thought of his own destroyed future and his own unlucky fate in matters of the heart, his own poor soul, so naive, sincere, and lyrical.

His bitterness disappeared when he thought of the horrors he had witnessed in Tomochic. Were the fanatics who were waiting for death and eternal life in paradise happier than he? He felt hopeless, crushed. And Julia, the lovely adolescent with her dark, melancholy eyes . . . a strange passion.

In his thoughts, he evoked their idyllic union again.

With just a few words from her, he had guessed her sad history; smiling beatifically, she had played the role of the martyr waiting to be escorted to heaven. How abjectly she had endured his drunken advances as he gave in to his most bestial passions and possessed her. It had come over him like a temporary madness. Worse, he had then absolved himself of all guilt. For her own part, she had succumbed to the young, virile Miguel. Then, awakening to her adolescence, she experienced her first voluptuous pleasures.

Suddenly the night was rent with the strident peals of martial bugles. A fantastical, almost unbelievably prolonged chorus then began: one bugle communicated to the next until the last position in the smoke-filled church had been alerted.

Finally the last few notes of the reveille, which also reached the ears of the handful of sublime fanatics, echoed through the mountains. In this remote corner of nineteenth-century Mexico, they belonged to the past: a heroic generation whose feats had been immortalized by yesterday's epic poets.

The young officer woke nervously from his reverie when the company's young bugler shot upright and played the return call into the wind. Now all positions were on alert.

Afterward Miguel returned to his private meditations, pacing under the light of a waxen moon as it was about to dip behind the mountain's crest. Julia! Was he truly in love with her or were his feelings a neurotic manifestation of something else? Perhaps he associated her with the tragic destiny of Tomochic? Who could say? He did know one thing: she still occupied a place in his heart. It tormented him that he had not gotten a good look at the abject women who had arrived that morning! When those unhappy souls had passed by, though he had not seen her among them, he realized he might not have recognized her.

Sitting or pacing back and forth, Miguel spent half the night absorbed in his wandering thoughts. At five-minute intervals the bugle played the reveille, sounding sorrowfully, rhythmic as a giant pendulum, in the stillness of the night. It echoed in the solitude of the moonless valley as well as in his dark, solitary soul.

CHAPTER 34

Praying, Singing, and Killing

It occurred at midnight. Although the moon had disappeared more than an hour ago, a few shadows could be discerned moving toward the river.

The marksmen surrounding the area opened fire. Echoing through the mountains again and again, the shots cracked open the dark's heavy silence. Within moments the Sonoran irregulars were on the scene. Although everyone had thought this must be an enemy foray, soon the shadows disappeared, replaced by two tanks of water.

By lantern light, the men could make out spots of blood in the brambles. "Pray to God that those poor devils got to drink one drop of water!" a compassionate voice murmured—a soldier's voice.

At dawn on October 28, the guards came back from the Medrano dwelling. Behind the dwelling a line of marksmen closely observed Cruz's home. From the roof the tricolor flag waved in the light breeze blowing from the northeast. That same morning members of the 5th Regiment escorted another convoy of provisions from Guerrero, bringing with them detailed instructions from General Márquez.

When the sotol that had arrived with the convoy began to flow like water, the ebullience and revelry of both troops and officers began to revive. The soldiers' songs once again burst from the adobe brick courtyard of the former dwelling of the Medrano brothers. Solemn Tomochic accordions accompanied the plaintive songs, as the fragrance of incense and funeral candles drifted on the wind. The melancholy tones of the accordions contrasted starkly with the happy, gluttonous faces and feverish din that rose in the crisp air beneath an immaculate blue sky. Though winter had barely set in, its stinging chill could be felt in the early mornings and at night.

Once again thick plumes of smoke rose from the cooking fires. The ragged *soldaderas* were frying pork, and in addition they had found chickens and turkeys in the corrals adjoining the deserted smoke houses of Tomochic. There was grilled meat, fried chili, grilled potatoes, salsa, and corn tortillas. Life was improving. Rarely had they eaten so well.

Someone who was listening very carefully might have heard a murmur emanating from the shed as a bored guard paced back and forth, rifle on shoulder, in front of it. Inside, the prisoners—women and children—prayed, coughed, and moaned.

At ten o'clock in the morning guerrilla contingents composed of thirty Pimas each slithered on their bellies through the fields toward Cruz's dwelling and the soldiers held prisoner in the shed outside. In the end, it was the Sonoran Indians who drilled through the wall and managed to save them.

Two prisoners had died of thirst. The others, including a second lieutenant from the 12th Battalion taken prisoner on October 20, managed to return unharmed to general headquarters, escorted by the valiant sons of Sonora. These rugged, tough Indians were worthy rivals of the mountain *criollos*[1] of Chihuahua.

Because the former prisoners had subsisted on nothing but a diet of toasted or raw corn for weeks, their food was strictly rationed. As for the Tomochic fighters, holed up in Cruz's house as though buried alive, they still had not uttered a single word. Proudly, obstinately they continued to defy death.

Everyone pitied and admired that handful of crazy heroes dying a slow death by starvation and thirst. Would they surrender? No, they were one with their sacred earth, praying, singing, killing.

The young officers could easily envision a group of men expiring in a dark, noxious space, with a rosary or small guitar in one hand and a loaded rifle in the other. Their remaining cartridges had been blessed by the Saint of Cabora and the leader of their earthly battles, he who in heaven would conduct them, as promised, to the right hand of God.

Against all odds, Cruz persisted, his will unbroken. Stalwart in his faith, he persevered alongside the decaying corpses of the latest victims.

CHAPTER 35

Chabolé from Sonora

Sporting a felt hat, twill jacket, and gray kerchief, the general paced back and forth beneath a small wooden archway in the Medrano dwelling. Pensive and restless, he beat the ground nervously with his staff.

Sometimes he chatted with Dr. Arellano and Lieutenant Méndez, while the Hotchkiss cannon, placed behind an adobe wall, aimed at Cruz Chávez.

It was necessary to take possession of the house once and for all. Otherwise they would have to wait until the last defender died of exhaustion or starvation to wind up this bloody expedition.

The general, speaking privately with several officers, admitted that he had never come up against such formidable foes in his long life waging campaigns. By way of comparison, a regiment of Zouave Indians had more than proved their mettle during the French invasion, and then there were the Indians from Juchitán, Oaxaca. In fact, both compared to the Tomochic fighters, now a force of no more than twenty-five.

Compassion for the remaining families inspired the general to attempt once more to force those haughty men to surrender; he would convince them that their obstinacy was not only cruel but blasphemous as well. Soon enough, he found that it was useless. He knew only too well that inside the Cruz barracks lives would not be spared. Whoever entered with that in mind would pay dearly. "Let Chabolé try to reason with them," he decided.

Chabolé was an old Indian chief from the Sonoran mountains, a fearless hunter of men and beasts. Give him a bit of *pinole*, a bottle of *bacanora*,[1] a loaded rifle, and he could do sixty miles a day at a fast clip through the mountains. Indeed, he and Cruz were well acquainted, having led mule teams to the U.S. border in amicable smuggling operations.

"Chabolé, would you try to talk to Cruz?" asked General Rangel as soon as the Indian appeared.

"Of course, general. On the double!"

Without further ado, the general imparted his instructions and Chabolé propped his rifle against the wall, along with the proffered bottle of sotol, and asked the first soldier he encountered to guard it for him. Then, to the astonishment of the entire camp, he serenely set off in the direction of enemy headquarters.

The Tomochic fighters permitted Chabolé to approach their half-destroyed fence. With a leap worthy of an acrobat, the old Indian jumped it and disappeared from view. After twenty minutes, fraught with high anxiety for those who had witnessed him disappear, Chabolé reappeared as calmly as he set out. Whistling a tune from his homeland as he approached the general, the old Indian shook his head and said, "They won't give in until God takes their last breath away."

Here is an account of that meeting.

When Chabolé reached the "little barracks," they shouted from within, "In the name of the great power of God, what do you want?"

Without a moment's hesitation, Chabolé retorted, "Listen, Cruz! Cruz! Do you hear me in there? It's Chabolé! I've come to embrace you, offer you a drink, and tell you to surrender!"

"Come on in, then!" came the response.

Chabolé waited for the door to be pushed open a crack. He entered, but the place was so dark he could hardly see a thing.

"Embrace me then, and give me the drink!" He heard Cruz say without losing a beat. While the two embraced in the dim light, the brave emissary noted that the openings in the wall had been covered. In that reeking purgatory there was no air and no light; corpses and wounded men lay in piles, and he heard women moaning and praying.

Chabolé felt Cruz take the bottle from him and heard him drink from it. Then, pushing Chabolé gently toward the door where the two comrades stood, Cruz said, "Okay, get out of here. Tell them we're not surrendering! First our Father in heaven will have to take our souls, and only then will the sons of Lucifer be able to take our bodies."

That afternoon an unexpected event caused a stir in camp. Among the prisoners who had emerged from Cruz's that morning was a public security forces soldier who had fallen into their hands on October 2. He had betrayed his own to go over to the enemy side. Traitor! Along with the others, the unfortunate man had put up a desperate fight in Cruz's home.

Using the pretext of looking in on some comrades, he had managed to get to the prisoners shed. Pleading with them not to rat on him, he waited along with the Tomochic prisoners for help to arrive. But the prisoners were indignant and informed on him. After a brief war council he was summarily sentenced to death.

At 4:30 in the afternoon the cowardly traitor faced the firing squad. After the military salute rang out, he was executed. Nobody pitied him. The women did not pray for his soul or invoke the Virgin of Guadalupe, and Cruz of Tomochic did not offer him a place in heaven.

CHAPTER 36

The Last Blaze

The posts of the previous night were occupied again, and Miguel was sent to a wing of the ruined church that had once served as a convent.

That day a damp, cold wind blew from the north on clouds billowing in a sky that was growing darker by the moment, an infinitely sad afternoon. A light rain began to fall on the gray, deserted valley. Thick smoke escaped through the broken beams of the church roof to mix with the clouds. The desolation rivaled the silence of death.

Miguel found decaying corpses on the path between the Medrano dwelling and the church. The hogs had torn them from limb to limb. A fetid stench filled the air. Flesh and clothing were completely covered with mud, and at first sight it was impossible to tell which band the corpses belonged to.

The section posted to guard the "little barracks" from behind the old convent walls came to a halt in the church courtyard while the rain poured down heavily. The lieutenant who commanded Mercado's section divided up his forces and ordered Miguel to lead several men toward the areas to the far left, which had already been destroyed. There, smoke no longer emanated from the roofless walls, whereas the dwellings adjacent to the church still smoldered in the rain.

The intense odor of rotting flesh led the second lieutenant to a pile of half-burned bodies that obstructed a doorway his troops had to pass through. First they hauled the corpses over a kind of bridge created with a section of beam, which the men then used to reach their destination and pass through the old rooms of the ancient cloisters. In a bygone era when mining thrived in these mountains, the Jesuits had constructed the convent in their efforts to colonize the Tarahumara Indians.

To the eyes of the hypersensitive officer, the ruins under the dull gray sky were cold and closed as a mausoleum. Although sometimes drawn to suicide, the second lieutenant was horrified by the senseless slaughter. What a grotesque afternoon: the freezing rain pelting down on the piles of rotting corpses and the smoldering remains of buildings that had been razed to the ground.

Violent gusts of glacial wind cut into the livid faces of the mute, despondent soldiers like knives. Wrapped in their blue greatcoats with their hoods pulled tight around their heads, they advanced slowly as monks in a doomed procession onto the grounds of the devastated, smoldering church. They meant to relieve a small detachment composed of men from the Eleventh who had been stacking corpses and then burning them with beams and rotten boards. However, this dark task turned out to be horribly ineffectual. They had also punched openings in the remaining standing walls and positioned soldiers behind each chink.

Now it was dark and Miguel was overcome with fatigue. He felt nauseated. He had a terrible taste in his mouth and a pain in his heart, and he was numb with cold. Soaked through and through, he sat down on a rock and observed the structure in front of him with increasing terror. Through sheer force of will, he managed to tame his fear.

The darkness was thick as paste. In the distance the faint aura of red eruptions and constellations of sparks were visible. Sometimes faint sounds could be discerned too: a piece of roof falling to earth, a wall collapsing, a beam giving way.

At eight o'clock the bugles broke the silence of that dark, rainy night, and the call echoed back and forth twenty times through the valley's invisible contours. Huddling next to the bugler in a corner, Miguel couldn't help nodding off. Then he would startle awake nervously, afraid of being caught dozing or being attacked by the enemy.

It rained and rained. It was still raining at two o'clock in the morning, the hour when the cold became unendurable. A few of those wretched boys began to whimper piteously as though their feet had already gone numb with gangrene.

Finally, at dawn, strong winds swept away the clouds and the rain let up, allowing the troops to light raging bonfires. After drying and warming themselves, the men took out their rations of meat to roast in the flames.

Soon the general's adjutant arrived with orders for the troops to seize the "little barracks" at ten o'clock that morning. The men occupying the church were to stay put and remain alert. Their only role was to make sure that the enemy didn't slip through the line of fire as they tried to flee.

Miguel prepared to witness the assault through the openings carved into the old convent walls. He felt himself becoming accustomed to every excess of horror, inured to all of it. Dispassionately he observed the smoldering ruins and even the pile of corpses. It was awe-inspiring yet familiar, like an impressive mountain range, a waterfall, or the rhythmic beating of the waves against the shore.

In Cruz's house the mortal silence that had reigned for the past few days continued. The young second lieutenant observed groups of soldiers lugging barrels of fuel, kindling, and dry branches. It reminded him of the assault on the church. Then the cannon in the Medrano dwelling fired three times. The assault! When the signal to attack was sounded, the soldiers rushed forward crying, "Long live the 11th Battalion." Carrying fuel and torches, they made a run for the "little barracks," where the openings in the walls filled with gunpowder. A few shots were fired in return.

Creeping along the fence that surrounded the "little barracks," the assailants crouched behind a pile of rocks to answer the gunfire, aiming at the openings in the wall in an attempt to quell the resistance. Then they charged, yelling slogans to arouse the soldiers. "Long live the 11th Battalion. Viva Mexico!"

As usual, from behind walls pockmarked with bullets, came the retorts, which promised death and retribution, sowing terror among the troops. "Long live the great power of God! Long live Holy Mary. Let the Eleventh come forward!"

While the troops' heavy gunfire bombarded the adobe bricks, three soldiers charged the corner of the house and began to climb to the roof. One on top of the other they grabbed at the loose bricks, lodging their knees in the crevices. When the first man hoisted himself up to the twenty-foot-high rooftop with his bloody hands, the men below broke out in wild bravos and vivas though it remained eerily quiet inside Cruz's house. Occasionally a few shots and shouts broke the silence.

Still, the assailants were apprehensive and momentarily vacillated. Then the first man to reach the rooftop held a hand out to the others, then those to still others. Steel pickaxes were handed up that the men used to open holes in the roof. Then the officers hefted themselves up, and a corporal tore down the flag waving on a pole along the edge of a wall. Soldiers on the ground threw torches, sticks and weeds, dry kindling, and fuel to their comrades above. The men lit them and then flung the burning bundles through the gaping hole in the roof, creating cascades of fire inside Cruz's dwelling.

Inside, the besieged were mute, hardly responding to the attack at all. Every now and again they fired a few rounds up the chimney. But the assailants redoubled their fire, spewing their blind bullets down the chimney chute and creating a horrific dull crackle.

Fetid black smoke wafted up out of the perforated roof. All gunfire ceased. Feeling the rooftop creak beneath their weight, the soldiers on top jumped to the ground. This time the Tomochic fighters had missed their mark.

Hunger and fire vanquished that impenetrable fortress. It was understood by all that anyone left inside the inferno was taking his last breath. At that point, the reveille sounded at general headquarters, reiterated by the different tones of the bugles that signaled the end of the campaign. In the midst of ruins, sadness, and ashes, in a valley rotting with smoldering graves and unburied dead, the bugles' vigorous martial notes rang out dismally.

The campaign was over. The last stronghold burned, engulfed in whistling flames fanned by the morning winds. The bugles' disorderly reveilles vibrated convulsively one after the other in the cold air, their thunderous martial joy contrasting darkly with the devastated landscape. Divisions of soldiers with improvised stretchers arrived at Cruz's house, where the flames were rising higher. The soldiers smashed the door with pickaxes, and a few Pima Indians made it inside that furnace. When they reemerged, blackened by smoke and ash, they carried the wounded Tomochic fighters in their arms like slabs of meat: semiconscious, bloody, half-charred human meat.

In the distance, a few soldiers from the Eleventh, the Twenty-fourth, and the corps of irregulars from Chihuahua mutely observed the tragic progress of the flames as they engulfed Tomochic's last bastion. As the wounded were brought out of the flaming house, a number of the men helped accommodate them on stretchers.

An officer arrived on horseback with a communiqué from General Rangel for the captain of the Eleventh (who had commanded the attack on the "little barracks"): as many lives as possible, especially among the women, were to be saved.

Once again the courageous soldiers shone brilliantly, displaying great compassion and heroism as they rescued the wounded in the most desperate of circumstances. While most of the Tomochic fighters died on contact with the cold air of the valley, others, breathing their last, gazed at their conquerors out of glassy, unseeing eyes. The strongest among them used their last strength to defy; sitting up, their arms held high, they waved their clenched fists menacingly at the soldiers. Some even managed to yell feebly, "Long live the power of God! Death to the soldiers!"

The corpses were tossed onto a pile and set afire with flaming beams. The wounded were transported on stretchers to the intact porch of a nearby dwelling. Not a single Tomochic fighter managed to walk on his own two feet. The four or five among them who weren't wounded were so weakened by hunger, fever, and thirst that they soon fainted, falling heavily to the earth.

The general refused to witness the terrifying spectacle. He sent the chief of the field hospital to take official notes on the disaster—to record why sending medics would be unnecessary. To take the last redoubt of the chief of Tomochic, they had waited until the death throes of its last defenders.

CHAPTER 37

Long Live Death!

Their faces ashen, the remaining seven Tomochic fighters lay face up under the porch, twisting and turning, drawing their final breaths. They had been placed perpendicular to the blackened wall, as though lined up for the dissecting room or displayed in a morgue. With their sightless, glazed expressions they seemed to be contemplating the grandeur of their beloved, sacred valley extending gloomily beyond them.

One woman lay wrapped in charred, stinking tatters that left her partially exposed. So, a woman had fought as well! With her thin, knobby arms outstretched, her hands scorched from gunpowder, the woman was taking her last breath. A bloody rosary could be seen beneath the empty black cartridge belt that crossed her naked breast.

A long tangle of frizzy curls framing his exposed head, the great chieftain, the heroic pontiff, lay at her side, his lanky body inert, one leg in the shape of a twisted rag, one arm bound in a large, blood-stained blue dressing. His black beard covered a thin, haughty face, making his aquiline nose seem even more imposing. Even among the thick skinned, this spectacle would have inspired profound pity, immense admiration. There he was. Sublimely, in the tragic attitude of a heroic gladiator, Cruz languished between his wife and a brother who had died of nothing more heroic than starvation. Well, that's what Miguel saw as he passed by with his troops.

Then the officer averted his gaze to avoid seeing living men in their death throes. How he wished they were already dead! Having thought himself inured to any and all horror, even Miguel had to look away.

"Oh, those pathetic men, second lieutenant, sir. How pitiful!" said a sergeant, his voice full of emotion.

"Yes, truly pathetic!" answered the second lieutenant.

As soon as the "little barracks" began to burn, the camp erupted in an outpouring of enthusiasm, shouting, and peals of laughter. It was the end of Tomochic! No more fear, no more exhaustion. There would be no more fighting. It was over! And they would be able to proudly tell their stories in the days to come: I fought at Tomochic!

The sotol was passed from hand to hand. High on their triumph, the troops—officers, locals, and soldiers—toasted their units and their commanders, their divisions, the Sonoran nationals, General Rangel, General Porfirio Díaz, and the government. They also drank to their dead and wounded . . . and to the souls of the Tomochic fighters.

With a stunned expression on his face, a somber Second Lieutenant Mercado contemplated the far horizon and the surrounding mountains, the dazzling blue sky stained here and there by smoke from the fires below. The Cruz dwelling was burning, and the surrounding houses were in ruins; in the distance, the indifferent river gurgled. At camp, Mercado was surrounded on all sides by the tumultuous sounds of the officers, Indians, and soldiers celebrating victory.

Then a gunshot sounded nearby, then another and another. The din ceased and was followed by a leaden silence. Coming back to reality as though from a long, confused dream, Miguel stood up. "What's happening?" he asked an officer who was whistling the tune to a lively zarzuela under his breath.

"Nothing, my man. Don't worry. Everything's over; they've just executed them . . . an act of mercy . . . to put them out of their misery!"

"But who?"

"Who do you think? The last of the Tomochic fighters."

And so it was. They were gunned down while drawing their last breath, their bleeding bodies and ragged clothes still smoking. "Blessed God!"

murmured one of the soldiers, sinking to his knees and making the sign of the cross.

With the death of the last Tomochic fighter, the Tomochic campaign came to an end.

That afternoon work crews were designated to incinerate the dead lying in the valley and the foothills of the mountains. They were piled one on top of the other and then set afire. The burning mounds spewed thick, foul-smelling smoke that invaded the entire valley of Tomochic. When the supply of kindling was exhausted, human oils kept the evil piles burning, scattering parts, transforming the incinerated bodies, blackening the naked skulls with their empty eye sockets and open mouths. Out of the dripping guts rose little violet-colored tongues of flame. The air smelled of rags and burned hair, fried skin, nauseating rot and human excrement. And instead of buzzards, pigs.

That afternoon, sickened and despondent, with his mind on Julia, Miguel was about to interrogate some female prisoners who were taking water to the sick women. But just then the forces of the Ninth were commanded to regroup in a house at the foot of the mountainside, outside the nucleus of ruins, at the far end of the valley.

The Eleventh, Twelfth, and Twenty-fourth and the general staff set up camp in spacious corrals near Cerro de Medrano hill. The Sonoran Nationals, the dragoons of public security, and the squad of men remaining in the 5th Regiment camped nearby. Meanwhile, the Fifth became responsible for rounding up the horses, mules, asses, cattle, and sheep recovered from the abandoned fields.

The women went into the houses destroyed by gunfire and bloodshed and fearlessly looted them, taking whatever they could get their hands on, even exposing themselves to the risk that a ceiling might come tumbling down on their heads. They had never been so happy! Predatory instincts set free, claws out and mouths agape, the heroines were transformed into harpies again.

Having been supplied with a horse and field saddle, Second Lieutenant Mercado was posted near the general. His mission was to deliver his orders that night to the new headquarters of the Ninth, located about a mile and a half from general headquarters.

To deliver the orders from the general, he had to pass straight through the ruins and smoldering fires of the destroyed city. Eyes wild, and with agitated abandon, Miguel contemplated the macabre scene, straight out of Dante's inferno, as he galloped along avoiding the piles of burning bodies. From time to time, from somewhere deep within, he felt a dark thrill at the sight of such desolation, such carnage.

Before setting out, Mercado had downed a half liter of sotol in two gulps. Mounted on a frisky horse that was raring to go at his slightest touch, he felt almost like a high-flying bird of prey cruising over the site of such catastrophe.

Half delirious on sotol and his quixotic nature, Mercado vividly remembered the Apache scalps hanging down from the lances of the Chihuahua horsemen. In a flash, he was riding in a nightmare.

The cold gusts of wind ripping by sang in Mercado's ears, and, as if infected with the madness of Tomochic, he ripped off his kepi. Inebriated, feeling himself to be the luckiest of men, the second lieutenant dug his spurs hard into the horse's flanks and flung his savage war cry into the lonely silence: "Sotol and kerosene! Hurrah! Long live death!"

CHAPTER 38

The Saint of Cabora

A ce of spades in the hole," the captain of the national troops said gravely. With my cards I'll finish 'em off."

Castorena shrieked, tapping out an obscene jingle while Mercado, seated in the middle of a tightly packed circle of officers, handed over a fistful of small bills.

"The luck of that hack poet," a lieutenant fumed.

"If that clown doesn't get out of here, we won't continue," growled the captain. "Out with the poet. Throw him out."

"Get out! Get out!" yelled several impatient officers in unison: the second lieutenant's histrionics were imperiling the game.

A smattering of officers, representing all divisions, had gathered to play monte. A gray blanket rolled out in the center of the large, dusty stable—the "senior officers' pavilion"—served as carpet. The eminent captain sat cross-legged on the carpet, guzzling sotol, one shot after another, and dealing monte to amuse the boys.

For the most part, the rascals arranged themselves in a circle on the carpet, sitting on sheepskins or on their own capes, while a few remained standing and placed bets. Among the latter, Miguel stood and sought out new thrills in the excitement of the betting.

A tipsy Castorena sprinted here and there, drinking, singing, and dancing all at once. Using Mercado to play for him, he was enjoying a streak of luck, which exasperated the old captain no end. Trimmed in gold braid, the captain's huge brimmed hat struck an exotic, colorful note amid the dusty flaps of the officers' kepis.

"One of my pesos is missing! One of my pesos is missing!" the poet shouted suddenly, leaving off his mad antics to count his bills again. "Hey, old philosopher, did you pocket it? Sir, one of my pesos is missing!"

"I'd say you have a screw loose somewhere!"

"Throw that sad hanger-on out of here!"

"King and a jack . . . Put your money out in the open, sirs. Please sit back from the table . . . money talks."

"The jack! The beautiful little jack." Enthusiastically, Castorena began to improvise:

> Sotol puts me right out of whack
> In the midst of my dancing and pleasure
> Good sirs, since my hand has the jack
> I'll bet all of Cruz Chávez's treasure.

Nobody laughed. The mention of the sad hero's name fell heavily in the midst of the pandemonium. Nor was the silence followed by the usual displays of bravado and peals of laughter, as had occurred earlier when the poet had coarsely toasted the destruction of the town. Rather, there was a mute show of respect for the unfortunate Cruz Chávez.

Miguel began to feel his anger rise and his repugnance for Castorena return. The second lieutenant now viewed him as puny and vulgar, an unworthy clown whose face was a grotesque parody. The man couldn't understand that the fleeting instant of death had transformed Cruz the rogue into Cruz the hero. "No one but a coward makes fun at the expense of a dead hero." The second lieutenant spat the words in Castorena's face.

"Brother, you may be right, but you know I'm tired of all the new work they're thinking up for us, like digging up the treasure of Tomochic as though it were another Tenochtitlán!"

Miguel, angry, was on the verge of moving away. The extinction of the Tomochic race made him tremble. Then Castorena, with a hint of affection for this poor devil, stopped the sad, pensive officer in his tracks, asking impetuously, "Do you want a drink of cognac? I mean the real thing, brought in specially for the general?"

"Cognac?" Miguel conceded at once, vanquished by his vice.

Pulling Miguel aside, Castorena produced a mysterious flask. The two officers took turns quaffing its contents down. "Oh man . . . it *is* cognac!"

"You better believe it. You can't get anything better, not even in Mexico City. Seriously, Mercado, I got me this fine poison in exchange for treasure from Tomochic that I found this morning on work detail at the church."

"Treasure from Tomochic?

"I swear to it! The Saint of Cabora! Not in the flesh . . . that would have been even better! But a statuary! A Pima guard escorting the convoy from Guerrero offered me the cognac in exchange for the icon from his homeland. Both of us came out ahead!"

Miguel, now a submissive captive to the man he had moments before dismissed as a fool, turned pensive when he heard that reverential name, Santa Cabora. It was her image alone that had inspired the obstinate, gritty people from Tomochic. They had claimed the right to thrive and prosper, to inspire other hearty Mexicans.

Teresita of Cabora! Mercado asked himself if her visions were hallucinations. The vibrant and above all tenacious girl with her disturbing eyes, stimulating and wild as a mixture of whiskey and gunpowder at times, at others benevolent, calm, and sleep inducing as opium smoke.

The Saint of Cabora! Had her burning, eloquent eyes—whose radiance shone like a halo round her face, instilling miraculous faith in the poor pilgrims from faraway mountain villages—incited the mountain peoples of Sonora, Sinaloa, and Chihuahua to spark rebellions and disturbances that could only be quenched in flames and bloodshed?

Was she nothing but a delicately wrought instrument, a mirror, manipulated in the dark by hidden hands, through whose sparkling play of facets and edges those strong, unschooled men—heroic, ignorant rustics—could unleash from their mountain fortress a terrible war of Mexicans against Mexicans in the name of God Almighty?

Santa Teresa of Cabora!

Little Teresita Urrea? Humble daughter of northern Sinaloa, born and raised in Sonora on the threshold of a dark theater of war with the hateful war cries of the rebellious Yaqui ringing in her ears. Was it she who later instilled mystic delirium in the naive, terrible soul of Tomochic, inspiring her people to pick up their Winchester rifles? Was it her madness that gave birth to that lunatic slogan, "In the name of the great power of God"?

What role had the poor hysterical girl played, her seizures instilling such warlike intoxication in the wild, solitary men of the mountains? In the primitive and mysterious Tomochic rebellion—a rebellion of epic proportions—what unconscious role had she played?

Teresita Urrea, Santa Cabora.

What twisted spirits had transformed that sweet, sick girl into a volcano spewing lightning flashes, cascades of blood, ice, tears, and venom, transfiguring her into a flag of hatred and massacre, a dangerous red banner signed with a black cross?

What unworthy Mexicans unleashed a civil war for purely selfish motives but weren't brave enough to fight in it? Could they even claim to know how to die for their cause?

This was what Miguel was thinking, to the astonishment of Castorena, who thought he had gone mad.

CHAPTER 39

Julia Was Dead, Then

Serving as an auxiliary, Second Lieutenant Mercado was ordered to do security guard duty at six in the evening. Accordingly, he reported to the courtyard and reviewed the troops detailed for the duty. "Attention, lookouts," yelled Mercado in a harsh voice. The order was repeated by a sergeant, his second in command. When the regulation review was complete, Miguel stopped at the gate.

October 30 was a splendid day. There had been heavy frost on the ground at dawn, but now the sun was shining in a pure blue sky—revealing the spectacle of disaster throughout the countryside. The second lieutenant felt sadder than ever as he looked out over the ruins. The desolate razed dwellings were abandoned to their fate, and the ruins of what had once been the church belched black plumes of smoke and silently burned away.

That same morning, after dining on a few pieces of beef with boiled potatoes and a meager cup of hot coffee (he bought the meals from the *soldaderas*), he led a contingent of twenty men to excavate the church in hopes of unearthing treasure among the church ruins. What they actually found, however, was mangled corpses, old bells, singed pieces of paper, portraits of the Saint of Cabora, and scraps of metal.

Another work crew was in charge of digging out the "little barracks." They unearthed the corpses of men, women, and children, as well as guns, rifles, bayonets, pistols, uncounted burned cartridges, and a lieutenant colonel's kepi. Without a doubt the kepi had belonged to Lieutenant Colonel Ramírez, taken prisoner at Tomochic. Later, in a brilliant move, the Tomochic chief had proudly set him free.

On the walls of the roofless dwellings the marks left by the lead bullets and the multiple pits left by the cannonballs were visible, showing that the projectiles from the little cannon were of scant use against thick adobe walls.

Considering the number of shells and boxes of grapeshot aimed at the town, the damage was relatively minor. Did the cannon have a corrosive effect on Cruz Chávez's morale? Not in the slightest, or maybe it had the opposite effect. It was rumored that Cruz Chávez had referred to the little cannon as the "devil's monocle." And Pedro Chaparro used an equally randy term when he spoke of it.

The devastation caused by the fire was by far the most depressing sight. Only two dwellings were still standing in all Tomochic—per orders from on high.

The slow incineration of the corpses ended with the winds raising the ashes and fanning the flames of the funeral pyres. Hungry pigs circled round, grunting dully, and eagerly set upon any unburned human flesh. The sight of the feeding pigs was so repugnant to the *soldaderas* that they refused to fry with pork shortening or eat pig meat: the pigs had consumed human flesh!

The second lieutenant recalled the Oaxacan sergeant's story. In his mind's eye he witnessed it all over again: the pigs and dogs clashing over the corpses in Tomochic. Now the scrawny, whimpering dogs wandered from house to house fruitlessly seeking their masters. Howling piteously at the soldiers, they ran in the other direction when they saw them, their tails between their legs. Nor were they seduced by the pieces of meat the soldiers threw to them. No matter how hungry they were, they refused to eat it.

Meanwhile, the 9th Battalion occupied former mayor Reyes Domínguez's place, which was located just outside the main hub. The dwelling had been left intact because Domínguez was one of the few who hadn't joined the rebel chief, although he was Cruz Chávez's brother-in-law.

Long before the conflagration, Reyes Domínguez had left for Guerrero City. Now he was living with his family and an old Frenchman who had once been schoolmaster in Tomochic. He too had fled a valley in the grip of frenzy and madness. When Domínguez was apprised of the war's outcome, he left for Tomochic immediately and reached his home in a day and a half. When he arrived, he found that his livestock had disappeared and his storehouse was empty. The general, however, generously repaid this exceptional citizen's intelligence reports.

Meanwhile, the troops recouped in their tranquil quarters. No more tumultuous festivities, no further mourning the dead. The men chatted pleasantly and analyzed recent events, their women at their sides, as though they were in their barracks in Mexico City. Several were taking this opportunity to honeymoon with the widows of the 11th Battalion, who were no better—and no worse—than the women of the 9th.

At five in the afternoon all the women and children who had been taken prisoner were transported to Reyes Domínguez's house. The sight of this procession stirred the men's compassion. Miguel began to tremble with happiness when he learned that the sickly flock was to be lodged in the house occupied by the Ninth. There would be news of his Julia! He would see her, perhaps even kiss her chastely and purely, not with his lips but with his soul, as he would kiss an unhappy sister.

To be as close to the parade of female prisoners as possible, Miguel Mercado positioned himself in the old doorway. Observing them, he could hardly contain his emotion. The pathetic women dragged themselves along but held themselves erect. At least they had eaten, washed, and dressed. And the wounded had been attended to.

Now General Rangel became magnanimous; a veteran of war, he was not ashamed to cry openly for these innocent victims of his men's madness. As general, he was implacable with the Tomochic fighters but as a man he was generous and solicitous of the war orphans and widows.

In the deepest recesses of his proud soul, Miguel expressed his gratitude to the general, for the sake of Julia. In his mind he substituted a sympathetic "Hurrah for General Rangel" for the "Hurrah for the 9th Battalion!"

As the captives passed silently by, a cold shock passed through him. Julia was not among them. He checked the women's faces as they filed past, fully exposed. No, he didn't recognize Julia. She had died, after all.

Bringing up the rear of the sad procession, two Pima Indians carried an improvised stretcher. "Who do you have there?" Miguel asked. "One of their women. She's dying," they responded. So Julia had died.

CHAPTER 40

Chapultepec, Chapultepec

At six o'clock that evening, Miguel relieved the guard on duty at Reyes Dominguez's house, which had been converted into a combination barracks for the 9th Battalion and sanctuary and prison for the surviving families of Tomochic.

The officers' correspondence had arrived from Concepción, Guerrero, an hour earlier; with the campaign at an end, normal life had resumed. In fact, an adjutant on guard duty delivered a letter to the second lieutenant. Who could be writing to him, he wondered? He had no friends, no creditors, no sweethearts.

By now night had fallen. In the dim glow of a lamp hanging from the high stone archway in the hall, he made out the writing on the envelope. "Mama, poor dear Mama," he whispered. Feelings of tenderness overwhelmed him and he felt his dark, fatalistic mood lift. Reproaching himself, he mused . . . so there was someone who was thinking of him, who hadn't abandoned him. He wasn't all alone in the world. Pulling his kepi from his head to better see the writing in the dim yellow light, he tore open the envelope and read:

Tenth of October, 1892

My beloved son,

I hope the change of garrison has cheered you some and that your health is better. They say that Chihuahua has a very temperate climate. How is your health? Are you all right?

At first I thought I shouldn't even write to you, only to make you feel more bitter, but sadly I have to confess that I owe allegiance to another. My husband Leandro has come back and he's very repentant. He is taking me abroad, far away from Mexico, God only knows where. Be good, forgive your mother who loves you with all her heart. I'll write to you. Reflect on God's goodness. It is the only consolation for those who suffer. Pray and have faith.

Your mother, Angela

Now my mother! Leaving me for that evil man who is not even my father . . . The pair of them leaving together! The unhappy second lieutenant felt as though the ground had given way beneath him. His chest tightened and his eyes clouded over as he began to sob. He continued to cry in a corner of the doorway behind the guard post. This was a crushing blow. Now there was nothing left in this world for him. Life itself was false, reality gruesome. His own mother was abandoning him to his own devices, all alone in the world.

Alone, what a frightening word! It conjured up the misfortune of his ill-starred life, the bitterness, disappointment, and infinite monotony he saw himself perpetually condemned to. Such an oversensitive young man, such a weak, emotional soul . . . vibrating like a snapped string, flung by fate who knows where? Scrambling through treacherous bushes and over boulders, he had been swept into the crater of the volcano, until he was staring down into the apex of horror. Duty, hatred, vice, war, love, and pain, all had forged him. Having the soul of a poet and philosopher, he felt how deeply he had sunk. Humanity nauseated and embittered him, and he heard himself repeating the familiar, gloomy refrain: it would have been better if I had never been born. Then he thought bitterly, "Nothing is sacred. Not the poetry of war or heroism, not even the poetry of motherhood . . . I'm all alone, totally alone! A curse on me!"

In his desperation, he nonetheless possessed the rare lucidity to understand that he was probably in the grip of madness. He took up his rifle, which was leaning against the stone archway under the lantern, and then mechanically put his kepi on his head. In a daze, having lost all sense of time, he felt for his cartridges and then stood listlessly watching the happy officers come and go.

"With your permission, second lieutenant, sir, it's time for the changing of the guard," said a corporal.

Miguel came to with a start. He felt fatigued and cold all over again. But he was accustomed to peremptory orders from above; after all, he had been educated in the iron discipline of the military academy. Miguel answered energetically, "Fine. And make sure the one guarding the female prisoners doesn't let anyone in, and that means the officers too. Understood?"

Second Lieutenant Mercado took leave of the guards and headed for the camp. Around a soothing fire, a handful of officers were conversing with the famous Reyes Domínguez, brother-in-law of Cruz Chávez and sole survivor of Tomochic. He was relating some of the sordid details of the insanity that had afflicted his homeland, which seemingly took hold of the dogs and even the stones.

As he listened to the torrent of words, Miguel learned more about what he already knew: it had been atrocious and terrible in Tomochic. It was the subject that everyone kept silent about.

The rebellion involved a handful of men. Although intelligent and strong, they were ignorant. They were short on education and long on iconography. These proud souls adhered to an odd religion that reached way beyond the bounds of convention to schism and lunacy. Then there was Teresa of Cahora, along with those who fanned the flames of her sainthood. There had been grand schemes within, though only a few sparks could be gleaned from the outside: excesses perpetrated by local authorities, sinister bosses, outrages committed by soldiers, and mysterious alliances.

Once again, Miguel realized that it was thanks to the strong arm of General Díaz that the nation had stamped out the rebellion with one brutal blow. The proud, mystical war cry of Tomochic, backed by audacity and a few Winchester rifles wielded skillfully in the depths of the mountains, had to be mercilessly smothered.

The second lieutenant tried to imagine the consequences of the Tomochic contagion spreading to Chihuahua, Sonora, north and south through the Sierra Madre. How much needless blood would be spilled then? How soon would the ambitious politicians, greedy and the hypocritical, have exchanged the "chilapeno" hats they wore in the uprisings for the top hats worn at official banquets?[1]

From Miguel Mercado's perspective, everything had been inexorably ordained by fate. If the people of Tomochic had been heroic, and if they had shown themselves worthy of a better destiny, so too had the troops and the heroic officers. The small tactical errors, the pathetic vices and routines revealed the outmoded Mexican military at its worst. All of it was a symptom of an evil that resided deep within the army itself. It was a manifestation of a systemic illness that would inevitably yield to the times.

This "rogue" officer would soon be out for good, thought Miguel. He was the worst of his kind, with his alcoholic breath, as quick with his bravado as he was to loot, proud of his vices and his ignorance, trusting in the cowardice of others more than in his own bravery—if he had any at all. Soon there would be no more rogue officers to make jokes at the expense of the strategies, mathematics, and clean uniforms of the students of Chapultepec military academy.

Chapultepec. The Aztec name vibrated in the thoughtful officer's unhappy soul. It was an epic poem, a glorious reveille that called one to the struggle, to duty, to life.

Chapultepec. That unforgettable, glorious place! In a flash it evoked the legend of Mexico in all its glory: the triumphant Netzahualcoyotl, Moctezuma's pomp and ceremony.

Chapultepec. It also signified the heroism of the child martyrs of 1847, who had illuminated the Mexican darkness with a rainbow of blood.

With the vision of the Chapultepec military academy resting on the presidential fortress of the victor, Miguel once again believed in redemption and triumph, in his country's future and in his own, for he too was a son of Chapultepec!

CHAPTER 41

It Had to Be

After moving away from the rowdy group of men surrounding Reyes, the officer on guard duty felt reality return. Leaning on his rifle, Second Lieutenant Mercado contemplated the farthest reaches of the valley below. The moonlight made it look as though sleet was falling over the desolate landscape.

The luminous red stains between the thick columns of black smoke rising from the burning structures were gone. Now the valley was teeming with scattered pinpoints of bright light, like the bonfires of a ghostly camp where mountains of human flesh burned silently in the gloomy peace of the moonlit Tomochic valley.

Impassively, Reyes talked about the fallen heroes. "Yes indeed, chiefs, they were honorable, manly, and loyal. Even the youngest and poorest spoke true. Their word was as good as a king's."

Miguel smiled. He knew just how far you could trust the word of the majority of statesmen, presidents, dictators, and kings.

Reyes continued. "They were hard workers. They'd have nothing to do with drunks or slackers. They threw that bandit Bernardo Carranza out on his ear. But first Cruz made full use of him, for he was gifted with a vast knowledge."

Once again, Miguel smiled. This wasn't the only noble Mexican caudillo who, believing he was defending a righteous cause, ended up using the traitors and the bandits, paying them more than he paid the faithful and true.

"Oh, how clean they were! They were very clean, my good sirs. Nobody went without shoes, nobody went around in their undershorts, even in the heat. Well, it's true they didn't shave and they didn't cut their hair. To them, it was a sin. You saw them here with long hair and big beards. Most of them looked like bears decked out as Christians. Then with their powerful voices, their haughtiness, their unflinching, steely gazes, never lowering their eyes. Add to that their terrible strength, a diabolical agility, a gift for aiming true, never missing their mark, and belts full of cartridges and a few Winchester repeating rifles, from twelve to eighteen shots."

"All right. Enough. We know about that much better than you do, my friend," interrupted Castorena. The bitter irony in his voice chilled all of them. A vision of those last terrible battles and comrades shot down by Winchester rifles passed through his comrades' minds. The old Remingtons the troops used were blunderbusses in comparison.

"And what women, eh?" commented Lieutenant Soberanes, a brave, gallant officer.

"Ay! Even good enough for us. The best . . . huge black eyes, a little sad, fine long hair, firm breasts. Obedient, quiet, good workers, wonderful women, and very pretty."

The words struck Miguel in his heart. So naive he couldn't hold his tongue when he felt something intensely, he exclaimed, "It's so true. I swear it is. Very beautiful and so kind. Beautiful!" The second lieutenant's words registered such sincere emotion that faces turned toward him with surprise and curiosity.

"Hey, you hypocrite. You've been holding out on us. Where are you hiding your Tomochic dove?" asked Castorena as he gave Miguel a not unfriendly slap on his shoulder.

"And what will the government do with all those poor orphans and widows?" a second lieutenant asked Reyes.

"They'll go to the most reputable families in Chihuahua, so that they can be used for the good of the state and bring forth more serviceable heroes."

"Those women deserved their men! I'll never forget how the last of them died with great dignity," said a lieutenant of the 5th Regiment.

"You know very well . . . I was there, I saw it all . . . O God, what horrors went on. Imagine! When we dragged them onto the porch, we laid them out in the open," and he gestured eloquently to a distant point. "We left them lying on their backs, and executed them just like that."

"Such brutality!"

"What do you mean, brutality?" interrupted the officer on guard duty. "If we had to shoot them in the end anyway, why wait for them to recover just to put the hood on them and prolong their agony? It was better this way. Yes, my good men, it was a humane act to finish them off the way we did!"

"The comrade is right," agreed the lieutenant who was telling the story. "We only gave them enough time for their last wishes. They'd already had plenty of time to pray and Cruz was expecting to go straight to heaven. He begged us to put him between his brother and his woman."

"Priestly etiquette. What the devil!" said Castorena, adding his two cents' worth.

"That's what we did. One Tomochic fighter who could hardly utter a last word managed to turn himself over and then twisted around to where they had laid the chief out, saying 'Cruz, Cruz . . . the powder.'

"'Give it to Nicolas,' said Cruz to a soldier of the Twelfth. This guy took him a scapular that had some of Teresa of Cabora's magical powder in it. They said you could use the powder to resuscitate yourself.

"I was with the dying men with a corporal from my regiment, and behind us was a firing squad of soldiers with their rifles loaded.

"'On your knees!' they said to the guy who was at the far end. Meanwhile, a trembling soldier approached holding his rifle up.

"'I can't.' He tried to stand up, but the soldier fired squarely into his mouth, tearing his skull to pieces, and scorching his hair. Then the corpse collapsed face down.

"At that moment another soldier, who had managed to get down on his knees, fired at Cruz, who fell backward, his chest pierced through, mouth agape, and eyes gazing up to the heavens.

"The last victim received two bullets because the hand of the soldier who was aiming at him was trembling. Pointing straight at the man's chest, he missed and hit him in the stomach. The Tomochic fighter then jumped up and yelled, 'Long live the power of God.'

"Then we saw the soldier load his rifle again, aim, and fire at point-blank range. The force of the bullet singed the man's beard, put out an eye, and scattered his brains all over the place.

"So that was how the last Tomochic fighter died. During nine days of tragic heroism, 103 of them had held out against the fire of 1,200 men equipped with a modern cannon.

"It was necessary to do away with all of them. It had to be. It just had to be!"

And all the young, high-minded officers in the group, true and disciplined sons of the military academy, were moved by pity and admiration. They unanimously agreed with the words of the officer of the guard. Leaning on his rifle for support, Miguel's eyes were vacant as he contemplated the sad, silent moon shining down on that cemetery.

CHAPTER 42

Alone

When the last of the officers had come in from outside where all had been conversing, the second lieutenant on guard duty ordered the corporal to bar the door of the improvised officers' barracks. Then Miguel sat down on a worm-eaten stool in front of the blazing hearth and contemplated the crackling flames, which sent blood red streaks of light zigzagging up the barrels of the rifles stacked against the rotten wall. Wrapped in their serapes, several off-duty soldiers from the guard corps lay snoring around the luxurious fire.

His hood pulled tightly around him, Miguel sat uncomfortably, both arms and legs extended toward the flames. Resigned to his woeful thoughts and misfortunes, he nodded off, fitfully giving into slumber.

As usual, the indistinct sounds of sobbing children and the weak voices of the elders praying for the souls of their dead emanated from the distant shed full of captive families. Meanwhile, in the dark courtyard, under the arms stockpiles, the troops stretched out alongside their women and gear. A few of the fires still smoldering to the east and west revived with the cool winds blowing from the north, the melancholy flames rising from mounds of ash and charcoal.

The guards passed the word along every five minutes or so, now that the enemy no longer existed. Their brusque voices rent the deep silence, "One, alerrrt! Two alerrrt! Three alerrrt!"

Suddenly the guard posted at the back of the courtyard called out, "Corporal?"

"What is it?" Shouted the corporal in return. Grumbling, he went to see what was the matter, then returned moments later and said to Miguel, "Second lieutenant, sir, one of the women is very sick and wants water. Apparently there isn't any. They say she's dying."

"All right, go with one of the *soldaderas* to get her some water. And quickly! Sergeant, I order you to proceed with the utmost caution. I'll investigate what's going on."

Miguel crossed the courtyard, tripping over soldiers lying on the ground, and when he arrived at the quarters of the female prisoners, he stopped on the threshold before going in. A dirty glass lantern sat on the ground and gave off a dim, yellow light that illuminated a long, low space. In the limited light Miguel made out a spectral scene: countless creatures swung listlessly this way and that projecting colossal shadows into the corners of the room, which reeked of human putrefaction.

A number of sleeping women lay wrapped in tattered sheets. Others sat upright in anguished immobility, like abject souls resigned to their martyrdom in purgatory. Purgatory and Limbo.

From a corner of the room came the plaintive, high-pitched whine of a child, while in the center an old hunchback was on her knees in front of an ancient chest. She probably fell asleep while praying. Her head lay in her folded arms and she was snoring.

Then he observed a woman stooping down to speak to someone writhing in agony on the ground. Miguel thought he recognized the voice. As he approached, advancing on tiptoe, he said in a low voice, "They're going to bring the water now. Who is dying?"

"Yes, yes, a little water, sir," answered a low voice that was full of sweetness. The young man stopped, struck dumb with surprise. In the darkness, he received such a shock to his system that he felt the hair on his head stand up. He tried to catch his breath. Julia! Just the thought of her!

Cold gripped his skull. His heart contracted and he couldn't breathe. Julia! He felt dread, pain, despair. He had found his Julia, alive but dying! He approached the pair. Mariana was standing. Julia was stretched out below her. "Is it really you?" whispered the second lieutenant softly. He leaned over, attempting to make out the face of the unfortunate woman. Abruptly the woman sat up and threw off her covering.

Julia's emaciated face was illuminated by fiery eyes, which shone from deep, black hollows and held him transfixed. Her shrunken breasts were visible through her torn, blood-stained shirt. No, this isn't Julia, it can't be Julia, thought Miguel.

She repeated, "Sir, I'm dying. I'm thirsty . . . water."

"Yes, Julia." Miguel could not for the life of him utter a single word other than the name of his strange love.

At that moment the corporal entered with a jug of water, which the second lieutenant grabbed from him. Then Miguel kneeled by the sick girl's side and, in the solicitous voice used with a child who won't take a bitter medicine, said to her, "Just a little, Julia . . . too much will harm you." Then she lay back again, her eyes wide; she was panting and spitting up black bile. Miguel asked the feeble Mariana standing at her side, "But what happened to her? What's wrong? Is she wounded?"

"A bullet pierced her chest," the old woman answered.

"Hush, Mariana, don't tell him, I don't want . . ." A violent cough cut her words short. Then exhaustion overcame her and she closed her eyes. Her breathing became more and more labored as she flailed her arms and brought them to her face as though trying to shield herself from morbid visions.

"Yes, sir," said the old woman at last in a sluggish voice that echoed gloomily throughout the cold, silent quarters. "Cruz gave her his rifle so she could help, then the other day he positioned her behind an opening in the wall so she could shoot from there." She nodded her head toward some indefinite place in the room. "A bullet entered, and that's how it happened. God will take her to him."

"I don't want to die . . . I'm bad, sir. I'll go to hell. I don't want to. No! Please forgive me," moaned the dying woman. Delirium was setting in.

"Julia, Julia, for God's sake, lie down! Don't you recognize me? Don't you remember, my love, my heart and soul." The officer choked back his tears.

With barely a stitch covering her, she sat up as though trying to flee from him. But Miguel gently restrained her. When he touched her, her flesh was burning with an intense fever. Julia looked at him absently and then laughed nervously, like an anxious lover.

"Yes . . . with you, yes, just with you, my love. Be gone, Don Bernardo . . . let him go to Tomochic. Do you hear? Such gunfire. Which one is my rifle? Death to the enemy! Give me your cartridge belt, Pedro. Long live the power of God! Death to the soldiers!"

Miguel kneeled by her side and tried to cover her breasts, but she flung the edge of the wrap away. Then she began to stutter incoherent phrases again, reaching with her arms, sobbing and laughing at the same time. The officer put his arm around the dying girl's shoulders and then listened quietly while she continued to rave.

Suddenly Julia fell silent. Staring straight at Miguel, she laughed in languid ecstasy. She brought his head down to her face and puckered her lips, asking for a kiss. Miguel did not kiss her on the mouth but placed a chaste kiss on her forehead.

"You . . . I'm always yours," she cried. For a moment she went limp. Then opening her eyes wide, in a high-pitched, hoarse voice imbued with a strange and powerful rage, she shouted, "Long live the great power of God!"

The officer loosened his grip on the girl as a shock of cold fear ran down his spine. Then the girl fainted, fell backward, and hit her head with a dull thud against the rock that had been her pillow.

A violent convulsion. She opened her mouth, then opened her eyes even wider, then died.

In his fiercest voice, a voice reserved for combat, Second Lieutenant Mercado ordered the corporal to open the door to the guard corps. The corporal was convinced that the second lieutenant was drunk.

Miguel went outside. It was four o'clock in the morning, the dead of night. The moon had disappeared and the stars glittered in their constellations. The nearby mountain peaks had faded away leaving only a black outline. In their shadowy recesses he could see luminous yellow smudges of smoldering bonfires. Soundlessly the corpses were consumed by the last of the flames. The cold winds off the mountains swept the ashes away, disseminating gusts of rot through the atmosphere. Even the dogs were quiet. Complete silence reigned.

"O Lord, my God! Alone! Alone! Where am I going next? Where will I go?" His kepi askew, Miguel sobbed as the icy breath of dawn swept over his exposed face.

Afterward he sat on a rock, cradling his head in his arms, which were crossed on the barrel of his rifle propped up on the hard ground of Tomochic. Finally he could cry. He cried as he had never cried before—at last, after so many bitter, violent years full of futility and utter despair. His tears flowed on and on, sweet and consoling.

When he raised his head and straightened up, he felt composed, strong, and capable. His sad eyes were still moist as he gazed down into a darkness broken only by deadly bursts of flame: piles of corpses continued to burn in the fathomless desolation of the valley below. In the east, dawn was breaking over the mountaintops.

Then Miguel Mercado cried out, "Bugler, play the reveille."

Editor's Notes

Chapter 2

1. This paragraph and the previous one contain obvious political irony; they were not part of the first edition.

2. This allusion to Díaz's motto doesn't appear until the second edition.

3. A silver coin that roughly equals a quarter of a peseta, a Spanish coin that has varied in value according to time and place.

4. At that time in the state of Chihuahua twenty-five- and fifty-cent bills were in circulation, issued by various banks.

Chapter 3

1. A type of rough-hewn leather sandal.

2. Small settlement or ranch.

3. A type of alcohol obtained from sugar cane or corn.

Chapter 4

1. A thick alcoholic beverage made from the juice of the Maguey cactus.

Chapter 5

1. A thick tortilla.
2. Small change.

Chapter 7

1. A stone used to grind corn and grains.

Chapter 8

1. Mexicans of European ancestry.

Chapter 12

1. Colorful woven blanket.
2. Vendors.

Chapter 15

1. An interjection such as "damn it!"
2. The seat of government.

Chapter 21

1. Chief.
2. A drink made from fermented corn.

Chapter 29

1. Napoleon's 1805 victory over the British, Austrian, and Russian forces.

Chapter 34

1. People of European ancestry born in Mexico.

Chapter 35

1. A drink made from maguey.

Chapter 40

1. This segment represents a true challenge to Díaz, his regime and his army. It appears in the 1906 and 1911 editions only. This is pointed out, as in other similar passages, not to discredit the authority of the writer but to clarify circumstances leading to the war council of 1893. (See the introduction.)